Wine Markets

Wine Markets

GENRES AND IDENTITIES

Giacomo Negro and Michael T. Hannan
with Susan Olzak

Columbia University Press   *New York*

Columbia University Press
Publishers Since 1893
New York   Chichester, West Sussex
cup.columbia.edu
Copyright © 2022 Columbia University Press
All rights reserved

Library of Congress Cataloging-in-Publication Data
Names: Negro, Giacomo, author. | Hannan, Michael T., author. | Olzak,
Susan, author.
Title: Wine markets : genres and identities / Giacomo Negro and Michael T.
Hannan with Susan Olzak.
Description: New York : Columbia University Press, 2021. | Includes
bibliographical references and index.
Identifiers: LCCN 2021022074 (print) | LCCN 2021022075 (ebook) | ISBN
9780231203708 (hardback) | ISBN 9780231203715 (trade paperback) | ISBN
9780231555197 (ebook)
Subjects: LCSH: Wine industry–Social aspects. | Wine and wine
making–Social aspects.
Classification: LCC HD9370.5 .N44 2021 (print) | LCC HD9370.5 (ebook) |
DDC 338.4/76632–dc23
LC record available at https://lccn.loc.gov/2021022074
LC ebook record available at https://lccn.loc.gov/2021022075

Columbia University Press books are printed on permanent
and durable acid-free paper.
Printed in the United States of America

Cover design: Elliott S. Cairns
Cover image: CharlieK / Alamy Stock Photo

Contents

CHAPTER NINE
Biodynamic and Organic Winemaking   157

Preface

In 1965, Bob Dylan—then a much idolized exponent of traditional folk music—unveiled his electric guitar and used it for three songs at the Newport Folk Festival. Many in the audience jeered. In a concert at Manchester in the next year, a fan yelled "Judas" when Dylan performed using his plugged-in instrument. Dylan retorted, "I don't believe you—you're a liar!" Dylan, who famously defined himself as a trapeze artist, was unfazed; he saw himself as an experimenter seeking to make original music. The audience at the time associated folk music with acoustic instrumentation and was confused and sometimes angered at the appearance of folk artists with electric instruments and sounds. During that period, the recording industry and the broader public were shifting their attention toward the newer rock genre. However, some folk-music performers and fans chose to stay with tradition. They considered performances like Dylan's at Newport stylistically unintelligible. They also reviled the electric guitar in the folk context as evidence of the tainting influence of commercialism (Weissman 2005).

The divided reaction of the audience to Dylan's electric turn highlights the contention arising from mixing genres, a core topic of this book. We see parallel concerns among winemakers. For example, in one of the cases that we study in the Langhe area in the Italian region of Piedmont during the 1980s and 1990s, innovative winemakers began to challenge the traditional genres of Barolo and Barbaresco wines. The appropriate type of barrels used for aging these wines became a source of contention. As in the case of generations of folk artists who had relied on acoustic instruments, traditionalist winemakers had been using very large barrels called *botti grandi*, which made wines enjoyable only after considerable aging. Some new winemakers started using small French barrels called *barriques* to make a more modern wine—an "electric" Barolo—drinkable after a short period of aging. One of these winemakers, Elio Altare, had taken a trip to Burgundy to learn about wine-making and convinced himself that the greatest wines in the world are made in *barriques*. When he returned home, he took a chainsaw and destroyed the *botti* in his family's cellar to make space for barriques. Elio's father viewed this act as an affront to the older generation and tradition. He disinherited Elio and did not speak to him for many years.

Why do audiences respond so strongly to choices such as what instrument to play for a certain genre of music or what barrel to use to age a certain genre of wine? Should they produce only in an existing genre and develop a clear identity as a proponent of tradition? Or should they seek to affiliate with foreign or newly emerging genres and become known as an innovator? Or should they hedge their bets by offering wines in more than one genre?

We need two theoretical notions to analyze these questions: *genre* and *identity*. At its core, the Dylan story has the following form: (1) the audience identifies the artist with a particular genre, and (2) the artist's performance combines this genre with another. Identification of the artist with the genre sets expectations for a performance, and the mixing of genre elements violates expectations. For this kind of response to be general, the members of the audience must agree about the genres.

What then is a genre? In short it is a mental representation—a concept—with a similar interpretation in an audience. The music genre labeled folk describes a set of choices on lyrical, acoustic, and performance dimensions. The collective concept tells what should be expected of a performance of folk music and what should not. In this book we show that genres matter for wine. In particular, genres affect how wines are interpreted and valued. They also serve as the building blocks of the collective market identities of producers. Producers are actively involved in these processes and in their communities, they have shaped the emergence of wine genres and their subsequent dynamics.

A major theme in our analysis of wine genres is uncertainty. Uncertainty arises when wineries and their wines are associated (or not) with genres. This is an instance of the general process called categorization. Some wineries/wines are easy for the audience to categorize, and others are more difficult. Some of this variation is associated with choices by the winemaker, for example, producing wines in different genres. We will show that these variations in uncertainty shape aesthetic reactions and valuations. To return to the Dylan story, his career was not, of course, derailed by the genre-mixing controversy. This might be in large part because his creativity was mainly lyrical. Indeed, he was awarded the Nobel Prize in Literature for the corpus of his lyrics. There is considerable sociological research on what happens when artists mix genres, as we describe in later chapters. In this book we explore what happens in the context of winemaking.

We sought to learn how producers thought about these questions and how their choices shaped their identities in the eyes of fellow producers, critics, and consumers. So we started by interviewing producers of the fine Italian wines Barolo and Barbaresco in an area called the Langhe in Italy's Piedmont. We started there because we had read about a raging contention over genres—modern versus traditional—and over the "soul" of these wines. We were following the sociological instinct that contention lays bare the underlying assumptions and meanings that are hard to grasp in a calmer situation.

We wanted another similar community of producers for comparison. We chose the Tuscan town of Montalcino and its surroundings to interview producers of Italy's other most famous wine: Brunello di Montalcino. We thought that the community of Brunello producers would provide a useful comparison because this wine was codified officially at roughly the same time as Barolo and Barbaresco. Indeed these three wines were the first in Italy to receive certification under the highest quality designation, *Denominazione di Origine Controllata e Garantita* (DOCG). At the time, Brunello had a roughly similar scale of production as Barolo/Barbaresco, received high levels of critical acclaim, and sold at roughly similar prices.

We knew less about wine production in Montalcino and did not know what to expect. As we will show, this turned out to be a fortunate choice because the social structure of the producers in this area of Tuscany is completely different from that in the Barolo/Barbaresco area. We learned that these differences shaped the degree of consensus among producers, which in turn shaped the forms of contention that emerged in each of these two settings.

Once we were well underway in studying the two Italian settings, we decided to add a third: the French region of Alsace. What drew our interest was the realization that many of the highest status producers in Alsace had moved almost en masse to a strange kind of unconventional farming called biodynamics. It seemed likely that biodynamic Brunello was emerging as a market identity. We wanted to compare this with its three other possibilities tied to different kinds of farming: conventional, sustainable, and organic.

The methodology that we adopted in this book combines intensive fieldwork and statistical analysis of producer populations. Our fieldwork consisted of interviews with winemakers, the editors and critics of wine publications, and people in wine retail (restaurants and wine shops). Our interviews with wine producers normally took place in their homes and cellars. Sometimes we also walked the vineyards.[1] These interviews were the most fascinating any of us have done because of the passion the winemakers expressed for their work and the close ties between this work and market identities. As much as it is feasible, we let these protagonists speak for themselves.

Our data come from transcripts of the interviews and notes that we took during interviews as well as from archival sources. We include the list of the main interviewees and informants in the appendix.

We also used the knowledge obtained from the fieldwork to structure systematic empirical investigation. Therefore our conclusions are also strengthened by statistical analyses. We collected archival data from materials in specialized publications that provide critical reviews and ratings, results of blind and nonblind wine tastings, retail prices at the winery, and methods of production. We supplemented this information with two telephone/email surveys, the first in 2009 in the Langhe and the second in 2010 in Alsace, to obtain additional comments and confirm information about winemaking practices with the wineries in our archival list.

In the interest of making this book broadly accessible, we have deemphasized technical details in laying out the theoretical approach and in reporting our empirical findings. In the text and notes we point readers to publications where to find these details.

Acknowledgments

This book is the culmination of a joint research project that over a decade has also produced a series of academic papers. Like the wines that we discuss in the next chapters, our ideas have been maturing for several years. And like the aromas of these wines, some aspects of these ideas have been retained while new ones have formed. We have tried to integrate them in a coherent intellectual product.

Many experts think that good wines improve with time, up to a point, of course. We hope the same can be said of our work here. The time is ripe to "pull the cork" and make a toast to the many people who have offered their time, helpful advice, and criticism during the writing of this book.

First, we would like to thank all our informants. These include the winemakers and winery owners with their collaborators in the three regions that we focused on—Alsace, the Langhe, and Montalcino—and also in other locations where we have had the opportunity to interview winemakers. These include Burgundy, California, Oregon, and Sicily. We are grateful to these people for spending their time reflecting on their work and in many cases sharing it for the first time with researchers—at least with sociologists! Often these winemakers welcomed us in their homes and shared life stories, meals, and friendship in addition to information and interview materials.

We also thank a number of professionals for their insights gained from working in the wine industry. This group includes wine critics and writers; wine magazine editors; and owners of restaurants and wine shops in Italy, France, and the United States. We are also indebted to the officials of the local producers' organizations that set the formal rules: the Consorzio di Tutela Barolo Barbaresco Alba Langhe e Dogliani, Consorzio del Vino Brunello di Montalcino, and the Camera di Commercio of Cuneo and Siena in Italy, who helped locate historical materials related to the development of the regulations for Barolo, Barbaresco, and Brunello wines. We also acknowledge the government officials who provided access to additional historical documentation at the Ministero delle Politiche Agricole Alimentari e Forestali (Archive of the Ministry of Agricultural, Food, and Forestry Policies) in Rome.

Parts of this research build on published work that we have developed with other collaborators: Hayagreeva Rao, Magali Fassiotto, and Ming Leung.[1] We wish to thank them for their contributions to the earlier work as well as planting the seeds of other ideas that germinated in this book. We also would like to acknowledge the helpful research assistance from some students at Bocconi and Emory universities: Agnese Orlandi, Elena Perondi, Severine Piot, Adrian Scott, Diane Valahu, and Abdul Zaheer.

We are very grateful to friends who provided detailed feedback on the penultimate draft of the book: Glenn Carroll, Greta Hsu, Özgecan Koçak, Dale Miller, Michele Piazzai, Amanda Sharkey, and Olav Sorenson. Many other colleagues offered helpful feedback on our prior research as well as this book or parts of it. The incomplete list of these colleagues includes Beth Bechky, Anjali Bhatt, Christophe Boone, Solène Delacourt, Jerker Denrell, Gary Fine, Amir Goldberg, Ming Leung, Wes Longhofer, Dave McKendrick, Pilar Opazo, Elizabeth Pontikes, Fabrizio Perretti, László Pólos, Ray Reagans, Chris Rider, Peter Roberts, Samira Reis, Jesper Sørensen, Anand Swaminathan, Peter Thompson, Jim Wade, and Ezra Zuckerman. Their comments improved our work. Food writer Christiane Lauterbach also provided useful reactions on an early draft of the book.

Finally, we acknowledge seminar participants at the many institutions in which we have been able to present the research related to this book. These institutions include Australian National University, Cambridge University, City University London, Durham University, École Politechnique de Lausanne, Emory University, Georgia Tech, London Business School, Massachusetts Institute of Technology, New York University, Northwestern University, Princeton University, Sabancı University, Stanford University, Université de Bourgogne, University of California at Davis, University of Groningen, University of Lugano, University of Maryland, University of Toronto, and University of Wisconsin–Madison. We are grateful to Goizueta Business School at Emory, the Stanford Graduate School of Business, EntER Bocconi, Durham Business School, and the Jemolo Fellowship at Nuffield College at University of Oxford, which provided financial and organizational support for parts of this project.

Wine Markets

CHAPTER ONE

Genres and Market Identities

AS WE EXPLAINED IN THE preface, this book examines the interplay of genres and market identities in the context of winemaking. In this chapter, we try to explain clearly what we mean by the words *genre* and *identity* and provide examples from the domains we study.

1.1   What Is a Wine Genre?

Attention to formal classification gives the misleading impression that genres have crisp boundaries, that each wine is either a full-fledged instance of a genre or not an instance at all. This is how regulations are written. They provide necessary and sufficient conditions for membership. That is, the wine genres and terroirs can be represented as sets of mutually exclusive concepts with sharp boundaries. These systems have an elther-or character. As with all "classical" concepts, any object either fits a concept fully or it does not—there is no zone of uncertainty. Think, for instance, of the concepts we learned in mathematics. For instance, any whole number is either a prime or not a prime.[1]

The assumption that people rely on classical concepts in organizing their worlds came under attack first in philosophy and then in cognitive psychology. The leading figure on the philosophy side was Ludwig Wittgenstein. In his *Philosophical Investigations,* Wittgenstein (1953) analyzed the social use of natural language and concluded that ordinary concepts do not satisfy the classical requirements but instead reflect what he called family resemblances.

Subsequent psychological research supported Wittgenstein's view on concepts expressed in natural (and not formal) language. The modern research tradition on the psychology of concepts began with Eleanor Rosch's (1975) examination of the relationship of subconcepts to concepts. Rosch's famous studies asked subjects to tell, for instance, how typical were certain types of fruits (e.g., apples, watermelons, olives) of the concept fruit.[2] Subjects report great differences in typicality among cases like these, and they agree by and large about the degrees of typicality: apples and oranges are regarded as very typical, watermelons and pineapples as only moderately typical, and olives as very atypical. Rosch and Mervis (1975) claimed that these replicable patterns of *graded typicality* reveal that concepts involve family resemblances.

Several major lines of work in cognitive psychology and cognitive anthropology have investigated these issues.[3] Although contemporary researchers disagree about the details of how concepts form and operate, they do agree broadly that concepts do not fit the classical picture of sharp boundaries.

We can clarify what it means to be typical by building a model in terms of a *space of feature values* (a so-called semantic space). For wine, relevant features might include

- The nature of the source material {European *vinifera* grapes, other grape species, rice, apples, berries, etc.}
- Alcohol level
- Color {red, rosé, purple, white, yellow, etc.}
- Effervescence {still, sparkling}
- Sweetness {dry, sweet}

Typical wine is fermented from vinifera (European) grapes, has a moderate level of alcohol (12.5–15 percent), is red/rosé/white, still (as opposed to sparkling), and dry (as opposed to sweet). We can regard each array of feature values as a point in a multidimensional feature space. (What matters are *particular combinations* of feature values, not the values of each feature taken one at a time.) The concept labeled cider can also be represented in the same feature space but with different values of some of the relevant features, for example, "fermented apple juice," replaces "fermented grape juice."

Concepts and Genres

Concepts are mental representations. They specify what to expect of something that is an instance of a concept. Research on concepts generally regards such expectations as specifying the *meaning* of the concept.

Typicality was the mainstay of research on the structure of concepts for at least twenty-five years after Rosch's initial work. Empirical studies elicited values of typicality by mentioning a concept, for example, furniture, showing a stimulus such as a drawing, and asking, "How typical is the object in the drawing as furniture?"

One can imagine doing this in a wine tasting, asking of each wine sampled how typical it is of some announced wine genre. Indeed, wine commentary and criticism very often addresses issues of typicality of a wine to some type or genre. The anglophone wine press frequently uses *typicity*.[4] The term is clearly modeled on the terms for typicality in the two most important wine growing regions: *typicité* in French and *tipicità* in Italian. Perhaps the best way to understand "typicity" is as typicality in the domain of wine.

What makes something typical of a concept, for example, a wine as an instance of a genre? Answers to this kind of question invariably point to the values of particular *features*, such as color and sweetness, to specify what it means to be a good example of a certain kind of wine. Typical wines have the expected values of the features.[5]

By *genre* we mean a concept whose interpretation is widely shared in an audience. In other words, a genre is a shared or collective concept. We think that the effect of even a collective concept works through individual cognition. The significance of wide consensus about the meaning of a label attached to a concept is that large portions of the audience tend to categorize and value objects similarly—the effect of concepts is magnified.

Some might find it odd that we use the term *genre* in the context of wine markets. After all, theories of genres in the humanities and social sciences deal with issues of categorization and interpretation of media works. Genre theory refers to analysis of media works that share particular conventions of content (such as themes or settings) or form (including structure and style). Genres such as western or horror in film provide frames of reference that help audiences to interpret the works. Similar to the approach we apply in this book, genre theorists have in recent years come to assume that the texts/performances/objects associated with a genre generally differ in how well they exemplify it—genres have a structure of graded typicality and cannot be defined by necessary and sufficient conditions.

Genres, like collective concepts generally, function as a shorthand to increase the comprehensibility and efficiency of communication between creators and audiences. When literary texts and art works show high typicality in a genres, they provide the pleasure of familiarity. Yet difference can also be essential in the appreciation of a work because it introduces elements of novelty that can stimulate the audience's attention.

Genre theory also distinguishes between semantic and syntactic elements of genres (Altman 1999). The former identify the basic building blocks that make up a genre, and the latter identify the structures and relationships among the elements. Genres have been theorized to evolve in relation to the semantic and syntactic: either existing blocks of elements are combined in different structures, or existing structures of elements take a new meaning. In the case of wine, one can recognize the short maceration and aging of grapes in small barrels in the cellars as producing a wine that is lower in tannins and drinkable sooner. At the same time, as we describe in the case of Barolo and Barbaresco wines in the Langhe region of Italy's Piedmont, the combination of these two practices contributed to define a modern wine that many viewed as commercial and breaking with established conventions in that region.

In genre theory, the bonds between elements of a genre are examined in historical context. In this sense, analyzing how elements of a genre have been used over time allows to understand the history of individual creators through their works, helping to delineate their identity.

Despite the differences between the empirical focus of genre theory and our work on the wine industry, we see both settings as posing issues of interpreting and valuing objects. We think that is is helpful to emphasize that markets, no less than art worlds, operate using collective concepts, categorization, and valuation.

Categorization

While concepts are abstract, the set of things that someone believes is an instance of a concept—called a category—is concrete.

For a wine retailer placing wines on shelves in a brick-and-mortar wine shop or attaching tags to wines in the database supporting online shopping, the decision of where to place a particular wine is a categorization decision. In the example of an online wine shop, the list of wines that one finds when clicking on a genre label such as organic wine is the category that the retailer associated with this concept.

Retailers, critics, consumers, and even producers have to make judgments about what wines fit what genres and how to categorize particular wines; for example, "What kind of wine is this? Is it a Chianti?" The so-called categorization probability is the likelihood that a person will judge an object to be an instance of a particular concept. Think of a wine tasting in which each taster takes a glass of wine and judges its color, aroma, and taste. Suppose that one of the possible categorizations is traditional Barolo. How confident is the taster that a focal wine is indeed an instance of the traditional Barolo genre? In the world of classical concepts, there is no uncertainty. The wine either is or is not an instance of the genre. As we described above, research in cognitive psychology reveals that real-world concepts, such as genres, have a probabilistic structure—there are no sharp boundaries. So it is meaningful to focus on subjective certainty. A person's degree of confidence about a categorization is what we mean by a categorization probability.

Categorization probabilities play a central role in our construction of the effects of conceptual uncertainty on valuation. Estimated categorization probabilities are equivalent to typicalities. We use measures of these probabilities to examine whether wines that are more typical of a genre receive greater critical acclaim and higher prices. We also use them to construct a measure of conceptual ambiguity—uncertainty about which genres should be used in interpreting and valuing a wine. We use this measure to examine critical ratings of portfolio of wines.

The Notion of Terroir

The somewhat mystical French notion of terroir dominates thinking about expensive ("fine") wines and forms the basis for some wine genres. The literal English translation of this term is "land." But this concept, especially as used in the wine context, means much more. It attributes special significance and quality to food products produced from particular sites, specifically soil, geology, topography, aspect to the sun, climate, and by people who work the sites and their characteristic cultural practices of production. The key idea is site-specificity: the claim that no other site can yield products with the same characteristics.

Claims to exceptional terroir are made for many kinds of agricultural products in Europe, not just wine. For France, for instance, the state officially recognizes terroirs for such diverse products as cheeses (starting with Roquefort in 1925), butters (e.g., Charente), lentils (Le Puy), honey (six varietals from Corsica), chicken (Bresse), and spirits (Armagnac, Calvados, etc.). For Italy, the list includes balsamic vinegar from Modena, mozzarella di bufala, San Marzano tomatoes, and olive oils from several regions. The European Union has encouraged all member countries to adopt a system of protected locations of origin. So now, for instance, Isle of Man Manx Loaghtan lamb, Stilton cheese, and Jersey royal potatoes have Protected Designation of Origin (PDO) classification in the United Kingdom, as do paprika of Szeged and onion of Makó in Hungary.

One cannot escape the concept of terroir in the fine-wine context. Members of the American wine industry tend to interpret the concept narrowly (and mistakenly in the French view) as purely material: soil, climate, wind, and so forth. That is, they ignore the cultural/historical concept, understandably given that the United States does not have a culture of wine-making of long standing. If we think about the exalted wine terroirs of Europe, they have not been identified by technical analysis of soils and climate. Rather, they have been singled out by a history of producing great wine. In the case of Burgundy, for instance, what are now regarded as the best terroirs are generally those that monks (especially Cistercians) had identified as ideal in detailed reports in the Middle Ages. For Bordeaux, the creation of the five-tier system of classification of quality was essentially a mapping onto prices in the market for Bordelaise wines in the mid-nineteenth century. We see this process repeated all over Europe.

The concept of terroir has special importance in wine industries not because it provides directly a system of classification but because it forms the philosophical and cultural basis of formal systems of classification. The classification systems, which we will discuss in subsequent chapters, specify terroirs and thereby allow categorization of wines as instances of terroir-based genres.

1.2   Producer and Audience Roles

In this book we focus on wine producers and their audiences. Consider first the producers. Almost all the producers that we study make wine from vineyards that they own. These producers grow grapes; harvest, press, ferment, age, and bottle their wines; and sell them under the label of the winery.[6] In most cases, these are family farms with small production by world standards. The Burgundian name for such enterprises, *domaine*, has gained broad usage in the wine world, and we will often use this label in referring to the family-owned winegrowers/winemakers. In each region we studied, a smaller number of wineries are organized as corporations. These are usually much larger than the domaines, and they often have outside ownership.

The characteristics of a wine, such as aroma, color, clarity, and taste, depend on hundreds, perhaps thousands, of decisions that are not easily observable to outsiders. These include how much care was taken in pruning and canopy management; how much was yield controlled; whether the harvest was timed appropriately; whether the grapes were properly sorted; how cold soaking was conducted; how fermentation, racking, and filtering progressed; whether anything (acids, sugar, oak chips or fluids, coloring agents, and so forth) was added to the product; whether the wine was ultrafiltered or put through reverse-osmosis. Also important is whether and how well the actions in the field and cellar were tuned to the peculiarities of the vintage.

The producers know these facts—exactly what they do in the vineyard and cellar—consumers do not. Producing wines that accurately reflect a genre depends on these myriad decisions. In other words, producing a genre-fitting wine depends on the goals, experience, and competence of the grower/producer.

The counterpart to the role of producer in the market is *audience*. The term *audience* refers to those who screen and evaluate the products and services offered in the market. Those who play the audience role hold key resources and allocate them to producers, particularly when they decide what to purchase. We refer to the various participants in a market in any role as agents.

Membership in an audience and producing in a market are *roles* in a market—not partitions into nonoverlapping sets. A role in its sociological meaning is a bundle of expectations, orientations, and obligations. Producers ordinarily supply goods, but they also evaluate those of other producers. For instance, scientists publish papers and also evaluate the work of other scientists in the role of "peer reviewer" of submissions to journals and grant agencies. When we visit the cellars of prominent winemakers, we frequently see bottles of wines by notable producers from other regions, and the winemakers readily give their views of the quality of these wines.

Diverse sets of agents play the audience role in markets. Consumers obviously do. We have mentioned that producers can also play such a role. Critics figure prominently in wine markets because of the diversity and complexity of the market and because wine is a so-called experience good, as we discussed in the preface. We have also mentioned that state authorities also influence the market. In France and Italy, the locations of our study regions, the state enforces rules of production that come largely from collectives of winemakers. In judging whether particular wineries or wines adhere to these rules, state agencies play an audience role, one that can decisively affect flows of resources to producers. Market agents in each role use concepts and categories to interact with other agents. The way in which concepts and categories are understood by individuals and communicated within groups, then, is very important to understanding market processes and outcomes.

Several subtypes of the audience for wine have a decisive influence: consumers, producers, and market intermediaries such as critics and retailers. The significance of the consumer audience is obvious. This group, in the end, decides whether to purchase a wine and reward its maker. How a wine from a past vintage tastes can prove a useful guide for the audience to assess current quality. But some producers change practices all the time in response to changes in climatic conditions or technical developments. Wine quality can only be assessed accurately in the act of consumption, and perhaps not completely even then (Nelson 1970; Darby and Karni 1973). This explains why critics have such importance, as we discuss below, as well as why information communicated through market signals has value for foretelling the quality of wines from new vintages, as we detail in chapter 10.

Producers routinely evaluate one another's work and sometimes act collectively to shape the accepted meanings of their wines. Intermediaries have a decisive influence on these matters, especially for fine wine. In the cases we studied, collectives of producers played the dominant role in establishing genres. As we noted above (and discuss in more detail in later chapters), the French and Italian governments delegated to producer communities the task of drafting codes to specify the official classifications. The national regulations generally endorsed the collective decisions of local communities of producers. More important for the focus of this book, communities of producers created various genres and fought to amend the official rules to accommodate the rules for their production.

The audience for wine also contains agents who intermediate between wineries and final consumers. In industries like wine the products are so-called experience goods, which, consumers have difficulty in evaluating or obtaining information on. A consumer can evaluate this kind of good only through consumption (after purchase). For such experience goods, critics provide three types of useful services (Caves 2000). One is gatekeeping. With a large number of products, like the thousands of wine labels produced every year, it would be impossible for consumers to gather information about each label or sample every wine. Critics select only few out of the many more options available to consumers.

Second, experience goods often include symbolic features and involve a complex social context that require expert knowledge to decode. In the cultural domain, think about the revolutionary approach of Cubism in visual arts. Artists like Pablo Picasso and Georges Braque pioneered a visual style in which they represented multiple views of objects or figures simultaneously in the same picture, resulting in paintings that appear fragmented and abstracted. Art theorists such as Albert Gleizes and Jean Metzinger helped to interpret this new style by connecting the work of the artists that used multiple viewpoints in their works to physical and psychological theories about the fluidity of consciousness.

Finally, critics provide quality judgments by certifying the value of the goods that they select and interpret for the consumers. The ability to distinguish quality and provide rankings of goods and producers—things like the list of top ten movie directors of all time or the best books of a year—is especially important in markets that contain many kinds of products and many items of each type. In such markets, consumers face choice of complex goods with uncertain value. Critics provide information, interpretation, and judgment, allowing consumers to rely on their expertise in deciding to purchase one product over another. Of course, critics can be biased and often do not agree with each other. So the availability of critical judgments does not completely solve the valuation problem for the consumer.

In Italy, the work of Luigi Veronelli and that of publishing group *Gambero Rosso* helped to shape the cognitive/cultural landscape of the new wine world. Veronelli was a pioneer advocate of Italian wine and food. A second intermediary in the Italian wine world emerged during the 1980s, the food and wine magazine *Gambero Rosso*, first published as an eight-page supplement of the critical, left-wing newspaper *Il Manifesto* in 1986.

Critical publications that focus on wines from a single country, such as *I Vini di Veronelli* or *Gambero Rosso* for Italy and *Vins de France*, tend to be more familiar with the local norms and history of winemaking. They gained national prominence and influence early on. As the wine world became more globalized and the U.S. market achieved more importance, we witnessed the rise of international critics such as Robert Parker and his *Wine Advocate* and U.S.-based publications such as *Wine Spectator* and *Wine Enthusiast*.

Intermediaries matter most when they are believed to be impartial. If they are not, then consumers could question the veracity of their expert opinion. This would devalue the role of the critic altogether. Robert Parker started his bimonthly wine publication *The Wine Advocate* featuring consumer advice in 1978. Parker claims to have been influenced by the activist philosophy of Ralph Nader, an American political activist noted for his involvement in consumer advocacy and credited with the passage of several landmark pieces of American consumer protection legislation. Parker saw a lack of independent wine criticism in a system in which the critical publications depended on advertising from wineries, brands, and distributors.

The new group of critics, including Parker and *Wine Spectator*, was based in the United States (the world's largest wine market), and these critics spoke increasingly for an international audience of wine consumers. Their independence, their use of innovative evaluation systems (such as numerical scores or rankings of wines and wineries), and the great diversity of wine regions around the world made these intermediaries not only useful for consumers but also highly influential. Being noticed and being rated positively by an expert in a crowded, complex market can translate into significant benefits for a small producer who has limited resources to invest in communicating with consumers.

Critics do not always agree. Indeed, during the period of contention over modern and traditional wine styles in Italy, *Gambero Rosso* championed the modernist wines and Veronelli took a more even-handed approach that slightly favored the traditionalist position. Basing decisions on critical scores is more complicated than it might seem.

1.3   Market Identity

Now we turn to the second main theme of the book: market identities. It can be easy to confuse the notions of market identity and brand. So we begin by distinguishing the two.

Wine Brands

The wine industry is organized mainly by price. Most wine sold in the world belongs to the low-price segment. In this segment, the product is a simple commodity, and price is all that matters to consumers (although they still must choose among red, white, and sparkling wines). At the next level up, once called the zone of the "fighting varietals," branding solves the problem of complexity. These brands increasingly claim affiliation with a lifestyle and make minimal reference to traditional wine distinctions such as the sourcing of grapes, winemaking, method of aging, and so forth. When successful, this strategy collapses the large number of possibly relevant dimensions to a small number—the features of the lifestyle.

Consider the case the brand called [*yellow tail*], one of the largest in the world. The story begins with Filippo and Maria Casella migrating from Sicily to Australia. The family began farming and made wine for family and friends. They eventually began producing bulk wine for sale to wineries. When their oldest son John took over the business around 2000, he wanted to enter the U.S. market. He did so in a joint venture with the U.S.-based distributor W. J. Deutsch. The first attempt failed. The second attempt, [*yellow tail*], became the fastest-growing brand in the history of the wine industry. According to the firm's website, John Casella wanted to

> create an approachable wine that everyone could enjoy. By doing so, he wanted to demonstrate that wine could be fun, easy to choose, easy to drink and easy to understand. (www.yellowtailwine.com/us/our-story/)

The wines were engineered to expand the appeal of wine beyond a small, highly informed consumer base. The strategies included reducing tannins (the source of the dry astringency that might be off-putting to those new to wine) and acid (to increase the sensation of sweetness), to produce a drink that non-wine-drinkers would like, making wine more in the style of a soft drink. New production processes eliminated variation in taste over long production cycles, including the effects of vintage variation. In short, Casella produced a Coca-Cola wine. In addition, the label departed greatly from the practice at the time: it featured an image of a yellow rock-footed wallaby (a cousin of the kangaroo) done vaguely in the style of aboriginal art with bands of neon colors to indicate the varietal (e.g., yellow for Chardonnay, red for Cabernet Sauvignon, etc.). The wines were priced in the $5–$7 range. This strategy succeeded spectacularly. Within three years, it was the largest wine import to the United States. It has become the fifth-largest brand on the U.S. market, with sales of 11.5 million (9-liter) cases.

Interestingly, the top-selling wine brand in the world, Barefoot (owned by E. & J. Gallo Winery), had followed a very similar strategy. It was founded in 1986 by the husband-wife team of Michael Houlihan and Bonnie Harvey with next to no capital or industry experience. They decided to build a brand with the motto "Get Barefoot and have a great time!" The label featured an image of a bare footprint. The wine and brand were designed to appeal to beer drinkers (Houlihan and Harvey 2013). The operation was still fairly small (with forty employees) in 2005 when they sold to Gallo, the world's largest wine producer. This appears to have been an effort to catch up with [*yellow tail*]. Using its scale in production and power in distribution, Gallo quickly caught their Australian rival and then came to roughly double their sales in the United States (22.5 million cases). Stephanie Gallo, the manager of the brand, in a visit to a class at the Stanford Graduate School of Business, referred to it as the "gateway brand" for the Gallo portfolio of brands and reported that about a third of its consumers were first-time wine buyers. Barefoot reduces the categorization problem to a list of click-through flavors for "Let's find your perfect wine", for example, blueberry, juicy, sweet, creamy, smooth, vanilla were displayed on the first page of the site (as of October 11, 2020); others could be accessed by clicking "more."

For our purposes, two aspects of branding are crucial. First, the brand is created by the producer or on behalf of the producer by an agency. Second, brands are fungible—they can be bought and sold, often by agents with no experience in the industry (as we will show in subsequent chapters). Identities are attributed to a producer by an audience. The audience "controls" the identity, not the producer. In contrast to brands, identities emerge from a bottom-up process in an audience and cannot be subject to market exchange.

Market Identities and Genres

Identities are rooted in concepts (genres here). They tell us what to expect of the person/thing that bears the identity. The identity of a person usually conveys some global set of expectations about that individual. In psychology, the study of identity refers to self-identity, a person's beliefs about himself or herself. In sociological research, identity usually refers to views by those other than the focal person. For a sociologist, a person's identity in some context are the expectations that people in the context have about the focal person (or collective entity). These are expectations about future behavior, not just summaries of past behaviors. The power of identity in shaping responses by others is providing a standard for evaluation of the extent to which future behaviors match the expectations.

Taking a context as fixed, social identity functions as a concept in that it provides expectations about the behaviors of the person to which the identity is attributed. Social identities apply to corporate entities such as wineries as well.

The expectations that get bundled into an identity can refer to all kinds of aspects. We want to narrow down these aspects to those that matter in a market context. To make this clear, we will refer to market-specific identities. The market sets the context and thereby makes certain expectations relevant to members of the audience for that market. In this book, the entities to which market identities are ascribed are wineries, winemakers, and the wines themselves. The agents who hold the beliefs that establish the identity are members of relevant audiences in the market, including winemakers, critics and other intermediaries, and consumers. The market identity of a winery/winemaker/wine tells someone what to expect when walking the vineyard, visiting the cellar, and tasting the wines.

For most wine producers, market identity consists of some genre affiliation (categorization), for example, traditional Barolo producer. These are *collective* identities. Consider, for example, Azienda Agricola Schiavenza. This family winery in the town of Serralunga was established in 1956 on land that had formerly been farmed by sharecroppers, *schiavenza* in the local dialect. This winery makes excellent wines that receive good reviews in the wine guides. The name of the winery suggests a certain modesty, given that almost all of the wineries in the region are named after their founders or current proprietors. When we asked Schiavenza's director Luciano Pira whether he regarded his winery as a traditionalist Barolo producer, he replied:

> I follow the example of producers like [Bartolo] Mascarello. Comparing myself to them would be an exaggeration though. Mascarello is more of a guiding light for producers who follow traditional ideas. Each of us also has our own identity, and we manage the business in our own way.

A basic genre-focused identity can be coupled with very specific expectations about the quality of an individual producer. Consider the highly regarded traditionalist Mauro Mascarello of Mascarello Giuseppe e Figlio winery. He makes a famous Barolo from the Monprivato vineyard (unusually in the Langhe, he is the sole owner of the vineyard—it is what the French call a *monopole*). Winemakers in Alsace and Tuscany have told us that Monprivato is their favorite Barolo. The latest vintage available when we write, 2016, retails for about $200 in the United States. Despite the winery's lofty reputation, everything about it and its proprietor suggest a single-minded focus on *craft*: winegrowing and winemaking. When we interviewed Mauro and his wife Maria Teresa, we sat across from them at a sort of picnic bench in the tasting room. The couple appeared to be uncomfortable in a meeting with academics and were quite taciturn. Realizing that this format was not likely to be productive, we asked if we could visit the cellar. As soon as we entered the cellar, Mauro became a different person—voluble, articulate, and self-assured. We came away thinking that Mauro was a traditional Barolo maker full stop, that the core of his market identity is also traditional Barolo maker. Yet his market identity surely takes note of his reputation for extremely high quality.

We can see the difference in the identities of the two producers just introduced also by contrasting the images conveyed on their labels. (Makers of these and other Barolos seldom change their labels.) Figure 1.1 shows one label for each producer. Notice that the winery's name plays a much less prominent role for Schiavenza. This label draws attention first to the wine type (Barolo) and second to the location of the vineyards (Serralunga d'Alba). Mauro Mascarello's label, by contrast, gives essentially equal billing to the famous vineyard and to the maker; "Barolo" appears in much smaller type.

As an interesting contrast, consider the late Bartolo Mascarello. As we will describe in the next several chapters, he was the leader of the mobilization of the traditionalist camp of Barolo makers. His market identity included the high craft skill of his nephew Mauro (Bartolo's daughter is also named Maria

| (a) Schiavenza | (b) Mauro Mascarello |

Figure 1.1 Labels from Schiavenza and Mauro Mascarello. *Source:* Photographs by Michael Hannan.

Teresa, like Mauro's wife). But it also encompassed a strong political identity. It was widely known that he had fought with the Partisans during World War II and then became a labor organizer on the docks of Genoa. When he returned to his home town of Barolo, he threw himself into winemaking. However, as the traditional way of making Barolo came under attack with the introduction of the French *barrique* (small barrel) and Italian politics became dominated by the conservatives led by Slivio Berlusconi, Mascarello adopted a hand-painted label with the motto "No *Barrique*, No Berlusconi" for his Barolo for several years beginning with the 1999 vintage (see an example in figure 1.2).

The late Teobaldo Cappellano, a much beloved Barolo producer, developed a similar—if less prominent globally—market identity. The most visible evidence again comes from his label, but this time from the so-called back label (the one on the back of the bottle) shown in figure 1.3. Cappellano was passionate about building community, fostering solidarity and the collective strength of small, local wineries and winemakers. His label mentions that he explicitly asked wine critics not to review his wines or even include him in quality rankings of wineries. He claimed that wine scores created divisiveness.

Finally consider Angelo Gaja. As we document in the next chapter, Gaja was by far Italy's most famous wine producer. As will be clear, he was

Figure 1.2 Label by Bartolo Mascarello. *Source:* Photograph by Giacomo Negro.

considered by many to stand apart from the category of Barbaresco producers. Indeed his market identity was unique and only loosely tied to that of Barbaresco producer. His easily identifiable label, shown in figure 1.4, again tells the story: his name completely dominates.

Clearly increasing prominence in a wide audience provides an opportunity for distinguishing one's market identity from its collective genre-based identity. But only in extreme cases like Gaja does identity get partly decoupled from the genres to which a winery/winemaker is assigned. More generally, market identity in the production areas we studied has a strong collective flavor, strongly rooted in categorical memberships, in genres.

As we noted at the beginning of this section, identities form around different units: wineries, family owners, winemakers, and so forth. Taking the view that identity lies in the eyes of the audience means we must allow for multiple possibilities. Some audience members focus more on the owners and others on the winemakers, for example. There is no single, objective "right" answer that one matters more than the other all the time.

Nonetheless, the context and the information available to the audience affect how market identities form for different "targets." To take a simple case, distant corporate ownership, as we see for some of the wineries we study in Tuscany, makes it unlikely that audience members will form a market identity

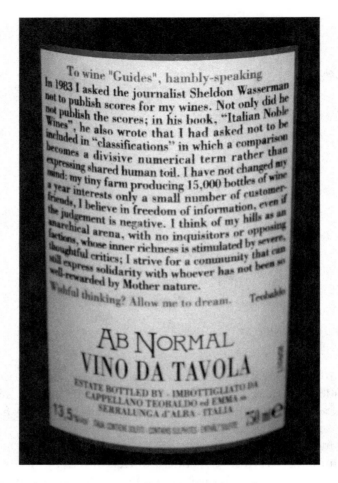

Figure 1.3 Label from Teobaldo Cappellano. *Source:* Photograph by Michael Hannan.

for the owner, at least for what concerns their wine business. One example is the famed Brunello family winery Cerbaiona. This winery, which was built from scratch by Diego and Nora Molinari, has recently been sold to an Oregon venture capitalist. In this case, this winery's new market identity comes much closer to the idea of a winery brand—depersonalized and fungible. When the owners hold multiple wineries from different regions in a portfolio, as we see for the Florentine noble families Antinori and Frescobaldi, the ownership group likely gets attributed some market identity. This is likely to take the form of a family wine brand of brands.

Figure 1.4 Label from Angelo Gaja. *Source:* Photograph by Michael Hannan.

Most of the wineries we study are owned and operated by local families; they are "farm wineries" or *domaines*. The examples given above—even Gaja—all fit this type. As we illustrated, some wineries do not stand out from the crowd, and their market identities are strongly bound to the collective wines of their zone. In many cases of stable family ownership and consistency in style and quality over generations, the market identities continue to persist as younger generations take control of operations. We see many instances of this kind in all three of the regions we study. However, we also see instances of two ways in which generational change disrupts identity. One is the sale of the winery to outsiders. This causes the identity that formed around the family owner to disappear, and the new owner has, at least initially, only the collective categorical identity. The second possibility is that the new generation radically revises the style and quality of the winery's production. The modernist revolution we examine in the Langhe and the biodynamic movement in Alsace (and Tuscany) followed this pattern. Clearly the members of the new generation sought to make different kinds of wine and thereby gain different market identities.

1.4   Genres and Identities in Collective Action

Our analysis of the dynamics of conceptions of winemaking and categorization of winemakers in three production areas emphasizes two interrelated sociological processes. Both concern the emergence of collective market identities as consequence of community solidarity and collective action. In this chapter, we cast these ideas in a broader intellectual context. By doing so, we hope to show that the processes that we have documented for several wine regions have general significance.

Community Structure, Identity, and Collective Action

We argue that solidary communities of producers likely come to agree about the meanings of the various aspects of their work and their products. Such consensus enhances the prospects that a collective of producers can take collective action in the interest of defining and defending their conception of their practices and products and demarcating boundaries. Success in such collective action sharpens distinctions in the market and causes other interested parties (audiences), such as critics, journalists, retailers, and consumers, to attribute a common identity to the collection of producers. We refer to this process as the emergence of a collective market identity.

The ways by which communities of wine producers establish consensus about meanings involves processes that are common to social movements in many domains. Gaining consensus requires that members of a collective come to agree that they share an identity, agree on a label for it, and develop a language that expresses the conventions that underlie that identity. Students of social movements refer to these actions as *framing* (Snow 2004).

In addition, creating a collective market identity requires developing consensus on categorization, on deciding what producers and products belong to it. Furthermore, success is most likely when the collective creates an organization to represent its interests and defend its boundaries.

Sociologists treat as nearly axiomatic the notion that collectivities with greater solidarity and denser webs of organization can better mobilize collectively. Although this intuition is likely correct, the notion as generally stated lacks predictive power. The difficulty is that *community* can mean so many things. People have multiple identities that tie them to many collectives. A person can be simultaneously a member of a gender, a nuclear family, a clan, an ethnic or religious group, an occupation, an industry, and so forth. People can choose whether or not to engage in collective activity on any one or more of these bases of identity. And the communities usually differ in solidarity and structure. Only after a mobilization has been observed does it become obvious which community has engaged in collective action. To be more useful, theoretical analysis of the emergence of collective action requires a priori specification of the likelihood of each of the possible forms of mobilization.

So the challenge is dealing with this kind of multiplexity. Sociologist Roger Gould used themes from social network analysis to provide a useful framework for dealing with the matter. In his view, the flow of protest depends on the flow of triggering events, any of which can make one or more partitions of the population relevant. As we will show in later chapters, a scandal about adulteration of some Italian wine in the region of the Piedmont highlighted the difference between artisan and industrial producers, and another scandal about mixing of grapes in violation of the laws covering the production of Brunello di Montalcino made central the distinction between family and corporate producers.

Whether collective actions result in reaction to events depends, in Gould's analysis, on the social realism of the partitions. In the political realm, ideologies map individuals to a partition, expressed by specific demands for progressive social change or its resistance. Here, market identities and the coexistence of supporting ideologies and practices help partition the cultural landscape. Whether an individual accepts the mapping and judges that it requires engaging in a collective action on behalf of the segment of the partition depends on whether the assignment fits the person's subjective experience. The framing perspectives in social movement theory refer to this as resonance. Greater resonance in turn increases a group's capacity for collective mobilization and improves the chance that such collective action succeeds.

As Gould (1995, 15) put it,

Collective identities undergird normative commitment to social protest, but are at the same time the product of the very social relations that are both affirmed and forged in the course of protest. The collective identity of workers *as* workers only emerges if the social networks in which they are embedded are patterned in such a way that the people in them can be plausibly partitioned into "workers" and "non-workers"; once this is possible, social conflict between collective actors who are identified in terms of this partition will heighten the salience and plausibility of the partition itself. The intensification of the boundary's cognitive significance for individuals will, in other words, align social relations so that the boundary becomes even more real.

When we describe the social structures of the communities of wine producers in Alsace, Barolo and Barbaresco, and Montalcino, we will see commonality and difference. To a large extent, the communities in Alsace and the Langhe have dense structures of interaction. In sharp contrast, the interaction within the producers community in Montalcino was increasingly bifurcated by the partition between family firms and corporate entities (often with outside ownership). The weak solidarity of the community in Montalcino impeded collective action in response to any kind of event, even those that challenged the official rules for the wine that benefited all. We see the same kind of process play out among a group of Alsatian producers. In this case, the extreme contrast involves the more cohesive biodynamic farmers and the less cohesive "sustainable" farmers, with organic farmers lying between the two.

Genres, Categorization, and Valuation

Social mobilization by producers, supported by a cohesive social structure, can shape the emergence and change of genres. Such changes in the "space of genres," in turn affects valuations of wines. Hannan, Le Mens, Hsu, Kovács, Negro, Pólos, Pontikes, and Sharkey (2019) have developed formal theoretical accounts of the effects of concepts and categorization on valuation. We follow these arguments here. They depend on two central mechanisms: typicality and conceptual ambiguity.

Research in cognitive psychology has demonstrated that people like and value objects that fit their conceptual distinctions. More typical objects are valued more than atypical ones. This pattern has been argued to depend on an effect of cognitive fluency. An experience with an object or situation is fluent for someone if they do not have to exert much cognitive effort in understanding and interpreting the object/situation. A high demand for cognitive effort (disfluency) generates negative affect, which can take the form of a low valuation. This completes a causal chain linking typical with positive valuation. Genres backed by strong consensus about meaning exert powerful control on producers in the sense that deviation from their conventions generally leads to devaluation.

There is another relevant form of cognitive effort: deciding which of several genres ought to be applied to an object in valuing it. Some wines, for instance, are clear instances of only one set of alternative genres. In this case, the step of deciding what genre to apply (how to categorize the wine) takes little effort. Alternatively, another wine might be judged to be, according to some measure, an inexact instance of two or more genres. In our language, such wines are conceptually ambiguous. Ambiguity poses demands for greater cognitive effort, which in turn is experienced as disfluency. So ambiguity also brings devaluation. Wines whose features sit between genres get doubly penalized: they are atypical of each potentially applicable genre and are conceptually ambiguous.

As genre distinctions change in the context we studied, some producers remained close to their original genre, others moved to a new one, and still others tried to span the genres. These spanners provide the empirical leverage to examine the effects of typicality and ambiguity on valuation (critical ratings and market prices).

CHAPTER TWO

Barolo and Barbaresco

In this chapter we turn to the first of the three wine regions we studied: Italy's Langhe. In particular, we focused on its iconic wines: Barolo and Barbaresco, traditionally called the "King and Queen of wines" in Italy.

The Langhe region sits in the southeastern corner of Italy's Piedmont region close to the French and Swiss borders in the foothills of the Alps. (*Langhe* in the local dialect means "hill.") It lies not much more than an hour's drive from Torino, the major cultural, economic, and industrial center of the region. The Alpine influence is strong, both visually and climatically. On clear days, the Alps appear very close. Many days in winter experience fog and sometimes snow from the mountains.

Barolo and Barbaresco are made here from the grape varietal Nebbiolo. People in the region generally assume that the grape was named after the fog, *nebbia*, which often rolls down from the Italian Alps. This grape varietal does not seem to do well anywhere but in the sub-Alpine zones of the Langhe and other nearby areas on mountain slopes in Piedmont and Lombardy. Attempts to grow and vinify Nebbiolos in California, for instance, have usually been disappointing, with a few newer, localized successes. So this varietal possesses strong local specificity.

The production zone for Barolo (the area in which the grapes must be grown and the wine processed) is quite small by national and international standards. It covers roughly five miles by seven miles, with fewer than 5,000 acres approved for production. Barbaresco has an even smaller zone.

We will analyze the shifting conceptions of these wines and of their proper production in light of the history and social structure of the region. So we begin with that.

Figure 2.1 Barolo vineyards with the Alps in the background. *Source:* https://www.maxpixel.net/Wine-Alps-Piedmont-Barolo-Vineyards-Langhe-Unesco-4836580 under license Creative Commons Zero.

2.1   Background

Wine production in the Langhe has a history extending from at least the onset of Roman domination. Growing and vinifying wine grapes in this region has long been the work of small, independent farmers. This history stands in sharp contrast to the history of sharecropping of agricultural production in other regions of the country, including Tuscany, as we will discuss in analyzing the production of Brunello in chapter 6. In Tuscany, the dominant system was sharecropping, in which nobles and other wealthy families owned the land, which was cultivated by the *mezzadri*, who paid rent in the form of half of the agricultural product from their labor. This system lasted until the land reforms in the post–World War II period. The story in the Piedmont was quite different, due perhaps to the stronger influence of Napoleon's republic there than in the rest of Italy. Between 1799 and 1804, the influence of the Napoleonic Code on the region effectively abolished feudal practices, including those in agriculture, and set the stage for the rise of small landholders.

To this day, most wine producers in the Langhe operate small farms that have been owned by their families for many generations. Until recently, most produced a mix of grain, vegetables, fruits, and nuts in addition to wine grapes. In fact, wine grapes often was not the primary crop produced by these farms.

We can get a rough idea of the scale of these farms from census information reported sporadically by the Chamber of Commerce of Cuneo, the provincial capital. We see that the wineries producing Barolo and Barbaresco are very small by international, and even national, standards. For points of comparison, consider Monin in the Veneto region, which alone makes more than 20 million bottles, and American producer Gallo, which produces roughly 75 million *cases*—which amounts to 900 million bottles—per year. When we started our research project, the most recent information covered the vintage of year 2000, and at that time more than half of the Barolo/Barbaresco producers farmed less than 3.3 hectares (8.1 acres) of vineyards. The average number of bottles produced for a vintage was roughly 25,000, the median was 15,000, and more than 90 percent wineries made fewer than 45,000 bottles. More recent data for the vintage 2013[1] show that the average size of cultivated land among producers has remained small, and if anything it has decreased slightly. Producers who make Barolo farm an average of 3 hectares, and their counterparts in Barbaresco, roughly 2.2 hectares. The median number of bottles per producer released in the market has increased, reaching 75,000 for both denominations. However, we must bear in mind that this bottle count includes other wines such as Barbera d'Alba, Langhe Chardonnay, and Roero Arneis.

So typical producers of Barolo and Barbaresco have stayed quite small. For example, some of the most renowned producers like Bartolo Mascarello, Giuseppe Rinaldi, and Roberto Voerzio produce roughly 30,000 bottles per year; Elio Altare and Giacomo Conterno produce roughly 55,000. Only eighteen wineries produce more than 500,000 bottles. The largest production of estate wines[2] comes from Fontanafredda: more than a half million bottles of Barolo and Barbaresco. In total, all the members of the Consorzio di Tutela Barolo Barbaresco Alba Lange e Dogliani (Consortium for the Protection of Barolo Barbaresco Alba Lange and Dogliani) make about 12 million bottles of Barolo and about half of that of Barbaresco.

In our study, we consider only wineries producing the region's preeminent wines, Barolo/Barbaresco, where we see mostly family-owned businesses; and nearly 58 percent of them are defined legally as *azienda agricola* ("farms"). Multiple family members work in the family's wine production and marketing. For about 65 percent of these wineries, the Chamber of Commerce identifies the same surname for owner, sales manager, and enological director, suggesting that key organizational roles were restricted to members of the family. In 2005, one source indicates that fewer than 5 percent of the wineries in Piedmont belonged to a corporate group, and about 4 percent were part of a cooperative (Delmastro 2005).

For many of the producers that we visited, the winery is integrated into the home. Often one walks down a stairway from the living room or hallway to enter the winery in the cellar (of course, there are entrances below for the movement of grapes, bottles, and machinery). In other cases, the winery building adjoins the family home. Over the time of our field research, winemaking has transitioned from father to children, women in many cases. All in all, these producers fit closely the notion of a family farm winery. Indeed, most of those we interviewed referred to themselves as contadini ("farmers").

Not all of the important producers of Barolo/Barbaresco fit the farm-winery notion. For one, there is the late Bruno Giacosa, who along with Angelo Gaja (discussed below), deserves pride of place in putting these wines on the world wine stage. His grandfather began a family business making wine from purchased grapes. Bruno joined the family business as a grape buyer at the age of fifteen. He mastered the skills of identifying the best vineyards and building ties with growers while he also learned winemaking from his father. In 1960, he started making his own wine from purchased grapes. Not long after, his 1964 Barbaresco Santo Stefano became arguably the first cru (labeled single-vineyard) wine produced in Piedmont. During the 1970s, Giacosa produced a series of legendary wines and became known as one of Italy's greatest winemakers. At this point, he was still what the Burgundians call a *négociant*, a market intermediary who purchases grapes, must (unfermented juice), or wine from other enterprises and makes/bottles wines that they sell under their names.

Toward the end of the 1970s, many of the farms that had supplied fruit for Giacosa began to produce their own wines. Moreover, according to Kerin O'Keefe's (2014) report of interviews with him, Giacosa had become convinced that the grapes he was buying were declining in quality due to the use of chemical herbicides, pesticides, and chemical fertilizer. So he began to purchase vineyards, beginning with the Falletto farm in 1982, and to produce "estate" wine. For the rest of his life, he produced both wines from purchased fruit under the label Casa Vinicola Bruno Giacosa and wines from his own vineyards under the label Azienda Agricola Falletto. So his operation was something of a hybrid. His winery, located in a charmless industrial building in the center of the town of Neive, produced on a fairly large scale by the standards of the region. Unusually for a maker of Barolo/Barbaresco, he also produced much more white wine than red. His long-term winemaker

Dante Scaglione told us in 2006 that only 20 percent of the 110,000 bottles produced at that time were Barolo or Barbaresco.

Another important variant on the organization of winemaking is the cooperative, in which grape growers organize collectively to create a wine production operation and make wines under the common label. Cooperatives play a very important role in the Italian wine industry and produce 60 percent of the country's wine, mostly for the least expensive segments of the market.

The most important cooperative in the Langhe is the Produttori del Barbaresco. This succeeded an earlier cooperative, the Cantine Sociali di Barbaresco, which was organized in 1894 by Domizio Cavazza, the director of the Royal Enological School in Alba. It began producing in the cellar of the church in the town of Barbaresco and bottled for the first time wines labeled as Barbaresco. Until that time, grapes from the area had been sold to production of Barolo. The cooperative fell on hard times during World War I and was finally abandoned in the 1930s in the face of demands by the Fascist government that grape growers shift production to wheat. In 1958, the local parish priest revived the cooperative under its present name in the hope of retaining young farmers in the region. The new organization was a great success. Today the cooperative has fifty-one member-growers, and it produces roughly 500,000 bottles per year. The organization stresses the identities of the members by placing on the back labels of the cru wines the names of the members whose production was incorporated. And its website (produttoridelbabaresco.com) contains individual photos of the members. Despite the difference in legal form, the Produttori operates in spirit close to the family winery given the prominence of the growers in the organization and its image.

Few estate producers of Barolo/Barbaresco have a corporate form of organization with nonlocal ownership. As we mentioned above, Fontanafredda has the largest production among the estate wineries. This winery traces its roots to the House of Savoy. Vittorio Emanuele II bought the estate in 1858 as a gift for his mistress and eventual wife, Rosa Vercellana, with the goal of creating Barolo production. Production began under the name Tenimenti di Barolo e Fontanafredda. After the king's death, his son Emanuele di Mirafore created a wine company called E. Mirafore. The new company flourished initially and employed modern methods of vinification and labor organization (O'Keefe 2014). The organization floundered during World War I. Then owner Gastone, the son of Emanuele Mirafore, began to sell shares in his company, and by 1927 the company was completely in the hands of outside owners. After several more changes in ownership, the company entered bankruptcy in 1930. The creditor bank, Monte dei Paschi of Siena, took control and maintained it until 2006. At that time the estate and winery was sold to a group of investors. One is the founder of the Eataly retail/restaurant chain.

The Prunotto winery began as a Cantina Sociale (an early cooperative), which had been founded in 1904 and liquidated in 1922. One of the members of this defunct cooperative, Alfredo Prunotto, purchased the winery in 1923 and began production of wines under his name. The winery was sold in 1994 to the Marchesi Antinori group in Florence, Italy's largest wine company. Prunotto is now one of the brands in the Antinori stable. It produces roughly 800,000 bottles per year. We know of only two other producers owned by outside firms. Enrico Serafino was sold to Gruppo Campari in 2010 and then sold again to Krause Holdings of Iowa. The same holding company purchased Vietti, a four-generation producer of Barolo in Castiglione Falletto, in 2018.

The smaller family wineries receive much higher esteem from critics, and they continue to shape the conceptions of how these wines are produced. Because terroir, family, and market identity have stronger connections for these small producers, compared with other types, it makes sense that any challenges to traditional identity would be met with fierce resistance from this group And, as we explain in the next chapter, it was the family wineries that fought publicly the so-called Barolo Wars.

In the next chapter, we argue that the overlap among family, market, and local identities reinforces a powerful notion that only local family wineries can produce a product that reflects the distinct terroirs of this region. These links help explain why family wineries led the movement known as the Barolo Wars.

2.2   Codification

Barolo and Barbaresco have an illustrious history. However, codification of these wines took place relatively recently. Historically the wine varietal Nebbiolo was used to make sweet wines, which were favored by the royal court in Torino, the House of Savoy. In the mid-nineteenth century, producers began to shift to a drier style. There is disagreement about the source of the adoption of this now-prevalent style. Early histories point to a Frenchman named Louis Oudart, who was brought by Juliette Colbert Falletti, the Marchesa di Barolo, to manage the family's wine production in the Langhe. Kerin O'Keefe (2014) marshals more recent historical work that points to indigenous leadership, namely, the Italian general Paolo Francesco Staglieno. The general, whose monograph on wine production from 1834 advocated complete fermentation of the local wines (that is, production of fully dry wines), worked for the House of Savoy's Carlo Alberto, the king of Sardinia and father of the first king of Italy. Whatever the origin of the connection, the concept of Barolo as we know it today was closely associated with the House of Savoy. This association is famously celebrated in its designation as "the King of Wines, the Wine of Kings."

Barolo and Barbaresco production is limited by regulation discussed below to grapes from the slopes of the Langhe, mostly facing south and west. By law, these wines must be composed entirely of Nebbiolo grapes. Other varietals, such as Barbera and Dolcetto, are grown in the flatter areas and the slopes with less favorable exposure to the sun. Almost all of the producers of Barolo and Barbaresco also make some combination of Barbera; Dolcetto; and perhaps other varietals such as Arneis, Freisa, and Gavi.

The wines called Barolo and Barbaresco, as we know them today, emerged from locally shaped regulation backed by the authority of the Italian government. Initial proposals to regulate the wine industry in Italy date to 1888, when members of the *Camera dei Deputati* (lower chamber of the parliament) pledged to fight wine adulteration and fraudulent activities. In particular, they wanted to target the illegitimate use of geographical denominations for regions of origin of established wine types such as Barolo, Barbaresco, Chianti, and Marsala.

Only in 1924 did the Italian government make a first comprehensive codification with a royal decree specifying the rules for "typical wines" (n. 497, dated March 7). A crucial formative event in the codification of these rules was the creation of voluntary producer consortia, including the *Consorzio di Difensa dei Vini Tipici di Pregio Barolo e Barbaresco* (Consortium for the Protection of Quality of the Local Wines Barolo and Barbaresco) in 1934.

The codification initiatives came to a halt during World War II and its aftermath. Two new bills were proposed in 1948 and 1953 but were never passed by the legislature. A broader change for wine production in Italy, and Europe more generally, came with the signing of the Treaty of Rome in 1957 and the creation of the European Economic Community (the organization later absorbed into the European Union). The Treaty of Rome was an attempt to tear down trade barriers and to create an international market where one had previously not existed. In 1959, the European Economic Community began the process of unifying the wine industry by passing the Common Custom Tariff (Meloni and Swinnen 2013). The act was aimed directly at reducing outside competition by placing customs duties on imported wines based on the type of wine, alcohol content, and sugar content. In Italy, a bill proposed in 1960 and approved in 1963 as a presidential decree (n. 930) instituted a system of granting legal standing to quality wines that conform to a system of rules called the *Denominazione di Origine Controllata* (DOC) (controlled designation of origin). As we noted above, this left to producer collectives the task of setting the rules.

The consortium proposed a set of standards for the production of Barolo and Barbaresco; the two wines gained DOC status in 1966. At this point, we have a full codification of rules for these two wines.

The 1963 law reserved a label for wines produced in explicitly recognized geographical locations that were also considered to be of *particolare pregio* (special, high value). These wines are designated as Denominazione di Origine Controllata e Garantita (DOCG) (controlled and guaranteed designation of origin). The special value is attributed to natural, human, and historical input factors believed to produce higher intrinsic quality. These regulations leave many of these quality-related characteristics undefined. The recognition of special value can also be attributed to renown and commercial appreciation at the national or international level. Barolo and Barbaresco have belonged to the class of DOCG wines since 1980, when the designation was first granted (despite being authorized by the law from 1963).

The process that codified the rules for production of Barolo and Barbaresco involved a combination of top-down and bottom-up initiatives. Specifically the national and regional governments authorized the creation of collective organizations of local wine producers (Consorzi), invited them to draft rules to guarantee quality. If the proposal was judged to have sufficient merit, its proposed rules were enacted into law. The most visible manifestation of the regulatory system to the consumer is a numbered pink strip attached to the neck of each bottle judged to conform to the rules.[3]

What became legally enforced rules originated as instantiations of producers' cultural conceptions, not dictated by either legal precedent or elite pronouncements. The crucial work of specifying the methods of growing and vinification were left to the producers. The specifications that they did propose built on the terroir notion discussed in the previous chapter. The collectives had to make explicit choices about what it means for a wine to be a Barolo (or Barbaresco). The requirements were put in place to guarantee this link to the territory. In this context, *territorio*, the Italian word for territory, can be read as terroir.

The current rules[4] specify that the wine be made exclusively from Nebbiolo grapes that are grown, vinified, aged, and bottled within a specified production area. Designation of the boundaries of the production zone occupies about a page and a half of the nine pages of the Disciplinare. The delimited zone follows an imaginary line surrounding three entire villages and part of the territory of eight additional villages. A meticulous definition such as

> follows the provincial road Alba-Barolo N. 122 North towards Alba up to Km. 5, where, near Cascina Giuli, takes the road for Case Borzone and Giacco and follows until it reaches, in the location Farinetti, the border between the towns of Grinzane Cavour and Diano d'Alba

is based on historical boundaries and their accepted use over time.

The rules also restrict some aspects of farming, including that vineyards must be planted on slopes with clay-calcerous soils at elevations between 170 and 570 meters above sea level. Maximum yields of grapes and of wine per hectare and the method of pruning are also regulated. Aging of the wine must last for thirty-eight months, of which eighteen must be in wood (originally oak or chestnut but not now specified). Finally there are a set of required *typical features of the wine*. Some of these rules specify allowed ranges of chemical parameters such as the level of natural alcohol of the grapes at the time of harvest and the minimum total acidity. Others are more subjective: the color must be garnet red (*rosso granato*); aroma must be intense and characteristic; and the flavor dry, full, harmonious. The Disciplinare specifies each of the properties already listed in further detail.

The rules do not restrict the methods used in vinification, for example, length of maceration, type of yeast originating on the grapes or from the cellar versus laboratory produced, filtration, and so forth. As we read the history of the situation, the winemakers who designed the rules took it for granted that Barolo makers (*Barolisti*) would perform uncontrolled fermentation, and long macerations, and age the wine in very large casks or *botti grandi*. The silence on these issues created the space for innovators to vary these practices while still maintaining fidelity to the official regulations, the *Disciplinare*, as we describe in the next chapter.

The attempt to write the rules to capture the essence of a particular terroir, in the broad French sense of the term, resulted in a complex set of rules stated with varying degrees of precision. Each rule controls one or more features that the local community of winemakers regard as important in specifying what it means for a wine to be a Barolo or Barbaresco. Only one rule dictates a single feature value: the grape varietal. As we noted above, other restrictions are given as ranges (altitude of the vineyard) or minimum values (pH and alcohol). And still others are stated in purely qualitative terms (color, aroma, and taste).

Suppose that the rules agreed upon dictated only grape varietal, vineyard altitude, and the location of activities. Then the Disciplinare would have the properties of a classical concept, one that can be stated in terms of necessary and sufficient conditions. Then any wine would either be a full instance of the genre or not an instance at all.

But as we mentioned, the rule-set does not end there. The inclusion of features such as color, aroma, and taste, designed to capture typicity (*tipicità*), makes the concept a fuzzy one, one with a structure of typicality rather than either-or distinctions. Some combinations of the feature values are regarded as prototypical, and others are seen as less typical to varying degrees. Such a concept when applied to the wines produced in a vintage poses a categorization problem: which wines pass the hurdle and merit the label Barolo DOCG. By the nature of the concept and the categorization process some of the wines with this label are fairly typical of the genre and others very typical. And the contention that we analyze in latter chapters centers on what is typical of the wines of the locality. If, as we argue in chapter 5, judgments of quality reflect typicality, then the probabilistic structure of the concept implies quality differences among wines with different configurations of the relevant features.

Significant differences in quality can still exist among the wines certified as an instance of particular DOCs and DOCGs because of differences in vineyards and skill in growing and production. Consider, for instance, the studies of Renato Ratti, a prominent producer of Barolo based in La Morra. In 1972, he published a *Carta del Barolo*, a map drawing the geography of the sites for making Barolo by compiling several previous viticultural studies. The map shows at least four levels of quality distinguishing growth sites within the Barolo production, in decreasing order: best subregions, special characteristics sites, historical sites, and the rest. The sites have different sizes and are scattered across the production zone, indicating significant heterogeneity in soil types and suitability for grape growing, which are also reflected in the perceived quality of the wines at least by experts like Ratti. These differences subregions, were not incorporated in the legal code, however, and all wines made within the designated production area would carry the same DOCG label. Nonetheless, wines whose labels indicated that the grapes came from one of these prestigious sites gained a clear advantage in the market.

As the practice of bottling cru wines (wines from designated vineyards) proliferated, many complained that the system of claims was incoherent. The Italian Ministry of Agriculture, responding to such complaints, urged communities of producers to rationalize what could be put on a label, the *Menzioni Geografiche Aggiuntive* (MGA), which translates roughly as "added geographical mentions." This awkward term is intended to refer to sub-zones with specific geographic characteristics that produce distinctive grapes and wines.

In response, the Consorzio during the 1990s encouraged the eleven villages that make Barolo and the four that make Barbaresco to come up with a list of agreed-upon vineyard names that could be listed on labels. After much discussion and local political mobilization, a set of rules were agreed upon in each village and given legal standing in 2010. The result for Barolo was a set of sixty-six MGAs. Locals think that this change in regulations simplified the system for the consumer. However, our reading of the dense analyses of the delimitations of each MGA and its claimed special properties (Masnaghetti 2015) does not support this view. There are strong differences in agreed-upon quality among the MGAs. So, to some extent, this new system captures what had been only implicitly recognized differences.

We find the process by which these wines came to be regulated to be interesting because the importance of bottom-up actions challenges the notion that institutional rules get simply dictated from above by state actors. The involvement of many small producers in the regulatory process also challenges the notion that policymakers get coopted to serve the political and commercial interests of a minority of powerful actors such as large firms.

The legal rules codified in the DOCGs for Barolo and Barbaresco enforced basic quality distinctions between these and other wines. These rules do not, however, convey clear information about specific quality differences between labels or producers within a DOC or DOCG. In an economist's terms, Italian and European regulation of wine markets reflected largely aspects of horizontal differentiation, such as location, more than quality differences. Goods are horizontally differentiated when buyers do not agree about which product is better. People value characteristics of the product, producer, and service differently. Some people like rock music and others like classical. If music albums are offered at the same price, some will buy rock and some will buy classical. The rules for DOC and DOCG wines also introduced dimensions of vertical differentiation, distinctions that reflect quality differences more explicitly. Goods are vertically differentiated when buyers agree about how to rank them in terms of perceived quality. Everyone, or nearly everyone, agrees that a room at a luxury hotel offers a better service than one at a budget hotel. If the prices of the two hotels were the same, we would all prefer the luxury hotel. When prices are not the same, buyers of vertically differentiated goods make different purchasing decisions because they have different incomes or value different criteria that lead to different trade-offs between price and quality.

Many goods, of course, combine elements of vertical and horizontal differentiation. Luxury electric cars provide an example. Nearly all buyers value the luxury components more than those of a utility counterpart. But only some prefer electric motors to internal combustion engines. Likewise, while most consumers prefer wine made from higher quality grapes and more skill in vinification, some prefer white to red, Spanish to Argentinian, and so on. Moreover, several dimensions of differentiation, such as gustatory characteristics or identity, remain unregulated by the law. For instance, many knowledgeable consumers prefer Barolos/Barbarescos that convey aromas of dried roses and tastes of baking spice or tar. However, the legal specifications do not refer to such gustatory sensations, other than to state the the aroma must be "characteristic." This situation creates an opportunity for the creation of unofficial codes that can replace or complement official ones. In the presence of complex official regulation, alternative systems of classification can prove more effective for buyers, intermediaries, and producers to guide their actions.

2.3   From Grape Growers to Winemakers

Before the period of contention on which we focus, Barolos and Barbarescos enjoyed high status compared to other Italian wines but not compared to the best French wines. Production was largely controlled by large firms located in the small city of Alba. According to our informants, these large firms generally purchased grapes on a spot market in Alba. Growers brought their grapes to the main square and negotiated with brokers. Because of the rapid spoilage of harvested grapes, the negotiation power lay completely in the hands of the buyers, who could wait out the sellers. For instance, Elio Altare (whose role we discuss in the next chapter) told us

> In 1975 I didn't find any wine buyer to sell my grapes to. For two weeks I stayed in Alba, and nobody bought them. After seven days, some broker found a buyer for his harvest. I asked him how much they would pay for this grapes. He answered me: "I'll take it at the price we were discussing last spring." . . . You can imagine my frustration.

Several factors contributed to changes in the activities of wine producers in the Langhe and to the response of the audiences in the market to Barolo and Barbaresco wines. The first was an event that caused public outrage, a scandal that broke out in March 1986 when a series of deaths were linked to the consumption of Italian wines, mostly from the Piedmont region, which had been adulterated with methanol.

The Methanol Scandal

Methanol, a natural component of wine, is formed in very small amounts during fermentation. In the body, methanol is converted into formaldehyde and formic acid, the toxin found in the venom of ants. So artificial increases in methanol content in wine, even in small amounts, creates harmful, even fatal, consequences for consumers. A modest quantity of methanol, above 25 ml (.8 ounce), can induce vision loss and metabolic acidosis that can lead to a coma.

The deaths of three men in Milan on March 17, 1986, for what appeared to be consequences of severe alcohol intoxication led to a criminal investigation. The magistrates released the names of the wines that were associated with the cases: a Barbera wine and a white table wine bottled by the Odore winery in Incisa Scapaccino in the Asti province. Laboratory analyses of samples of the wine bottles found by the deceased men and of wine collected at the winery revealed the presence of methanol in greater amounts than allowed by law.

A new national alcohol tax enacted in 1984 increased levy on ethyl-alcohol but reduced it on methyl-alcohol. Critics argued that the law was intended to favor chemical manufacturers that utilize large quantities of methyl-alcohol, but unfortunately it might have triggered perverse incentives for use of methanol in other contexts (e.g., Corbi 1986). Increasing methanol content also increases a wine's alcoholic content. Unscrupulous businesses could take advantage of this cheaper solution to increase the commercial value of grapes too low in quality to obtain the desired alcohol percentage.

After the suspicious deaths were reported, an Italian wine tanker was seized by the French authorities in Sète. The wine, transported by a company based in Mandria in the southern province of Taranto, was suspected also of containing illegal amounts of methanol, and laboratory analyses found that it did. A few days later, the owners of the Ciravegna winery in Narzole in the province of Cuneo—bordering on the towns of Barolo and La Morra—were arrested for supplying the adulterated wine to the Odore winery.

Twenty-six deaths were linked to the methanol adulteration, and a number of people lost their eye sight. It was later found that four large wine producers and as many as thirty other producers in four Italian regions, including Piedmont, were involved (*New York Times*, April 9, 1986). The

Italian government reacted to the scandal by introducing ordinances to ban the commercialization of wines made by the wineries under investigation and by wineries whose samples indicated higher, illicit content of methanol. A new law introduced a public registry, maintained by regional authorities, of all businesses involved in the production and commercialization of grapes and derived products, including wine. Financial resources were allocated to launch a campaign to inform consumers of the health risks associated with wine adulteration.

Despite these efforts, the methanol scandal had immediate disastrous effects on the Italian wine industry. Several countries placed bans on the import of Italian wines, and exports plunged 39 percent in the first eight months of 1986, according to the data compiled by the Italian Statistics Institute. Total exports for alcoholic beverages (and vinegars) went from the equivalent of €972M in 1985, to €762M in 1986, and even in 1987, exports remained below the level of three years earlier, at €813M (coeweb.istat.it). (Over the period we studied, the euro/dollar exchange rate ranged from 0.85 to 1.6, with an average of 1.2.)

The methanol scandal turned out to be a watershed event. It did more than cause an economic crisis in the wine industry. According to Claudio Conterno of Conterno Fantino winery, the scandal "completely destroyed all of the links that existed . . . I can assure you that those six months were months of confusion and rage."

When a social context undergoes major upheavals, as was the case with this scandal, established procedures get greater scrutiny. Under these conditions, consumers lose trust in products. The scandal increased consumers' attention to quality and the identity of producers. Buyers came to understand that high-quality wine also meant higher prices and that buying from established winemakers was an important guarantee of quality that ensured that the wine was actually made only from grapes, and certain grapes at that. When we interviewed Italy's most famous wine producer Angelo Gaja in 2006, he recalled that "we started to make money with this business only after 1986, after the methanol scandal. Before that . . . money was made by merchants, not by the estate wineries." In this sense, the methanol scandal destabilized the industry structure and relations. At the same time, it produced a new context in which producers were held more accountable for their production decisions. For some, this meant pursuing more successfully individualistic and differentiated goals. For others, it meant taking hold of and preserving the traditions of the region.

The Wine Guides

A second factor that contributed to change in the wine world was the emergence of specialized market intermediaries, particularly wine critics and publications. In the first chapter, we described how the work of Luigi Veronelli and *Gambero Rosso* defined important factors in the development of the new wine world in Italy. After that, international publications such as *Wine Spectator* and critics such as Robert Parker started to pay more attention to the changes in winemaking that were occurring in the Langhe.

We mentioned earlier that Luigi Veronelli was an early wine and food expert. From 1971 to 1976, he presented a TV show, *A Tavola alle Sette*, which showcased food and wine from the different Italian regions. His writings on wine, which he began in 1959, set the standards for future wine guides. In 1988, Veronelli started to publish an annual selection of Italian wines entitled *I Vini di Veronelli*, and in 1991 he started using star ratings to classify the labels included in his guides. Venerable wine producer Bruno Giacosa was quoted as saying that Veronelli was:

> the first person to teach us that a great wine was born in the vineyards. He was the first to point out the absolute necessity of carefully selecting grapes in the vineyards, the importance of terroir, of realizing the potential of one vineyard or cru over another. (O'Keefe November 30, 2004)

Around the same time in which Veronelli published his first comprehensive guide to Italian wines, another key intermediary entered the market. In 1987, the food and wine magazine *Gambero Rosso* published its first guide to Italian wine, titled *Vini d'Italia*, which in a short time became the most influential critical guide in Italy. The guide was closely affiliated with the Arcigola movement, the forerunner of the Slow Food organization, which has since spread globally.

The methanol scandal and its aftermath and the development of market intermediaries took place alongside other factors that brought about change in the wine industry in Italy. After a period of economic and political turmoil and social unrest in the 1970s, the country introduced a recovery plan, which led to increasing gross domestic product (GDP), lower inflation, and increased production in agricultural and industrial output. The economy grew rapidly, and in 1987 Italy became the sixth largest economy in the world. In regions like the Langhe, grape growers took advantage of the positive economic outlook and, increasingly, they started making their own wine and bottling it with their labels, becoming independent firms.

Beyond these contextual factors, another factor emerged in the mid-1980s as a motor of change in the wine industry in the Langhe. It was the movement of modernist winemakers. We turn our attention to this movement next.

CHAPTER THREE

The Barolo Wars

What became known as the Barolo Wars began as an attack on the prevailing methods of production. Makers of Barolo and Barbaresco had long relied on very long periods of maceration, the period in which the juice remains in contact with the skins and seeds after pressing. Because the skins contain much of a grape's tannin, long maceration yields very tannic wines. The conventional approach also lacked methods for controlling the sometimes very high temperatures reached during fermentation, which can cause loss of color and desirable aromas. Moreover, the approach did not promote a secondary malolactic fermentation, which converts astringent malic acid with a green-apple taste to rounder tasting malic acid. Nearly all red wines now undergo such fermentation. The convention was to employ *botti grandi* (very large casks) for aging. Figure 3.1 shows casks in the cellars of Fontanafredda. The white label on the cask at the far right indicates that its capacity is 140 hectoliters (hl)—equivalent to 18,667 standard 0.75 liter bottles.

Moreover, true to the mentality of traditional farmers, wine growers in the Langhe had sought maximal yields. The wine world nearly universally believes now that this practice reduces quality. These old practices in the vineyard and the cellar produced very austere wines; they were very tannic when young and realized their full potential only after considerable aging.

3.1 The Modern Turn: Gaja and Altare

The various rule systems in Italian law described in the previous chapter impose tight constraints on some aspects of production but allow discretion on other key choices made during vinification, such as duration of maceration, whether fermentation relies on the naturally occurring yeasts of the vineyard

Figure 3.1   Botti grandi in the cellars of Fontanafredda. *Source:* Photograph by Giacomo Negro.

and cellar or on laboratory products, and whether fermentation temperature is controlled. These options became subjects of some contention when producers began to vary these techniques to produce initially a French style of Barolo/Barbaresco and later an international or New World style.

The formal rules also leave open the kind of barrels used for aging. Choice of storage vessel matters because it affects color, aroma, and taste. The barrels/casks have a noticeable presence in the winery over the whole production cycle and can be seen by visitors (such visits can be an important marketing tool for wineries). The type of aging vessel became the main focus of the dispute between producers in the Langhe. Figure 3.2 illustrates the scale difference for the two types of barrels. The large cask on the left has a capacity of 75 hl (a hectoliter is one hundred liters, equivalent to 26 gallons)

Figure 3.2 A wine cellar containing both botti grandi (on the left) and barriques (on the right). *Source:* Photograph by Giacomo Negro.

and the standard Bordeaux (barrique) barrel on the right has a capacity of 2.25 hl.

Angelo Gaja

The person credited for initiating the changes that set off the period of contention we study is Angelo Gaja. According to wine writer Nicolas Belfrage (2006, p. 84), "A legend in his own lifetime, Angelo Gaja deserves and receives much of the credit for dragging the wines not only of Barbaresco but of Alba—of Italy!—to the top of the world wine tree."

The Gaja family winery, founded in 1859, is the oldest in the Barbaresco zone. Indeed the grand winery structure has pride of place on the main street in the center of the tiny village of Barbaresco. Angelo's father had already purchased many top vineyards and had developed a reputation for very-high-quality wines. Angelo told us that his father was the industry leader and that "there were no wines from Piedmont, no Barolo or anything, with a higher price than Gaja's Barbaresco."

Figure 3.3   Angelo Gaja. *Source:* https://search.creativecommons.org/photos/08e3128f-3306-4a1a-8c1c-9ef53f10b43d under license Creative Commons Zero.

So when Angelo entered into the business with his father in 1961 at the age of 21, the firm was one of the country's leading wine producers. Nonetheless, he managed, in relatively short order, to push it to new heights. The first step was to introduce what winegrowers call a green harvest, which consists of cutting some of the unripe grape clusters to reduce yield.

> When I joined in 1961, we reduced the number of bunches per plant by 50 percent... it was a shock for both the men who worked with us and for my father... My father had been mayor of (the town of) Barbaresco for 25 years. I remember that the municipality counselors, who were all wine-producers, said to me: "Look, you're wasting it all. This is a decision only a novice can take, a student."

The next step was to introduce aging in barriques, the Bordeaux barrels of 2.25-hectoliter or 225-liter capacity, because

> The barrique is first of all a color fixer. Nebbiolo has anthocyans that can decay easily. Barriques add wood tannins that form more dense molecules. This adds intensity and stability to the color of Nebbiolo... Second, barriques can obtain in two years the results of the aging process that my father obtained in 4, 5, 6 years.

Alessandro Torcoli, the publisher of the leading Italian wine magazine *Civiltà del Bere*, recalled that Gaja realized that international high-end restaurants were not interested in very tannic wines that took a long time to soften and become enjoyable:

> He needed a winning wine, one which would ingratiate itself. I mean a wine seeking the *captatio benevolentiae* from the market... The consumer would not need to follow it; rather the wine would get closer to the consumer.

Indeed Gaja has a very strong consumer orientation, citing the market response to wines as a justification of practices. As we will see, not all of the leading producers in the region agree that the market should be accepted as the ultimate arbitrator of quality. Interestingly, given the focus of our cognitive models on typicality, Gaja expresses disdain for the notion of typicality. When we asked his views on this matter, he answered:

> Please don't use that word. It is difficult for me because being typical is a concept that is evolving. I mean that in the past wine defects were accepted as part of typicality, like the *puzza di merdino* that French people called *merde de poulet* (chicken shit)... So we need to be careful when we talk about being typical because we make mistakes.

Gaja believed that typicality could be bad. He also acknowledged that the schema of typical Barolo or Barbaresco was changing but not that it was unimportant. Gaja had great influence on wine producers in the region. For instance, Domenico Clerico, whom we discuss below, told us that "I have three teachers: Angelo Gaja, Angelo Gaja, and Angelo Gaja!" Despite his great influence, Gaja held himself apart. He told us that he had not interacted much with other winemakers in the formative period. Elio Altare, who became the leader of the modernists, told us that he did not know Gaja personally when he began his experiments with modern methods. Nonetheless Gaja's radical break with traditional practices had a strong influence on other young winemakers, none more than Altare.

We can interpret another important decision made by Angelo Gaja in the context of a market orientation. First, he released single-vineyard Barbaresco wines. Gaja recalled that until the end of the 1960s the family mixed Nebbiolo grapes from different vineyards in different areas. This was a practice followed generally in this region. Merchants who purchased grapes from multiple growers used to make wine like that, with grapes that came from different places and not a single vineyard. This practice had been challenged by the wine critic and activist Luigi Veronelli. According to Gaja, Veronelli looked at France and concluded that it was a mistake to mix grapes from different sites and call the wine simply Barolo or Barbaresco, especially when the wine included grapes from the greatest vineyards (or crus, to use the French term that has gained wide use in the world wine industry).

Veronelli proposed that wines from the greatest vineyards be vinified separately and be labeled with the names of the source vineyards as a way to emphasize their unique characteristics. Gaja argued that these characteristics would also be reflected in price compared with the situation under the Denominazione di Origine Controllata e Garantita (DOCG) rules that permitted the use of only two labels, Barolo and Barolo Riserva (with a parallel pair for Barbaresco). To return to the distinction between horizontal and vertical differentiation of goods, releasing vineyard-specific wines and gaining agreement among consumers that these wines have distinctive qualities increased horizontal differences. When horizontal differentiation increases, each good becomes more different, less comparable to the others. These are not differences in terms of higher or lower quality but differences that map onto preferences for certain characteristics of the good, for example, color, sweetness, geographical location, and so on. The demand for two goods is related when consumers perceive the goods as close substitutes so that if the price of one good increases, they can buy the other good and be similarly satisfied. With increasing horizontal differentiation, the demand for one good becomes more independent from the demand for another. When that is the case, changes in prices for one good do not result in changes in demand for another good. For example, consumers with a preference for wines with firmer structure and stronger tannins prefer wines classified as Serralunga Barolo and think that they are quite different from those categorized as Cannubi Barolo, which arguably show more elegance and fruitiness. The consumers who like one type will likely stick to it, and a bottle of the former does not exactly substitute for a bottle of the other. Producers of both types can in theory increase their prices because the consumers will not switch type if the price of the wine that they prefer goes up a bit. Above and beyond this, if consumers believe that certain production zones yield higher quality than others, then the prices of wines made in these zones can increase further because all consumers will agree that these wines are better.

Gaja explained that his winery made a first step toward (horizontal) differentiation in 1967 when they vinified a single-cru called Barbaresco Sorí San Lorenzo and released it in 1970 labeled as such. After 10 years, the Gaja winery was releasing four Barbarescos, not only the historical one called simply Barbaresco but also three single crus: Barbaresco Sorí San Lorenzo, Barbaresco Sorí Tildìn, and Barbaresco Costa Russi. The decision to release single-vineyard wines met with great success, and Gaja's Barbarescos have become iconic in the international market. Their prices in the retail market have increased steadily. Prices for the 2015 vintage of Sorí Tildìn average $500, based on data we collected in May 2021 from winesearcher.com.

For some years, Gaja "declassified" the single-vineyard wines. From vintage 1996 to 2011 these wines were not officially labeled as Barbaresco anymore. While he was convinced that the vineyard-specific designation was the "correct marketing concept . . . and there was nothing I could do," Gaja explained the decision to declassify the single-vineyard wines to us as follows:

> A prejudice originated against the Barbaresco without vineyard name, which is the wine of our history. Americans started to call it "regular"— "regular!" And I say, [expletive deleted] I don't do anything regular!

When Gaja declassified his wines, he gave them the designation of *Indicazione Geografica Tipica* (IGT) (rough translation: wine typical of the region), the tier above the basic table wine often used for wines that did not meet the regulations for the Denominazione di Origine Controllata (DOC) or DOCG category. Due this change in classification, these wines would not be included in the category with other Barbarescos, which belong to the DOCG category, in professional tastings. They would be tasted with other Nebbiolo wines in the IGT category. This way, the Gaja Barbaresco could compete and be recognized well in its own DOCG category, and the three single-vineyards could compete and be recognized in the IGT category.

Another reason for this decision might be that Gaja made these wines using grapes other than Nebbiolo, particularly Barbera. The Disciplinare requires Barbaresco to use only Nebbiolo grapes. Gaja chose the appellation Langhe for their single-vineyard wines, which allows up to 15 percent of other grapes. As a matter of fact, more recently the winery announced that they were refocusing on Nebbiolo-only single-vineyard Barbarescos and would not be using Barbera grapes anymore in these wines, implying that they had been doing it in the past (Sanderson 2016).

Elio Altare's Chainsaw Massacre

A few years after the innovations developed by Angelo Gaja, Elio Altare became, according to Belfrage (2006, p. 65), "the most cogent and radical voice of the modernist school, a fanatical experimenter in pursuit of quality."

He came from much humbler origins than Gaja. His family owned a mixed farm founded by Giuseppe Altare (Elio's grandfather) in 1948 as Cascina Nuova. The family produced wine but also grew fruit, wheat, and other crops. This farm was typical of those in the region.

Altare became profoundly dissatisfied with what he regarded as the low quality of the family's wine.

> In 1960 the production here was five tons per hectare. With fertilizers the production increased four times. And the quality went down. In the old days, we would cut the Nebbiolo, forget the grapes inside the barrel, and start doing something else . . . after [doing] all these things we would press the grapes. That is not a good idea if you want to make good wine. This kind of tradition is not the right way to make good wine . . . He [my father] made it that way because it was easy.
>
> The second problem was the use of big and old barrels . . . For my father, and the others like him, the important thing was not to make good wine, but to preserve the wood of the casks because the wood was a resource. That was the traditional way of thinking. When my father made great wines, it was not because he was a good producer; it was just because he was lucky.

So Elio set out on a course of experimentation.

> In January 1976, I went to Burgundy to understand why the customers could spend 10, 20, 50 times more than for my bottles. What justified that price? I was really ambitious, and I still am. If you are ambitious, you seek to compete only with the best. I asked myself, "Who can forbid a young producer to compete, to make investments?" Who can tell you, "You don't change because I am Barolo! There are rules!"?

A key component of his experimentation concerned the length of the period of maceration during which the juice remains in contact with the skins. Altare described the experiment as follows:

> In 1982 I made a Barolo with two-week fermentation on the skins; it had horrible tannins. In 1983 I made only a one-week fermentation, but I made a rosé (the wine had suffered from high temperature and lost its color). In 1984 I made a sixteen-day fermentation—too long. In 1985 twelve days— too long; in 1986, eight days—too long; in 1987, six days. In 1988, four days—I thought the wine was fantastic: drinkable, well-balanced. We used barriques and botti. I saw that wine as a compromise. I made a compromise

Figure 3.4 Elio Altare (first from right) destemming grapes with his team, including daughter Silvia (third from left). *Source:* Photograph by Jeff Bramwell.

because I had bought only a few barriques: it was very expensive and my father had not given me enough money. Thus I used barriques only 50 percent. Parker gave me a 96 score. Wow—it was a scandal!

The scandal was mainly that he adopted the small Bordeaux barrels (barriques) for aging.

Why do I use barriques? Not because it is a trend, but because I use common sense. I was wondering: which wines are the best in the world? Which one is made without the barriques? None!

Elio's father would have nothing to do with his son's ambitious plans. As was the case with Gaja, Altare's father objected strongly to a green harvest (the removal of some immature grape clusters, or crop thinning). The industry now regards this practice as essential to high-quality wine production, as we noted above. But it turned out that the most contentious issue was the use of barriques. Altare undertook a notorious radical act that symbolized the cultural break in the region and put the focus squarely on the choice of barrel. In 1982, his frustration with his father's refusal to allow him to purchase barriques led him to destroy the family's botti grandi with a chainsaw. He told us that he began using the chainsaw to cut down the family's fruit trees after his father had sprayed chemical insecticide, which had previously sickened Elio to the point of needing hospitalization. Then he spontaneously carried on with the botti. This act led his father to disinherit him entirely. Elio's daughter Silvia told us:

> When Elio started to make all these changes, my granddad stopped talking to him. He was so disappointed he even stopped going to church because the people in the village thought that my father was crazy. My grandfather was convinced that my father was wrong. Only in 1985 when Elio started being a little successful, he said to him: "Elio, you're right. I'm sorry."

The vintners who eventually were called modernists did not simply argue that winemaking practices could be reformed by adopting technical innovations under the cover of the legitimacy of traditional practices. We find it revealing that the participants in this Italian wine world use the French name for the small barrel, especially in light of the fact that the Italian language has a word for it: *fusto*. Rather, the use of the term *barrique* challenged the legitimacy of the old ways and symbolized a break with the past.

Young People Become Attracted to Winemaking

Encouraged, at least in part by the success of Gaja and Altare, a new generation of producers reversed a trend of abandonment of farms and refocused on grape growing and winemaking. Even the most partisan traditionalists acknowledged this benefit of the modern turn. For instance, die-hard traditionalist Giuseppe Rinaldi, who we discuss in the next chapter, said of this development:

> We had many producers that produced in the Gaja way. It must not be interpreted only as a bad thing because a lot of young people started to produce, to really make, something with their hands. The entire Langhe developed further and in a way it had a positive impact on local culture because it prevented the extinction of wine producers.

The late Domenico Clerico, one of the leaders of the new wave of modernism at his eponymous winery, recalled the context in which he became involved in winemaking:

> We had a farm with cows and grew wheat. We also had a vineyard, but wine was not very important. At that time, planting vines was more important than making wine. The wine market was different, wine was sold in bulk . . .

Being the son of a farmer thirty years ago was a dishonor. In the 1970s many people left to work in factories and then helped out in the vineyards as a secondary job. But this meant that there was no passion, no real interest in winemaking.

Other producers started out after leaving more secure jobs in other industries. The late Elio Grasso, proprietor of the eponymous winery, had worked for a bank in Turin for ten years before he started making wine. He shared similar views to Clerico's:

When my father died in 1979, I felt an urge that I had to keep doing what he had done after living here for 92 years. So I decided to continue his activity... All of my family was against my choice—my brother, my wife— except for my mother. At that time people focused on getting a proper education and felt ashamed to work the land. That drive to continue my father's work was important, probably more important than the money I could make selling a bottle of wine.

Several producers suggested that, after the methanol scandal, the relationship between customers and producers in the wine market changed. Clients started visiting producers regularly and sought to understand the relationship between a winemaker and his vineyard. According to Clerico, "What changed was that people started to feel the need of drinking good wine, local wine thanks to more informed consumers, to restaurants, and the wine guides that talk about producers."

3.2   The Barolo Boys

By breaking with tradition, this initial group of young, innovative wine producers, later called the Barolo Boys, began to establish a new network of winemakers who were open to novelty and experimentation. A loose-knit web of social ties arose in which members met together to discuss new techniques and organize tastings of each other's wines. Marc De Grazia, an early participant in the rise of modernism in this community as a wine broker and exporter, described the exchange of ideas:[1]

Before the 1984 vintage was released, Clerico and I organized a tasting meeting. We invited something like twenty winemakers... This was a memorable meeting... It was the very first time that producers started to talk to each other about their work; before that they did not necessarily like each other . . . We got along so well that a wine dealer, who owned a wine shop in California, coined the term "The Barolo Boys." And when we went to visit him there, he gave us T-shirts with our names on them. There is also a local [La Morra] soccer team called Barolo boys.

This group created a new platform for disseminating information about local wines, effectively raising the visibility of Barolo and Barbaresco. According to Claudio Conterno of the Conterno-Fantino winery, who participated in these events:

This big group of twenty to thirty producers changed the history of this region in the sense that they made people talk again about Barolo and, most important, they made people open bottles of Barolo again.

The networks of communication among winemakers in this group helped create new shared conceptual understandings of quality winemaking in this region. In other words, this informal network also aided the construction of *collective concepts* for modern Barolo and Barbaresco. As we will argue in chapter 11, the creation of collective concepts is an important stage in the development of a social movement's identity, as in the case of the modernist movement in Barolo and Barbaresco.

Altare stressed the importance of such consensus:

We are together also to give a unified message. Because if you come to me, I'll tell you my philosophy, and if you go to my neighbor and the philosophy changes, you will be confused.

In contrast, we find that institutional sources (especially academic ones) had less influence on this movement than the informal gatherings did. For example, in the town of Alba, an enological school has been training enologists and winemakers since its foundation in 1881. The connection between that school and winemaking in the Langhe was long-established; for example, the founder of the Cooperativa Produttori del Barbaresco, Domizio Cavazza, was the headmaster of the school in 1894. But few of the producers developing the new genre attended that institute or claimed to have developed their ideas through formal training in school.

We can get a better sense of the modernist movement by considering what we learned from three of the most prominent Barolo "Boys" (one was a "girl"). Recall that we characterized Domenico Clerico earliler as a key activist in the formation of the modernist movement. Like Altare, he took

Figure 3.5 Domenico Clerico. *Source:* maccaninodrink.com.

over a family farm (in 1976) that had engaged in mixed agriculture and grew grapes. Clerico decided to move the estate fully to wine production. He described to us his experience in learning by doing with feedback from peers:

> We did a lot of experiments... We made mistakes in choosing the containers to age the wine. We spent a lot of money on barriques, but at that time maybe we were not good at using them. We chose to use barriques to give new wood to the wine, going against the concept of typicity [*tipicità*], which has no meaning for me. I don't care if a wine is typical if it's full of defects... I use only barriques, and I have never used big barrels.

Clerico continued to innovate. In 2005 he showed us that he was trying even smaller barrels, which he called cigarillos, with a capacity of 130 liters. He also managed to purchase a series of very-high-quality vineyards over the years. And he produced cru wines from each.

Chiara Boschis, the female member of the "Barolo Boys," came from the family that owned the historic Borgogno winery in the center of the town

Figure 3.6 Chiara Boschis. *Source:* blinkingcity.com.

of Barolo. After Boschis graduated with a degree in business and economics at Torino, she took a job in management consulting. Then, when the owner of the E. Pira winery died with no heirs in 1981, Boschis convinced her parents to buy the winery, now called E. Pira—Chiara Boschis. Members of her family managed the winery for several years before Boschis took over, the first female winemaker in the region. She had been strongly influenced by Giorgio Rivetti of La Spinetta in the modernist approach[2] and followed that path. Like the others in the movement, Boschis told us of the importance of the collective effort.

> Together with other winemakers, we started to do brainstorming... we realized that our wine had a great potential, but we were unknown, and the wine was still too rustic... we realized right away that we had to become better farmers, better winemakers. So we invested a lot, we started to reduce the crop in the vineyard, to have better concentration, more expression of the wine, to invest a lot in the cellar. Even if we didn't have any money, we got rid of the old stuff, all the barrels that were really never changed because the people didn't have the money.

As the only female winemaker in the region at that point, Boschis might have confronted even more obstacles:

> Being a woman I had to work even harder because I didn't want people to say, "Oh, she's a girl, she takes short cuts, everybody is kind to her." No,

I really wanted my wines to stand out in blind tastings . . . I had to work even harder to be taken seriously . . . and the most important thing for me was first to develop a reputation among the other winemakers.

She succeeded: her first wine, the 1991 Barolo Riserva Cannubi, won the coveted *tre biccheri* rating from *Gambero Rosso* and she became a star winemaker and a member of the "Boys."

The late Roberto Voerzio of Cantine Roberto Voerzio, more than any other of the modernists, did extensive experimentation in the vineyard. He led the way in dense planting of the vines to encourage competition of the roots as a way to keep yields low and concentration high.[3] He varied the way in which the vines were trained. And most famously, he radically reduced fruit clusters with an extensive green harvest (eliminating bunches during the growing season). When we walked one of his vineyards with him, he reported that he had learned that the optimal grape production for Nebbiolo was a total weight of one kilo (about 2.2 lbs) per plant, indeed a very low yield.

In the cellar, Voerzio's practices were more similar to the other modernists. As he described:

Until 1995, I used botti of 15 to 25 hl together with barriques. From 1986 to 1996 I changed among five different ways of aging. But nobody noticed it. For instance, in 1995 I made the Barolo Capalot with thirty

Figure 3.7 Roberto Voerzio. *Source:* thedrinksbusiness.com.

Figure 3.8 Giorgio Rivetti in the barrique-filled cellar at La Sinetta. *Source:* skurnik.com.

months in wood, fifteen months in new barriques and the rest in botti of
15 hl. When the botti were new, I used new botti and old barriques. When
the botti became older, I did the opposite. The barrique and no-barrique
distinction always made me laugh.

Even if the distinction made Voerzio laugh, it became the core of the new
cultural distinction between modernism and traditionalism in the Langhe.
And the exact details about the mix of barrels did not seem to matter for
interested outsiders—as long as it contained barriques. Of the Barolo Boys,
Boschis, Clerico, and Giorgio Rivetti of La Spinetta used only barriques.
Altare, Enrico Scavino, and Voerzio used barriques for the first period of aging (usually a year) and then decanted the wine to botti for the remainder.
And Luciano Sandrone used only *tonneaux*, small barrels with a capacity of
500 liters, roughly double that of a barrique. Nonetheless, all were categorized as modernists. What mattered was *any use* of small barrels for aging.

3.3   The Market Reacts to the Modern Genre

The modernist interpretation of Barolo and Barbaresco rejected the long-
established practices of winemaking in the region on multiple grounds. Some
of these reasons were technical. Modern producers aiming to improve the
quality of the grapes grown in the vineyard as well as the wine made in the

cellar. According to the modernists, this strategy was in part driven by necessity. Domenico Clerico recalled to us in 2005 that, until the mid-1980s, Barolo was not appreciated and many producers could not make enough money to support their business: "Drinking was not a pleasure. People drank wine just to get some strength or because there wasn't anything else to drink."

The modernists realized that they were challenging traditional practices in the region. But they were motivated to make a product that consumers would like. In Elio Altare's view:

> You don't drink culture, and you don't drink tradition. It's easy—if you don't like it, don't drink it. It must give you pleasure. If I find a taste that is good for this moment, I have to follow it. I can be nostalgic for the horse or the cart; but now it's better to buy a car for transportation.

Our informants also suggested that producers believed that a new, modern genre could also help elevate the market position of all Barolo and Barbaresco wines. During a discussion in 2017 Chiara Boschis recalled:

> We were comparing our wine to the great French wines—so charming, so clean—and we understood that our wine was really unsophisticated a little bit dirty, with animal sensation... Some people thought this was typical, but it's not. We wanted to add finesse to our wine so we realized we had to change.

Many also hoped that these efforts would bring success to their wineries and to the region. According to Boschis:

> We also wanted to be really successful. We couldn't stand that when traveling the world... you could only find French wines. Barolo was *never* there. We had to change that. So, it was a sort of pride; we wanted to be famous and put Barolo on the map.

Silvia Altare (Elio's daughter), who has been involved in operating her father's winery since 2000, described her father's motivation in similar terms. She told us:

> My father does not work for money but for glory. I think he cares more about a page on a newspaper, but he doesn't like to do shipping, payments, and so on. I look after the orders, I do all this stuff. When he sees that his group is successful, and the tourists come here... he's happy.

Responses of the Critics

The critics responded very favorably to the new genre of Barolo/Barbaresco. In head-to-head competitions, critics repeatedly preferred these new-genre wines over the old-genre ones. These preference might have arisen due to the nature of the tastings, with many wines tasted in a brief period. One wine journalist explained that, when fifty or more wines are tasted in a day, those with soft tannins and a fruit-forward taste stand out as more pleasurable than than austere wines.

Gianni Fabrizio, chief editor of the *Gambero Rosso* guide, discussed the importance of barriques in shaping the wine to the taste of the critics:

> According to the modernists, the biggest problems of Barolo were the lack of color and the presence of too strong tannins. These characteristics were perceived similarly by critics. They thought that the public wouldn't love this [the old] kind of wines.

The new wines were not only different in taste. At a more symbolic level, the innovation involved created a sense of genuine novelty in the wine world. In the words of Aldo Vacca, director of the Produttori del Barbaresco cooperative, "This is the land of tradition. If you change genre [*stile* in the Italian original] in Australia nobody cares. The grape here is unique and change is a big deal."

Some influential critics wrote scathing reviews of what many regarded as iconic traditional Barolos. Perhaps the most notorious is a review by the highly influential American wine critic, James Suckling, of a wine by the leader of the traditionalist camp, Bartolo Mascarello. Suckling wrote of Mascarello's 2001 Barolo in *Wine Spectator* that the wine was "Very funky. Smells like a warm room with two wet dogs in it... Drink now." Besides ridiculing the wine, the review is notable for recommending that the wine that Mascarello intended for long aging be drunk immediately upon release. Suckling gave Mascarello a score of 84 out of 100 points. At first look this number does not appear especially negative. However, critics rarely use the full range of available points. In the data that we collected for statistical analysis from the *Wine Spectator*, a score of 84 lies below the 15th percentile of the observed distribution. It is indeed a very low score.

Given that most consumers lack detailed knowledge about the methods used to produce the wines that they might consider for purchase and given the very large number of alternatives, critics' reviews unsurprisingly have a disproportionately large influence on market outcomes. In short, critical praise translates into success with audiences in the wine industry.

One of our data sources, *Vini di Veronelli* (1991–2019), provides detailed information about the aging method used by each winery for all wines. In this way we were able to identify Barolo and Barbaresco wines made using exclusively the traditional large botti versus wines made using barriques. We compared the average scores for wines aged only in botti and wines aged at least partly in barriques as assigned by *Vini di Veronelli* and two other guides. These are *Vini d'Italia* (*Gambero Rosso* Slow Food Editore, 1987–2012) and *Wine Spectator* (Wine Spectator 1984–2018). The three publications use different scales to award their ratings. *Vini di Veronelli* (VV) uses stars (*stelle*) from one (good) to four (extraordinary), *Gambero Rosso* (GR) uses glasses (*biccheri*) ranging from 0 to 3, and *Wine Spectator* (WS) uses a 100-point scale. Table 3.1 gives the results for the vintages from 1982, the year of Altare's chainsaw massacre, through the 1990s. It shows that wines made in the modern genre (with at least some barriques) obtained consistently higher scores, on average, about one-standard deviation above the wines made with only botti.

Market intermediaries appear to have the most influence when consumers agree less and rankings are in flux. Corsi and Ashenfelter (2001) point out that expert opinion has strong effects on prices while wines age and consumers have not yet had direct experience of actual quality (see also (Hadj Ali et al. 2008)). An editor of the *Gambero Rosso* wine guide discussed the consequences of assignment of the guide's highest rating, *tre biccheri* (three glasses):

> After they receive the *tre biccheri*, some producers raise their prices a lot ... When the list is official, former friends who didn't win are not friends anymore. This gives me a great responsibility because I know that my evaluations will affect these producers and their businesses.

We examined the correlation of critical ratings and prices, specifically the release retail prices[4] provided by WS. We find that ratings and prices show a positive and significant correlation of 0.48 during the period 1982–1999. Second, wines with higher ratings receive substantially higher prices. On average, a wine that receives one star from VV sold for $39, and a wine with four stars sold for more than double, at $94. The difference for glasses used by GR is also significant, changing from $42 for the lowest score to $86 for the highest. The difference in winemaking genres we have described was also converted into substantial differences in market responses.

Table 3.1 Average scores of wines by genre in major wine guides

	VV Stars		GR Glasses		WS Score	
Vintage	Botti Only	Some Barriques	Botti Only	Some Barriques	Botti Only	Some Barriques
1982	2.1	2.1	1.8	2.5	88	88
1983	2.2	2.0	1.6	2.3	87	92
1984	n.a.	n.a.	1.7	2.3	82	82
1985	1.9	2.2	1.7	2.1	86	92
1986	1.8	2.7	1.6	2.2	87	91
1987	2.1	2.3	1.4	1.7	82	88
1988	1.8	2.1	1.6	2.0	85	88
1989	1.8	2.1	1.8	2.1	85	92
1990	1.9	2.3	1.8	2.1	86	90
1991	2.0	2.3	1.5	2.0	82	84
1992	2.4	2.6	1.4	1.7	82	85
1993	1.9	2.2	1.7	2.1	84	87
1994	2.2	2.3	1.4	1.7	82	84
1995	1.9	2.2	1.6	1.8	86	89
1996	1.9	2.3	2.0	2.1	89	90
1997	2.1	2.3	1.9	2.1	89	92
1998	2.2	2.5	2.1	2.3	89	91
1999	2.4	2.7	2.4	2.6	89	90

3.4 Traditionalism Awakens

The modernist insurgency embodied strong critiques of traditional practice, as we saw in quotes from Gaja and Altare. Many others, both winemakers and critics, claimed that old-genre Barolo/Barbaresco was bad wine—too tannic, unbalanced, and oxidized, and containing off-putting aromas. Gigi Piumatti (at the time of the interview another chief editor of the *Gambero Rosso* guide), told us over lunch:

> Producers started using barriques because of the bad smell that the large wood casks can produce. Often these casks were left uncleaned. Barolo was considered good only if it smelled like *merdino* (manure).

His colleague Gianni Fabrizio added:

> This was the typicality that was not good ... It was the bad smell that you could find in 95 percent of Barolo. The most important innovation ... was the use of barriques as a solution to get rid of this bad smell ... but unfortunately these barrels give a lot of wood flavor.

The modernist insurgency flourished with the support of critics and consumers. As the modernist genre took over, old winemaking traditions and knowledge might have lost their historical importance. One seemingly natural outcome of the market success of modernist wines would be that all producers of Barolo/Barbaresco would follow the new genre. The market response was another significant incentive to move away from tradition. However this did not happen.

In fact, the diffusion of the modern Barolo and Barbaresco, particularly the use of barriques for aging, eventually fueled a backlash. It caused some winemakers to recognize and defend an identity as traditionalist. While these vintners had long been using what we now call traditional practices, the producers did not refer to themselves with this label. Until the modernist insurgency gained ascendency, the traditionalists identified themselves as Barolisti (Barolo makers). What was new after the insurgency was their insistence that they were Barolisti tradizionali. And journalists agreed with them. In short, their market identity changed.

Traditionalists began to insist on a sharp genre distinction and to insist on the authenticity of their traditional interpretation of the wine. They argued publicly that the modern wines were no different from international wines and were very similar to Californian wines. They claimed that the new-genre wines were therefore atypical and inauthentic as Barolo or Barbaresco because they did not reflect the terroir and traditions of the region.

The discontent among those that held with old practices broke into the open in the second half of the 1990s. For instance, Turin's daily newspaper *La Stampa* (March 7, 1997, p. 73) reported

A bad mood meanders through the Langhe regarding the production methods of Barolo; and producers are by now split. The heart of the matter is a small 225-liter barrel that came from France about ten years ago, the mythical barrique that, with its young wood, transfers sweet perfumes and tannins.

During the course of 1996 the dispute between the two sides has come to the fore during the meetings organized by the Consorzio in the context of a revision of the Disciplinare. The dispute has become so fierce that the director of the Consorzio, Giancarlo Montaldo, has sent a letter to all producers in the area (dated February 21). The call to producers was clear:

"What is wrong and dangerous is to criticize the work done by colleagues because it is deemed too old-fashioned or, on the contrary, because it is excessively cast toward the future."

At about this time Teobaldo Cappellano, a staunch traditionalist, debated Carlo Petrini, the president of the Arcigola (the forerunner of the Slow Food Association), in the columns of a local weekly about the merits of the barrique for aging Barolo. In the same year Bartolo Mascarello wrote an open letter to the Barolo Consorzio criticizing "French-Californian models" and proposed that wineries be allowed to put *metodo classico* (classical method) on the labels of Barolo made using traditional techniques. Mascarello interpreted the adoption of small Bordeaux barrels as a challenge to face from inside the community. He issued the clarion call, "There is one and only one Barolo, defend it!" And he started adding the handwritten label on his Barolo: *"Il ne faut pas faire des barriques mais des barricades!"* (Make barricades, not barriques.)

In the next chapter, we examine in detail the dynamics of the collective response to the rise of modernism in the Langhe by traditionalist producers of Barolo and Barbaresco.

CHAPTER FOUR

Mobilization of Collective Market Identities

TODAY WE SEE A RENEWED interest in traditional, classic—but somehow forgotten—practices of making wine in many regions. Consider California's Ridge Vineyards, one of the country's preeminent wineries. Paul Draper, who ran the winery and directed its winemaking over four decades, claimed to be engaged in "preindustrial winemaking." The goal was to produce wines that are less ripe, have lower alcohol, and have more complexity and minerality than is typical for California wines. This new trend aspires to bring Californian wines closer to the techniques used in California in the nineteenth century as well as their original European roots. In another New World wine country, Chile, winemakers like Derek Mossman Knapp are developing a genre and a movement that focus on old vineyard sites and natural practices. Their approach emphasizes uniqueness rather than the "big" extraction and concentration for which Chilean wines are known.

As we see it, the movement to rediscover—or perhaps reinvent—the past for winemaking began in the Langhe. As we describe in this chapter, a dispute arose between two conceptions of how to make Barolo and Barbaresco during the 1980s and 1990s and continued in the next decade. One conception was termed a modern genre. As we detailed in the previous chapter, the followers of this genre gained critical and market success in Italy and especially in the international market.

This chapter tells the story of the oppositional response by some producers of Barolo/Barbaresco. This group of producers defined themselves in opposition to the modern genre and, in so doing, discovered a traditionalist market identity in the following sense. Their perception of a threat to the established way of making Barolo/Barbaresco activated a collective market identity that had been taken for granted. As the modern genre of making Barolo became prevalent, winemakers, critics, and consumers had to answer the question: what is the "real" Barolo? This is a question about a concept, about the meaning of a label.

The rise of the modern genre is an instance of what we call a *reinterpretation* of the concept of Barolo/Barbaresco. That dispute about the proposed reinterpretation became intense and had some long-term effects. Three decades later it has crystallized into two distinct market identities.

As we noted in previous chapters, the traditional and modern genres and associated market identities refer to a cluster of practices (type of barrel, length of maceration, degree of control over fermentation, type of yeast, dense planting, green harvest, and so forth) that evolved as two genres. Even if some producers do not explicitly acknowledge significant distinctions between the genres, acts such as Altare's destruction of his father's botti surely focused attention on the choice of barrel as central to the difference between the genres. As we explained in the previous chapter, the choice of barrel/cask persists during the period in which the wine ages for three to five years in the cellar. Therefore, this choice can be easily observed by the frequent visits to the winery and its cellar. Other aspects of production techniques can be observed only during brief periods in the processes of growing and vinification. Perhaps this explains why they became less central in the concept formation we are discussing.

The evidence we collected suggests that the barrique/botti distinction became a test for assessing market identity, somewhat like the reaction of the audience to Bob Dylan's decision to use an electric instead of an acoustic guitar. One of our informants, the prominent traditionalist producer Mauro Mascarello from Monchiero, made the point succinctly: "The difference between modern and traditional is actually in the cellar processes."

Knowing only that a producer used the French barrels led producers, buyers, and critics to assume by default that they also use most, if not all, of the modernist practices of vinification. The nature of this test is specific to winemaking in the Langhe, but the use of minimal tests to assign membership in a genre is not (Hannan et al. 2007). For instance, sociologist Diana Crane (1987) noted that in visual arts incorporating an attribute that signals a genre—for instance, gestural brushstrokes and spontaneity in abstract expressionism—increases the categorization probability of an artist in that genre.

During the 1980s and 1990s, producers, critics, and consumers interpreted the use of barriques as a practice that determines market identity in the Langhe. From interviews with wine merchants and sommeliers in Alba and Milan, we learned that these key market intermediaries perceived cultural fault-lines that coincide with the traditionalist/modernist divide and that they rely on the use of the barrique for categorization. For instance, the wine carte of the elite restaurant Aimo e Nadia in Milan listed on separate pages the Langhe wines aged in botti grandi and those aged in barriques. The restaurant's sommelier told us that the listings are based on production methods and "if there are intermediate situations, we put producers in one of the two categories according to our judgment." Another sommelier remarked, "The difference is between those that make wine exclusively in large barrels, the traditionalist producers, and those that employ small barrels, who are more innovative."

Traditionalists resisted the siren song of the market and emphasized their loyalty to their old market identity. Why? We examine this question next.

Two interrelated premises motivated the modernist revolution: first were the widely held beliefs that the wine industry in this region required technical/sanitation improvements and second was the assumption that Barolo and Barbaresco would gain from establishing a new market identity. Defenders of the region's winemaking traditions organized their critical response to modernism along these lines. Some producers, whom we call arch-traditionalists, made primarily *moral* objections to the market orientation of the protagonists of the modernist genre. Those we call the pragmatic traditionalists focused their response on the practical, technical questions about the strategic value of moving closer to French and American practices but did not embrace the ideological antimarket sentiment.

4.1 Bastions of Tradition

The proponents of the arch-traditionalist (who some of our informants called fundamentalists) took a clearcut position: there is tradition and everything else. For them, the modern and traditional genres stand in stark opposition. Many told us that Bartolo Mascarello, Giuseppe Rinaldi, and Teobaldo Cappellano are prototypes of this traditionalist position.

Maria Teresa Mascarello, who succeeded her father Bartolo in running the family winery, connected the change in winemaking practices to the demands of the international market: "The trend in the use of barriques has been encouraged by a model of globalization. The U.S. market, for example, demands a standardized and homogenized taste. The barrique helps with that."

Maria Teresa is a fourth-generation winemaker. In the early 1900s her great-grandfather, Bartolomeo, ran the cellar of the Cantina Sociale di Barolo, the local cooperative. Bartolomeo trained his son, Giulio, who made

Figure 4.1 Bartolo and Maria Teresa Mascarello. *Source:* italianwinemerchants.com.

the strategic decision in 1919 to start his own wine production from the grapes purchased from a few local winegrowers. Giulio bottled part of this production and sold the rest in bulk in demijohns (bottles with 54 liter capacity - about 11.3 gallons). In 1930 he bought his first parcels of land in various locations, including the core portion of Cannubi, a vineyard just north of the town of Barolo famed for its quality. Having land in multiple locations, Giulio blended Nebbiolo grapes from multiple vineyards for his Barolo. He became one of the very first producers to grow and bottle Barolo. Bartolo joined the family winery in 1945, and in the 1960s he decided that they should bottle their entire production. He continued with the practice of blending from multiple plots. Bartolo believed that combining grapes from different areas improved aroma, complexity, and balance of the wine. He openly rejected the idea of single vineyard cru promoted in the context of the modern genre of Barolo, which did not belong to the tradition of winemaking in the Langhe. He was quoted as saying that the Italian language did not even have a word for *cru*.

In the 1980s and 1990s Bartolo became a staunch defender of what he called *Barolo classico*. In his later years, and before Maria Teresa took over in 2005, Bartolo began hand-painting his wine labels. A famous one, reproduced in the first chapter, featured a headshot of the media tycoon and Italian prime minister Silvio Berlusconi wearing a bandanna under a flap with a ladybug (Bartolo's symbol). The manifesto "No barrique, No Berlusconi" was emblazoned on the front label. In this way Mascarello challenged both the philosophy of modern Barolo and that of modern Italian politics, both of which he viewed as motivated by profit.[1]

Giuseppe (Beppe) Rinaldi was another leader of the traditionalist counterrevolution. Rinaldi, who passed away in 2018, also represented a long family

Figure 4.2 Giuseppe Rinaldi. *Source:* Photograph by Donatella Arione.

history of four generations of Barolo making. After training as a veterinarian, Beppe took over his father Battista's winery in 1992. He farmed his land organically. His practices in the cellar were decidedly old-fashioned. He fermented with the indigenous yeasts for roughly a month in ancient upright oak vats with no temperature control. He performed the punch-down process[2] by hand and aged his wines in botti grandi. Like his cousin Maria Teresa Mascarello, he followed the tradition of blending Barolo from different sites as a way to obtain a balanced wine. Rinaldi believed in the traditional genre of winemaking. As he explained to us, he did not try to make an "easy" wine.

Food writer Edward Behr, who interviewed Rinaldi for the magazine *The Art of Eating* in 2001, quoted him as saying that he wanted his Barolo to be a wine that demands research.

> It takes time. You have to study, to think, to understand, like all of art. It isn't simple but complex; it doesn't please right away. It's the opposite of a mass-produced product. It has angles, not curves. (Behr 2001, p. 20).

Rinaldi stressed to us in conversations in his cellar and over lunches and dinner (with Mascarello) that the violation of historical practices of winemaking, if unchecked, would result in a loss of identity for the wines, and for the region:

> The value of Barolo is in its difference ... They [the modernists] made it into a typical mass product instead of distinguishing it from the others.

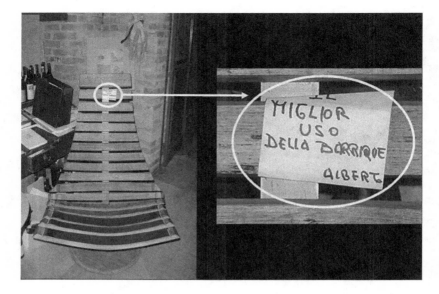

Figure 4.3 Giuseppe Rinaldi's chair made from a barrique. The sign says (in translation): "the best use of barriques." *Source:* Photograph by Giacomo Negro.

A land like ours, with a history, a tradition, and an old identity, erased everything it had to be more attractive on the market.

Rinaldi's disdain for barriques could be seen in the photo of a chair in his cellar made from the staves of a barrique (figure 4.3). The barrels in Rinaldi's cellar used to age Barolo were instead botti grandi (figure 4.4).

Maria Teresa gave us an account of identity that strongly parallels that of her cousin Beppe: "Winemaking for me is not improvisation. It is the work that my father had transferred to me, so it is part of my identity. I don't want to erase my roots, my history."

Some in the arch-traditionalist group perceived that their adherence to old-school winemaking invoked scorn from others. For instance, the late Teobaldo (Baldo) Cappellano (then proprietor of Dott. G. Cappellano–Fondata nel 1879) remarked, "It is incredible. Today people are really sure that it is impossible *not* to use the prototype of the multinationals." And Rinaldi told us:

The battle is still unbalanced because out of 250 to 300 labels the traditionalists are maybe fifteen. The press is attracted to the modern wines, and we have been attacked systematically.

Figure 4.4 Botti grandi in the cellar of Giuseppe Rinaldi. *Source:* Photograph by Donatella Arione.

Yet the data we collected indicate that the number of traditionalist wineries was not as small as he recalled. About half of the wineries in the data that we analyzed were and remained traditionalists. This assessment that the traditionalists were a tiny minority adds credibility to our claim that the traditionalists and arch-traditionalists saw themselves as a beleaguered group.

In Cappellano's view, wine that tastes of wood (from aging in barriques) is not a good wine: "I've never heard somebody say that a good wine tastes like wood." Most likely he did not mean that all wines made using barriques taste of wood. However many—the traditionalist producers but also wine experts and consumers—found that Barolo and Barbaresco made in the modernist genre had oaky flavors. Marco Boschiazzo of Bovio,[3] a modernist turned traditionalist, told us:

> Around the early nineties, when we started using barriques, we used them in a very wrong way, doing some terrible things, in my opinion. We made some wines that were too oaky—much, much more oaky than the Californian wines of that time.

The arch-traditionalist producers shared the view that the success of the modernists posed a threat to their collective identity. In situations like these, the group whose identity feels challenged and disparaged can sometimes transform these negative feelings by using them as motivation to organize collectively. In this way, an attack on one is viewed as an attack on all.

Figure 4.5 Teobaldo Cappellano. *Source:* Photograph by Giacomo Negro.

Cappellano told us in 2006 of a group that he joined with other traditional producers in the Langhe, including Giuseppe Rinaldi and Teobaldo Rivella of Barbaresco: ViniVeri (Real Wines). This group did not focus specifically on opposing the modern genre in Barolo and Barbaresco, but it works toward related goals of promoting natural wines and brings together like-minded old-school producers.

As Cappellano described it, ViniVeri shares some of the values described by the arch-traditionalist position, particularly their antiprofit orientation. He posted a manifesto on the group's website (www.viniveri.net/ta/en/consortium/manifesto/) on August 23, 2012, which reads in part:

> In a world where everything has a label, ViniVeri has chosen to remain loose in its definition. Even the group's motto, Vino Secondo Natura (Wine By Nature), leaves one questioning. To some this is a useful tool; to others it sends a negative message.
>
> For this reason, I will try, if possible, to explain the philosophy of this group of anarchical naturalists.
>
> In 2004, a group of four small organic winemakers—who had already been working this way for years—found itself tired of participating in wine fairs where the . . . packaging became more important than content.

Even before our first official meetings, we realized that we were all doing the same things in the vineyard, that our wines all expressed the same care and dedication and that we treated our clients with the same respect and warmth. We became fast friends. We all have the same sensibility and approach to the land. We all believe that our value is based on what was given to us by the earth and what we are able to give back to it in return. It came as a pleasant surprise that all of us felt so foreign when compared to the rest of the market.

So here is what we are (not). We are not organic, even if the rules of our consortium are even more restrictive in terms of both the vineyard and the cellar than those pertaining to organic certification. We are not biodynamic, even if many of us follow Steiner's philosophy. We are not any of these things because we know that, unfortunately, rules often become trends and rules are made to be broken.

It is easy to take advantage of the naiveté of others. We realized this when we were told that if we made certain compromises and used industrially produced chemicals, we would get "quick" results and would not impoverish the land or our own minds. We were no longer learning from nature and growing more knowledgeable because, at some point, we were offered a perfect little package with simple instructions for how to grow grapes. We decided to revolt and to return to making wine as it had been made in the past. We pledged to not simply accept what we hear, but to question and study what is around us. This is ViniVeri.

Cappellano told us that the group had decided to remain small: "We need to be an ideological movement, radicalize. It is difficult to become larger and remain close to our ideas."

Like other consortia, ViniVeri provides joint marketing programs that build awareness of the members and their wine region, ultimately stimulating interest and demand; education and research programs that help members to produce the best quality product; and in some cases, legislative support to advance member rights. Despite the early decision to remain small, ViniVeri had grown in 2019 to include 152 wineries and eight growers.

4.2   Pragmatic Traditionalists

Not all the traditionalist producers that we interviewed shared the clear-cut, ideological positions of the arch-traditionalists. Some continue to use the traditional winemaking practices for practical and technical reasons more

Figure 4.6 Roberto Conterno of Cantine Giacomo Conterno. *Source:* Photograph by Giacomo Negro.

than for ideological ones. Roberto Conterno, who runs Cantine Giacomo Conterno, proudly showed us the large casks in the cellar in which he ages his wines, including the iconic Barolo Monfortino, and told us:

> Our botti are more than fifty years old and we are thinking of replacing them because they have already been put through a lot of use ... It is almost against my will because they have become a part of my life. Our forefathers knew what they were doing and we are only improving what they were already doing well ... We follow tradition in this winery, but being traditional doesn't mean that we have to be close-minded because sometimes that term gets misinterpreted. We conduct studies to improve on what our forefathers had already figured out through experience. Maybe they didn't know why a certain technique worked, and we study the technique and confirm its validity scientifically.

We also discussed these issues with Roberto's cousin Giacomo Conterno of Poderi Aldo Conterno. Their respective fathers—Giovanni and Aldo— were sons of famed wine producer Giacomo Conterno, who began bottling his own Barolo as early as 1920. Aldo and Giovanni worked together at their father's winery until 1969, when a disagreement about genre[4] led them to split the business in two. Giovanni continued with the original winery under its original name (Cantine Giacomo Conterno). Aldo founded a new winery, Poderi Aldo Conterno, now run by his three sons: Franco, Stefano, and Giacomo. Giacomo (the son) described his interpretation of tradition to us:

> The reason we don't use barriques for Barolo is simple... the taste of the wood, especially chocolate and vanilla flavors, is invasive... A small barrel has more contact with the wine, and the impact of oxygen is strong. Nebbiolo makes a wine rich in tannins... but I don't need to make it stronger. I need to balance the wine and I prefer the smooth tannins of the big barrel.

He connected the technical impact of the method of aging barrel to obtaining a product that is typical of the locality but cannot be reproduced elsewhere:

> There are a lot of good wines. You can even buy a good bottle for three euros because the techniques in the cellar help you do what you want, but most of these wines are what I call Coca-Cola wines. If you buy Coca-Cola in Atlanta is not going to be any better than the Coca-Cola you can buy in any other place in the world. These wines taste good everywhere and they don't taste like the soil they have been made in. You don't know if they come from France, Spain... They are just huge, pinky, tasty, big, chocolate, and vanilla wines.

The protagonists at traditionalist wineries like Cantine Giacomo Conterno and Poderi Aldo Conterno have views about winemaking genres that center on the product. Their choice to maintain traditional winemaking comes partly from consideration of the technical qualities of the wines and partly from valuing the wine region's uniqueness. Aldo Vacca from Produttori del Barbaresco also made such a pragmatic argument:

> The modern genre [*stile* in the Italian original] is a way to make good wine but not necessarily better than the old one. Moreover, the modern approach will produce wine more and more similar to the wine from other parts of the world. Because the more oak you have in the wine, the more the oak is going to cover the natural flavor of the grapes. Then you make a wine similar to wine made in California or Australia. You would lose your power: uniqueness.

The pragmatic view differs from the arch-traditionalist one, as we saw in a discussion with Giacomo Conterno. In his view:

> There is a distinction between being traditional and being radical like a Taliban. Some do this job just because they were told so, and they get angry when other people say: "Let's try something different and create an opportunity." I don't use a large, fifty-year-old cask just because my father used it. The most important factor in the cellar is how the oxygen helps the wine to develop in the casks. I change most casks every ten years. If a traditional producer says that you have to use very old casks because they do not want to spend money on new equipment . . . it's their problem, not mine.

He concluded the discussion by saying that winemakers just make wine: "We're not worshipping a religion. We worked years for this wine. But we are not a church. We're just trying to enjoy something."

Alex Sanchez, who works alongside his spouse and her sister to run the Brovia winery, argues that consistency in methods is essential for developing a clear market identity:

> To believe in you, the client needs history, quality, and needs to see you, your winery, as someone reliable . . . I don't consider a winemaker an artist, but there is a similar sensibility in the way we look at our work . . . You can change approach once or twice, but if you are just looking to follow a trend, you are not looking to attract people who believe in you; you are looking to attract the people who follow that trend, which is different. You cannot build strong relationships in the market that way.

Some traditionalists simply wanted to follow tradition and did not offer either ideological or pragmatic justification. They took for granted that what had been done in the past was what they should follow. For instance, Elio Grasso had always used large casks to age his Barolo.[5] When we asked him what were the advantages of making Barolo in botti grandi, he gave an interesting answer: "I don't know the advantages! My philosophy is to continue the work of my father, and my father always used big barrels for Barolo." These traditionalist producers did not question the legitimacy of existing practices. They hew to tradition because it seems the right thing to do, and they do not seem to engage in a calculation of the outcomes or advantages that maintaining a traditional approach can bring.

4.3 Defections and Stabilization

Now we examine shifts in market identity from traditional to modern. As we have discussed above, we assume that choice of methods of aging was a strong indication of market identity during the period we studied.

The number of traditionalist producers represents about half of the wineries that produced Barolo and Barbaresco within the period of interest. We base this estimate on records of the types of barrels used for the set of wineries that were ever reviewed in the Veronelli guide.[6] These annual publications provide information about the barrels used to age each wine in each vintage. The crucial information comes from indications for each wine listed, whether it was aged in (1) botti only, (2) barrique only, or (3) a combination of the two. The coverage of much older vintages is less systematic, so we consider vintages starting with 1982. We coded information from the editions of *Catalogo Veronelli dei Vini d'Italia* (1988–1990) and *I Vini di Veronelli* (1991–2019), which together cover the vintages of 1982–2014).

Roughly half of the wineries in the data used barriques and (by our assumption) therefore made wines in the modern genre at some point in their existence. Of these, two-thirds started out in the modern genre, and a third switched from tradition and started using barriques at a later time. These numbers represent about one-third and 17 percent of the total number of wineries, respectively. The remaining wineries started out by using traditional botti and continued to do so. These numbers imply that between 25 and 30 percent of the wineries working in the traditional genre switched to the modern camp.

Figure 4.7 shows, for each year in the data, the number of wineries that used only botti in one vintage and adopted barrique in the subsequent one. The number of such genre switchers increased from the early 1980s, and the rise continued throughout the next decade. This is the time when contention between modernism and traditionalism peaked.

We also see a similar pattern for initial genre choices by new wineries. For vintages before 1990, only 25 percent of the Barolo/Barbaresco producers reviewed for the first time used barriques. During the years 1990–2001, 40 percent of the wineries entering the guide used them. The data indicate that the modernist category continued to gain ground and attention during much of the 1990s as the critics raved about the new-genre wines.

Isabella Boffo of historical producer Poderi e Cantine Oddero recalled about that period:

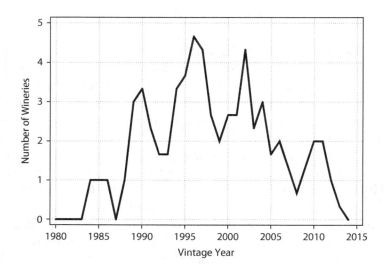

Figure 4.7 Number of wineries that changed to using barriques in the Langhe by vintage year.

In the 1980s and 1990s, it was hard to sell a light-color Barolo with strong tannins. People were looking for soft tannins, big concentrated wines, darker color, and more fruity aromatics. But we didn't change our wine-making and aging. We have always been traditional. We suffered for some years when we had fewer requests, mainly from export markets.

The number of producers changing for the first time to the modern genre began to decrease in the 2000s (figure 4.7). We described above how the traditionalists reacted to what they viewed as a threat to their market identity and started to defend their approach actively and what it symbolized. We think the mobilization of the traditionalists helped to inhibit further erosion of their category.

We can get another vantage on these issues by examining change over time in critical reactions to the two genres. To do so we coded the ratings assigned to Barolo and Barbaresco wines reviewed by our three sources: *Gambero Rosso* (GR), *Wine Spectator* (WS), and *Vini de Veronelli* (VV). Before getting to the results, we need to provide some information about these data. These publications use different scales to award their ratings, 1–4 *stelle* (stars) for VV, 1–4 *biccheri* (glasses) for GR, and a 100-point scale for WS. We give the distributions of the ratings for these publications in figure 4.8.[7] GR and WS rate using blind tastings, and they do not know the identity of the producer.

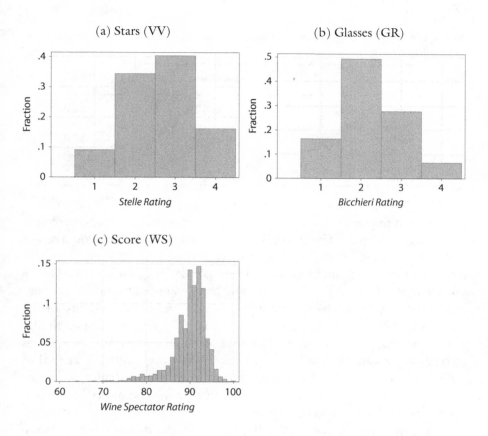

Figure 4.8 Distribution of ratings for three guides.

Instead, the VV editor told us that they conduct tastings at the winery and that the star ratings they assign express a general evaluation of a wine's features, or, as the editor put it, "the wine's speed cruise."

Now we turn to examining whether changing from traditionalist to modernist affected average ratings. Table 4.1 summarizes information about ratings of producers of Barolo and Barbaresco reviewed by these sources for the vintages 1982–2000, the period of the Barolo Wars. We distinguish average ratings for producers that changed from from traditionalist to modernist before and after the change. We compare these ratings to those of producers that had always been traditionalist and those that were always modernist. We see two main patterns. First, the critics awarded higher ratings to modernist producers, whether or not they tasted blind. Second, the producers that changed to the modern genre received higher ratings after they changed,

Table 4.1   Average scores for subsets of producers in major wine guides for vintage years 1982–2000

	GR Glasses	VV Stars	WS Score
Always traditionalist	1.75	1.86	86.0
Traditionalists that changed genre			
Before the change	1.66	1.89	85.0
After the change	2.00	2.14	87.6
Always modernist	2.23	2.53	90.3

even though their ratings remained slightly lower than those that entered the market as modernist.[8] Thus reactions to genres by GR and WS would reflect only differences in capabilities between producers. The VV ratings can also entail reactions to identities associated with genres. The numbers in table 4.1 suggest that, while it is possible that using barriques might produce "better" wines, the higher ratings can be partly due to the market identity of the genre, and it becomes somewhat self-fulfilling if the tastings are not blind.

Change brought some benefits for traditional producers, at least in terms of receiving greater accolades from critics. From our fieldwork as well as studies of the influence of critics in markets with intermediaries, we know that positive critical ratings generally also improve the commercial success of wines among retailers and consumers.

Clearly the market was responding positively to modern wines. If the traditional producers were driven only or mostly by expected commercial benefits, then the traditional genre of Barolo/Barbaresco and its associated market identity might have slowly disappeared. Moreover, if defectors from tradition receive positive valuation from the audience, then the publicity associated with the changed valuation can set off motivational cascades and inspire others to breach.

We can get a sense of the strength of the temptation to move in the modernist direction from accounts of three winemakers from highly esteemed estates: Fabio Alessandria of Comm. G. B. Burlotto, Valter Fissore at Elvio Cogno, and Franco Massolino of Vigna Rionda Massolino. All three told us that, as young winemakers in well-established traditional wineries, they were excited to experiment with barriques during the mid-1990s, the high point of the modernist surge.

Comm. G. B. Burlotto is one of the historical wineries of the region, founded in 1850 and already bottling Barolo by the late nineteenth century.

Fabio Alessandria is the fifth-generation winemaker. Today the winery makes only traditional wines. Indeed Alessandria and his crew crush the grapes for its flagship Barolo Monvigliero by foot. Nonetheless, he told us of his flirtation with the small barrels:

> When I finished my technical [enological] school in Alba in 1994, everybody spoke about barriques—journalists, winemakers, everybody. It was something new for the area, very attractive, also miraculous. I was young, and I decided to try. For a few years we aged our Barolo Cannubi in barriques... After a few years we found that this was not so miraculous for our wine... but [the experiment] was important for me—I was young.

Vigna Rionda Massolino was founded in 1896 by Giovanni Massolino. His son Giuseppe was one of the founders of the Consorzio. The family firm, currently run by brothers Franco and Roberto Massolino, today produces traditional Barolo. Yet Franco Massolino told us a story strikingly similar to Fabio Alessandria's:

> In 1990 we decided for our Barolo Parafada to experiment with aging in barriques to understand what happens if one of our Barolos is aged in a different way. It was an interesting experiment. We produced the Parafada with this kind of aging and then decided to go back to a traditional way because this is what we prefer.

The Elvio Cogno winery is much younger than Burlotto and Massolino, having been founded in 1991. However, Elvio Cogno, its founder, had co-run another winery (Marcarini) for many years. His son-in-law Valter Fissore, who now manages the estate, had worked for several years at Marcarini and learned traditional practice. And the winery today is regarded as highly traditional. As in the other cases, the young Valter Fissore also experimented with barriques for a small portion of his Barolo production:

> When I started with my father-in-law in 1991, I wanted to see what was happening with using the small barrels... The world—everyone—was talking about it, and I wanted to understand how it worked. I was 28 years old and this was my first vintage on my own.

It is easy for us to imagine that, absent the mobilization in defense of traditional Barolo as part of a proud local heritage, the dabbling with barriques would have turned into a more serious focus of these winemakers. Clearly they were excited to learn about the new possibilities. As young winemakers they also felt less constrained by the local tradition.

The counterrevolution turned the tide. The defenders of tradition argued publicly that those who defected from tradition were responsible for diluting the preexisting identity of Barolo and Barbaresco. These issues became contentious because producers in both genre camps use the same category name (Barolo and Barbaresco). Such a situation provided fertile ground for some producers—in our case the traditionalists—to attempt to reduce the ambiguity caused by the multiple genre interpretations. The reaction of traditionalist wineries developed on the premise that the modernist genre risked ignoring the uniqueness of Barolo and Barbaresco relative to other wines and the long history of winemaking in the Langhe, of which they and their families had been part. Traditionalism for them was an identity of which to be proud, not ashamed.

Studies of contemporary markets reveal that consumers increasingly value consistency and reliability. Moreover, they value loyalty to a philosophy and authenticity that is supposed to reflect the place where a product originates (Appadurai 1986; Verhaal and Carroll 2019). Protagonists' recasting the shift to modern winemaking in terms of authenticity raises the stakes. This framing makes the category boundary between modernism and tradition consequential for market identities beyond consideration of the technical details of production. Here the calculus of choice of category members changes from one of consequence to one based on identity and appropriateness: one chooses an option not because it will lead to good expected consequences but because this is what people with a certain identity are supposed to do (March 1994).

Some producers reacted to the multiplicity of genres by hedging their bets and producing one or more wines in each genre. Creating ambiguity might hedge bets, but it comes with a price, as we show in the next chapter. The prevalence of genre straddling decreased after the end of the 1990s. This change came up during our interviews and also in the data that we collected from the wine guides.

One way to look at this issue in greater detail is by measuring the relative prevalence of the tradition. To do so we use the data culled from the VV guide to show the average proportion of wines made using only botti, as shown in figure 4.9. The figure shows a slow and modest initial decline in the proportion of Barolos/Barbarescos made in the traditional way in the period before 2000 and a significant increase afterward.

The response of traditional wineries was strong in part because the rules of the *Denominazione di Origine Controllata e Garantita* (DOCG) for Barolo

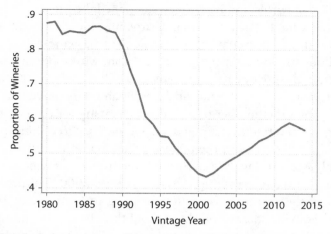

(a) Average proportion of botti-only Barolo and Barbaresco by vintage year.

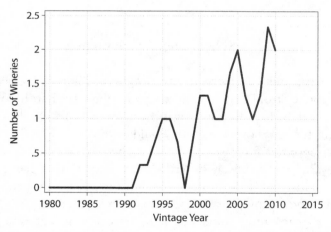

(b) Number of wineries that changed to using botti for Barolo and Barbaresco by vintage year.

Figure 4.9 Evidence of the resurgence of use of botti only for Barolo and Barbaresco.

allows both traditionalists and modernists to label their wines as Barolo with no qualification (the same is true for Barbaresco). Consumers would need to search for additional information to understand the genre in which a wine was made.

The genres have become more distinct in recent years (figure 4.9). We think this is because the response of the traditionalists in defense of their interpretation of Barolo and Barbaresco sharpened the genres' boundary and made it more salient. Their success in sharpening the distinctions likely discouraged producers from trying to straddle the two genres.

What about straddling in the other direction, with modernist producers changing from the use of barriques to the use of botti? Figure 4.9(a) displays change in the prevalence of traditional Barolo and Barbaresco wineries. Figure 4.9(b) shows the number of producers changing for the first time from the modern to the traditional practices. We notice three things. First, the pattern looks different from the pattern of adding barriques to a portfolio of botti-only wines in Figure 4.7. Second, the number of wineries changing camps is more limited, averaging zero or one until 2000. Third, we observe an increase in the number of wineries changing to botti grandi only in the last decade. Some modernist producers sold their barriques and reverted to the traditional ways, but only in recent years, when the tide seems to have turned, and the wine world began to attribute value to the traditional genre.

4.4   Subsequent Developments

When we began our interviews in the Langhe in 2005, most people with whom we spoke strongly downplayed the notion of a Barolo War. Many modernists told us that this notion was the invention of journalists and that, in any event, the sense of contention would dissipate.

In some sense this forecast was correct. The modernist view on practice in the vineyard won decisively in terms of the use of green harvest, denser planting, and low yields. Any differences were overtaken by a concern with sustainability and a growing swing toward organic practice.

Moreover, many modernists began to retreat from extreme practices. Some reduced reliance on new barriques, which impart oak tannin that can overwhelm the wine. Others who used only barriques have followed Gaja and Altare and now employ a mix of barriques and botti. Fewer producers now use rotofermenters. And the wines are now less dark. In these and other senses, the extreme modernist wing has moved toward the center.

An interesting example of the movement from modernism toward tradition involves Chiara Boschis. In the first years of this century, she began reducing her use of new barriques from 100 percent. When we visited her in 2017, she told us that she had learned that the optimal approach uses one-third new barrels, one-third one-year-old barrels, and one-third two-year-old barrels. What was striking to us was that she showed us botti grandi of

20 hectoliters that she purchased in 2010 because she wanted to make a wine that combined production from most of her vineyards (an "assemblage").

> [In] choosing to make our Barolo Via Nuova as an assemblage, so as a more classic way of doing the Barolo, I thought, "Okay, also another aspect important of the traditional winemaking was the use of the larger barrel. Let's use botti then."

Another prototypical modernist and member of the Barolo Boys, the late Domenico Clerico, went even further. According to his successor as wine-maker, Oscar Arrivabene, whom we met in 2017, by the time of assembling the 2014 vintage, Clerico had decided to change to a traditional genre. He had been retasting older wines by Bruno Giacosa and remembered how much he liked them. He ordered botti and adopted traditional practices.

The critics seem to have moderated their enthusiasm for modernism. For instance, the editors of the influential GR guide, which had championed the modernist movement, told us in 2005 that they had concluded that their tasting methods had unfairly penalized the traditional wines. In tastings that mixed (young) traditional and modern wines, the sweet fruity taste of the latter would stand out. These editors told us that they had begun to have separate tastings of the two kinds of wines. Moreover, perhaps in what many regarded as a mea culpa, they awarded the title of "best Italian wine" over the twenty years of publication to Aldo Conterno's traditionally made Barolo Granbussia 1989. This was notable because this guide had always given the highest scores to Gaja and Voerzio.

Using data on critics scores in our three data sources, we coded ratings for botti-only wines and wines that used at least some barriques. Figure 4.10 contains line graphs of the predicted average scores for each of these critics for the period from the 1980s to 2018, the last available year of these publications at the time of this writing. The graphs depict scores by vintage. The curves in the graphs are smoothed to make it easier to see the trend.[9] The figure shows two recurring patterns. First, for most of the 1980s and 1990s, modern wines received higher scores than wines in the traditional genre. Second, in the last decade the gap between the scores for modern versus traditional wines has closed, and in very recent years traditional wines seem to be gaining higher accolades. Remember that due to the Disciplinare restriction for the minimum period of aging, any given vintage is reviewed three or four years later.

The three sources differ in terms of what genre they seemed to prefer initially, with VV showing some slight preference for traditional wines in the

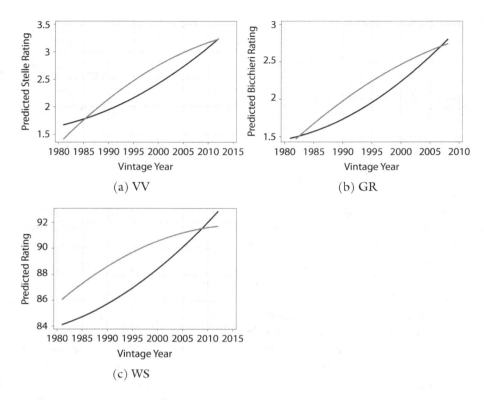

Figure 4.10 Predicted values of average ratings by three wine guides for botti-only wines (black line) versus wines with some barriques (gray line) by vintage year.

early 1980s, and WS awarding higher scores to modern wines instead. At the very beginning, GR does not show a significant preference for either genre. In any case, the pattern of higher scores for modern wines for a prolonged period and a comeback of traditional wines in recent years apply across all three critics. This is also interesting given that the methods of tasting and evaluating wines are different (with GR and WS using more systematically blind tastings while VV assigns their stars unblind).

We also conducted regression analyses of individual ratings and explored whether the penalty for wines made using botti changed over time. The regression models estimate the rating for each wine, holding constant the fixed characteristics of each winery that produced the wine, the town of production, the quality of the vintage in which the wine was produced, the years of experience of the winery since first bottling, and whether the wine is a regular release or a reserve wine. In each of the data sources, we find that botti-only

Table 4.2 Ratings for botti-only wines compared to wines made using barriques

	VV Stars	GR Glasses	WS Score
Botti-only wines			
Vintages 1980–2005	−0.30	−0.34	−1.92
Vintages 2006–2014	−0.12	−0.17	−0.66

wines received lower ratings, but this penalty was reduced by about a half in the more recent period, which we started in the year 2006. Table 4.2 summarizes these effects. For example, for WS, botti-only wines received roughly two points (−1.92) less than wines aged at least partially in barriques. This negative effect was reduced by more than a half (a positive coefficient of 1.26) in the more recent decade. The other two data sources show similar patterns.

Other Media

Has the categorical distinction between modern and traditional winemaking genres lost its relevance more broadly? The view that the dustup has faded and no longer holds relevance strikes us as inaccurate. O'Keefe (2014, p. 42) summarizes the recent situation in a way that conforms to our observations:

> Before the first decade of the New Millennium was over, an unofficial cease-fire gradually took hold in Barolo and Barbaresco, helped along by the emergence of a middle-of-the-road genre that is now widespread in both denominations—so much so, in fact, that a number of recently arrived wine writers even question if the Barolo War ever actually took place. But yes, the war most certainly did take place ... the two distinct genres that battled for survival for decades are both alive and well, although the producers are more at ease with this coexistence, and most no longer insist that one genre should dominate.

The categorical distinction traditional/modern has, if anything grown stronger in the market. For instance, when we began our study, American wine shops and websites paid almost no attention to the distinction. Now the distinction seems pervasive in restaurant wine lists and descriptions given by retailers. The contention that we have described had the long-run consequence of changing the conceptual landscape.

We checked our impressions based on field observations with an analysis of mentions of the distinction in the press. We used two general-interest media, one international—the *New York Times*—and one domestic—the *Corriere della Sera* (of Milan), the largest-circulation daily newspaper in Italy, and one specialized publication in the wine industry, WS. For the *New York Times* and WS, we computed yearly counts of the phrases "traditional Barolo" or "classic Barolo," and "modern Barolo" or "international Barolo." For the *Corriere* we counted occurrences of the equivalent terms in Italian. Figure 4.11 shows the pattern over time. Each point in a figure corresponds to the number of articles in each publication that mentions the category labels. The curves in the graphs indicate smoothed trends over time.[10]

We observe two things. One is that there is considerable year-to-year variation in the use of category labels as indicated by the points. The other is that the fitted local polynomial function that smooths values over years shows mainly increasing use of the genre labels. (We see a similar but less pronounced pattern for the use of "modern" or "international" Barolo.) Overall, we do not find evidence that the categorical distinction has eroded in the press.

Marketplace

In the previous chapter we described the activation of traditional producers in defense of their practices and identity. The market response to the revival of traditionalist winemaking genres was also positive, revealing an upward trajectory in demand and prices. According to Isabella Boffo of Oddero, "I think that now the consumer's palate has been changing and people are more and more interested in discovering the real Barolo, the real Nebbiolo expression. I just think it's a natural evolution."

A number of wine journalists have also noted that the prices of traditional Barolo/Barbaresco in recent years have increased sharply relative to their modern counterparts. We did an analysis to check this observation using release prices from WS and information about the aging method of each wine from VV. We compare the average prices for botti-only wines and barrique wines each year in figure 4.12. The curve in the graph indicates the trend over time (again using a smoothed polynomial function). Similar to the graphs of critics scores already presented, we observe that modern wines at slightly lower prices on average in the early 1980s. Then, these wines increased their prices above the traditional wines during the late 1980s, 1990s, and early 2000s. The price gap gradually closed, and the prices for traditional wines

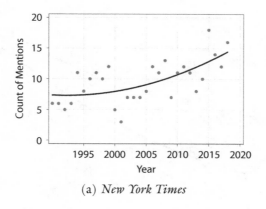

(a) *New York Times*

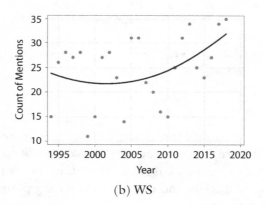

(b) WS

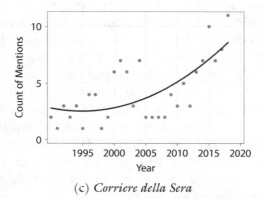

(c) *Corriere della Sera*

Figure 4.11 Yearly counts of mentions of "traditional Barolo/Barbaresco" ("tradizionale" for *Corriere della Sera*) or "classic Barolo/Barbaresco" ("classico") in three publications, 1990–2018 (with fitted local polynomial given by the solid line).

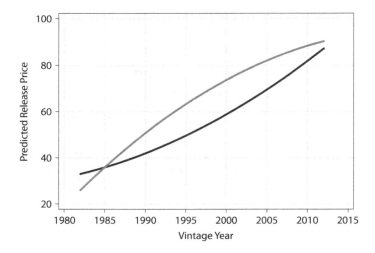

Figure 4.12 Average release prices for WS for botti-only wines (black line) versus wines with some barriques (gray line) by vintage year.

are comparable to their modern counterparts for the more recent vintages in the 2010s. This pattern supports the idea of a comeback for the traditional genre. The pattern in this figure is strikingly consistent with those showing a convergence in ratings, due no doubt to the strong positive relationship between ratings and prices.

In addition, we chose a set of exemplary producers of the two genres and their iconic wines and recorded from WS their release prices at time of introduction to the U.S. market for two great vintages, 2001 and 2004. Then we recorded their average prices at retail in December 2015 from wine-searcher.com. Finally we calculated (nominal) price appreciation using the ratio of the price in 2015 to that at year of introduction (2005 for the 2001 vintage and 2008 for the 2004 vintage). Table 4.3 shows what we found. Prices surged over this period for the traditionalists, with those of Rinaldi leading the way. Interestingly the 2001 Bartolo Mascarello, which James Suckling's WS review in 2006 gave a shockingly low score of 84 points and described it as "smells like a warm room with two wet dogs," rose in price by 46 percent since the review was published.[11] Prices were either flat or declined for the modernist wines and fell for those that span the categorical divide. These data too suggest that the categorical distinction retains its potency among U.S. consumers.[12]

Table 4.3 Changes in prices for Barolo and Barbaresco by notable producers from arrival in the U.S. market to 2015

Producer	Wine	2001 Vintage			2004 Vintage		
		2005	2015	Δ	2008	2015	Δ
Traditionalists							
G. Conterno	C. Francia	100	168	152%	150	269	79%
	Monfortino	425	758	78%			
B. Mascarello	Barolo	115	168	46%	95	222	134%
G. Mascarello	Monprivato	65*	212	226%	125	201	61%
Produttori del Barbaresco	Asili	55	99	80%	80	96	20%
G. Rinaldi	Brunate -Le Coste	57*	207	263%	96	225	134%
Modernists							
E. Altare	Arborina	105	101	−4%	155	135	−13%
D. Clerico	Mentin -Ginestra	83	96	16%	120		15%
Gaja	Barbaresco	230	197	−14%	180	204	13%
	Sorí Tildin	350	368	5%	416	386	−7%
La Spinetta	Campé	131	113	−14%	160	158	−1%
Spanners							
Einaudi	Cannnubi	95	110	−7%	100	83	−17%
Marchesi di Gresy	Camp Gros	70	68	−3%	86	80	−7%

Δ equals one minus the ratio of the price in 2015 to the initial price.
* indicates that we used the retail price paid by one of the authors.

4.5 Understanding Collective Interpretations

In a broader sense the reinterpretation of Barolo and Barbaresco and the opposition it sparked identify a mechanism through which organizations and consumers can create diversity and complexity in the concepts used to distinguish products and producers in the market. Early on, there was a clear separation between the modernist and traditionalist camps in Barolo/Barbaresco. Clusters of producers in each camp were very distinct from each other. The new genre found favor with critics and consumers, and producers that embraced it enjoyed higher prices, as we showed in the previous chapter. Unsurprisingly, given the economic incentives, some traditionalist producers switched sides. The producers that remained traditionalist regarded such moves as risking confusion in the market about the meaning of Barolo and Barbaresco. Traditionalists also tended to view conversions to modernism as disloyal to the identity of the region, as moral defections. Had the producers completely abandoned traditionalism, then the new modernist market identity could have supplanted the traditionalist one. But this did not happen.

When does tension between competing visions and practices like the one that we observed in the Langhe between traditional and modern winemaking genres yield a persisting categorical opposition? To answer this question, we paid attention to the response of the traditionalists to increasing ambiguity about genres of Barolo and Barbaresco, which they viewed as a challenge to their own collective market identity. We focused on two factors that appear to be associated with varying degrees of confusion about genres that result in different effects of genre reinterpretations in markets (Negro et al. 2011). One is the identities of the agents responsible for the change, insiders versus outsiders to the category. The other is the kind of claim that these agents make: replacing an existing genre and its identity or introducing a new, distinct genre.

Consider first the source of the change. Change that comes from outside the group of producers can be problematic but perhaps not as much as change that comes from inside. When outsiders bring change, such as innovation in winemaking practices proposed by university laboratories, they can be ignored, challenged, or assimilated. These outsider actions can also generate oppositional identity movements, which could unite the insiders and reduce factions. The actions of outsiders can be difficult to accept, but they are typically easier to understand as being generated by external forces or conditions.

When insiders initiate (or participate in) a new genre, the dynamics are generally more complicated, and it is more difficult for the system to reach an equilibrium. One reason is that the producers whose market identities are tied to the old genre share some common features, including history, geographical provenance, social ties, and broad market identity, with the some of the partisans of the new genre. This situation is unstable because audience members will likely conflate the identities tied to the two genres. We expect that incumbents will react more strongly when insiders create and promote the new genre than when the new genre comes from outside.

Sometimes a new genre arises with a new label. In such cases incumbents might not respond favorably because they are satisfied with how things have always been done. But the different label will not create confusion between the new genre and the old one. If a consumer sees that one wine is labeled as produced in California and another as produced in South Africa, they understand that these are different kinds of products. Consumers interested in trying a Californian wine can choose the first, while consumers interested in a South African wine can select the second. Wines from these areas can compete for the attention and tastes of different audiences—or even the same critics and buyers—but they will not risk being mistaken for one another.

A more problematic case is when a new genre arises and gets associated by its partisans and market intermediaries to the label already associated with an existing genre. This increases ambiguity about the meaning of either genre. In such cases tension likely arises between the partisans of the two camps. Such a concern will create pressure on all sides to reestablish more clarity in market identities.

In particular, those whose market identities are tied to the old genre generally worry that they will be interpreted as proponents of the new genre even if they oppose it. Greater ambiguity about the genre will motivate incumbents to clarify the boundary between the genres. For these reasons we expect that the response of the incumbents to a new genre that uses the existing label will result in stronger—even oppositional—reactions. In the case of Barolo and Barbaresco, we see that the modernist genre was embraced by established insiders, like Gaja, and by newcomers, like Clerico and Boschis. The rules of the game, as codified in the Disciplinare, allowed the new genre to claim the old labels Barolo/Barbaresco.

The confusion about genres for these wines was heightened by two other factors. The first concerns the dynamics of change. Many who sought the market identity of modernist had once had the other identity. The second is what we call genre spanning in the next chapter. Some producers produced wines in each genre. Both of these factors threatened to blur, and perhaps erase, the boundary between the genres. Our analysis revealed that this threat prompted winemakers with strong ties to the traditionalist market identity to mobilize strongly against the new genre and its associated market identity. We have seen that the collective reaction of the traditionalists, which we call the counterrevolution, resulted in slowing down the flow of producers to the new genre and encouraging a counterflow.

CHAPTER FIVE

Genre Spanning, Ambiguity, and Valuation

IN THIS CHAPTER WE ADDRESS some of the ways in which categorical memberships can influence judgments of quality and valuation. These issues are complicated, and it is difficult to make progress in addressing them without relying on a model. With colleagues, we have built such a model (Hannan, Le Mens, Hsu, Kovács, Negro, Pólos, Pontikes, and Sharkey 2019). We rely heavily on that work, but we do not explicate the technical details here.[1]

We organize our analysis around the notion of what sociologists call category spanning. This term refers to the choices that producers make that cause audiences to categorize them one way or another. The choices are those that cause products, such as wines, to be regarded as instances of more than one genre (concept more generally). When this line of empirical work began, the research community did not distinguish between concepts/genres and categories. The language of category spanning gives the sense that the issue is the *categorization* of an object as an instance of more than one genre (or the claim by an agent that a firm or other entity is an instance of more than one genre). This view is too limiting. Issues of ambiguity arise even when objects have not been categorized. The issue fundamentally concerns the consequences of having a profile of feature values that makes it likely that a product might be seen as an instance of multiple genres. Nonetheless, it is hard to avoid using the language of spanning in discussing the focus of this chapter: conceptual ambiguity.

5.1   Conceptual Ambiguity

Uncertainty about categorization affects how objects are perceived because it creates some ambiguity. An object is ambiguous for someone if it is hard for her or him to figure out what kind of object it is therefore what to expect of it. In other words, an object is ambiguous if it is difficult to categorize it straightforwardly in the relevant concepts. A film that might be action, comedy or sci-fi is ambiguous relative to a film that is clearly action only. Likewise a winery that is in some sense traditional and in some other sense modern is also more ambiguous than one that clearly belongs to only one of the genres.

Ambiguity is a subjective experience. From an outsider's perspective, an object is judged as ambiguous if it has been categorized as an instance of *multiple* concepts in the set of available concepts.[2] Where do these categorizations come from? Sometimes they come from direct experience with the object, for example, a tasting and tour at a winery. Other times they come from accepting the categorizations by others, for example, consumers following critics.

In our empirical investigations, we do not have access to the individual cognitions of the members of the relevant audience. So we infer likely categorizations from the values of key observable features. For instance, in the previous chapters we learned that a crucial feature in the wine regions we study is the kind of barrel used to age a wine. We can measure this feature for many wineries over many years. We assume that these measurements reflect how audiences would assign membership. It is not certain that everyone would accept unquestioningly our categorizations. For these reasons, we chose to assume that categorical memberships have some uncertainty for those who make the critical valuations we measure.

Our measurement of ambiguity assumes that *an object is ambiguous if its relevant feature values (its position in the semantic space) do not suggest a particular genre assignment.*[3] Our measure of conceptual ambiguity is close to zero for an object that has a very high categorization probability in a particular concept and very low probability of categorization in any of the other concepts being considered. Conversely, the measure of ambiguity is high for an object that has an even distribution of categorization probabilities. That is, an object that is, in some respect, an instance of every concept has maximum conceptual ambiguity.

When we implement this notion with our empirical materials, we face a choice of exactly what genres to consider as relevant. As we have discussed in previous chapters, we learned that producers and critics treat the practice of aging in barriques as the key indicator of making modern Barolo and Barbaresco. In other words, knowing that a winery has aged a wine in barriques leads to the belief that it also used a set of modernist practices such as very short periods of maceration. So we obviously need to distinguish wines aged in botti from those aged in barriques. But this does not settle the matter because some wines are aged initially in barriques and then latter in botti. Are there three genres corresponding to these alternatives, two clear genres and a hybrid?

We concluded that it makes the most sense for our analysis to consider only two genres, modern Barolo and traditional Barolo, for several reasons. Most of our informants (producers and market intermediaries) discussed the matter in these terms. And, as we showed in the previous chapter, journalistic treatments of these wines continue to refer to the traditional/modern distinction. In our 2009 telephone survey of producers of Barolo and Barbaresco, we asked respondents to tell us who they regarded as most typical of modernism. By far the plurality of mentions were Altare and Gaja. This is interesting because both used a combination of barrique- and botti-aging. Finally, we are not aware of any agreed-upon label for a third genre. Therefore we think that the meaningful distinction is between tradition (as indicated by sole use of botti) and modernism (as indicated by any use of barriques).

These distinctions apply to what we call *labels*. We have been able to categorize all of these labels produced by each winery. The labels, such as Burlotto's "Barolo Monvigliero," are the wine products of the winery. Some of these labels refer to the vineyards from which the grapes were obtained; others refer to some other distinction made by the producer. At the label level, there is no ambiguity, as we see it. Instead ambiguity arises at the level of the winery.

Crucial to our analysis is that audience members form mental representations of wineries (producers). We assume further that these representations are influenced by the genres of its products. Some producers have made only traditional wines. For example, Fratelli Cavallotto has produced in the years we studied Barolo Bricco Boschis, Barolo Riserva Vigneto, and Barolo Riserva Bricco Boschis Vigna San Giuseppe—all traditional. Podere Rocche dei Manzoni produced (among others) Barolo Perno, Barolo Big, and Barolo Big 'd Big—all modern. In an example of mixed production, Poderi Luigi Einaudi produced Barolo Terlo, which was modern in all the years we coded, and Barolo Cannubi, which was made in the traditional way in some years and in the modern way in others.

Wine *producers*, as Einaudi illustrates, can work in one or both genres, which gives rise to the possibility of genre ambiguity. Given our assumptions, a wine producer can be categorized in just one of the following:

- traditional only (t),
- modern only (m), or
- both modern and traditional (mix).

We calculate conceptual ambiguity using the proportions of a wine producer's labels that fall in the three types. For example, suppose that the same person has equal subjective probability (1/3) of assigning the winery to each option; then the entropy measure for this set of categorization probabilities equals 1.1, the maximal value of ambiguity with three possible assignments. At the other extreme, if all the subjective probability is assigned to one possibility, then ambiguity equals zero. To consider an intermediate possibility, suppose that these genre categorization probabilities were $P(m) = 0.5$; $P(t) = 0$; $P(mix) = .5$; then conceptual ambiguity equals 0.69.

5.2   Ambiguity and Valuation

We see valuation as inextricably linked to concepts. People are generally "information misers;" they try to get by with minimal cognitive effort. So people generally do not attempt to discern every single feature of an object.[4] People do not possess mental representations of the relationships between all the possible features and their values (e.g., about the extent to which movies that contain more love scenes also tend to have more suspense). Rather, the concepts people have in mind shape "on the fly" feature inferences.

A person's set of genres (concepts), together with the context, dictate what features are germane, and it draws attention to those particular features. In other words, even if a person were to evaluate an object on the basis of its feature values alone, the concepts that the person holds determines what features are used in the assessment.[5]

That concepts can shape how people affectively respond to what they encounter is evident from both casual observation of the world and scholarly work. We emphasize two facets of affective response or valuation. The first involves the affective reaction to the concepts themselves, what psychologists call *valence*. Concepts can have positive or negative valence. A nice illustration concerns the so-called *Sideways* effect. The Academy Award–winning film *Sideways* was among other things a celebration of Pinot Noir. In a memorable moment in a restaurant scene, the lead character in the film played by Paul Giamatti proclaimed, "No! If anyone orders Merlot, I'm leaving. I am *not* drinking any fucking Merlot!" This diatribe is directed at a varietal, not a particular wine or winery; it ascribes negative valence to a genre. It turns out that the film affected the valence of both wine types, with sales of Merlot declining and Pinot Noir rising after the release of the film (Cuellar et al. 2012).

The second facet concerns the valuation of particular instances of concepts, in our case of wines and wineries. The models developed in Hannan et al. (2019) build on the intuition that objects inherit some or all of the valence of the concepts that apply to them. Working out this idea requires making a number of distinctions about the information available to the evaluator.[6] Valuation generally entails both categorization (what kind of object is this?) and the assignment of value based on fit to a category (how appealing is the object in light of the relevant concepts?).

To begin with the simplest possibility, consider contexts that make only one concept relevant. Such a possibility would be a standard wine tasting in which it is announced that the wines to be tasted are all instances of a particular genre. Then there is no subjective uncertainty about what is the relevant concept. Hannan et al. (2019) argue that the valuation (e.g., score) assigned to a wine in this context is given by the product of the valence of the genre and the typicality of the wine for that concept. A prototypical instance (one with typicality of one) gets the full valence of that concept. Wines of low typicality will receive lower scores. For example, if the wines being tasted are Napa Merlot and you agree with the Giamatti film character, you will give low ratings to the highly typical wines in that tasting. On the other hand, if the wines are Santa Maria Valley Pinot Noir, then the prototypical wines will be rated highly and the less typical ones less so.

Suppose instead that the genre is not announced or that the evaluator lacks confidence that the organizer of the tasting uses the genre labels in the same way that she does. Either case introduces some *uncertainty* that is reflected in valuation. Now the valuation is the product of three terms: valence, typicality, and the categorization probability. The greater the uncertainty (the lower the categorization probability), the lower the valuation *ceteris paribus*.

Sometimes multiple concepts come into play. We once participated in a game with critics from *Gambero Rosso* and wine educators from the University of Gastronomic Sciences in Pollenzo in Bra, a town in the Langhe. In this game, each person in turn went to the cellar with the restaurant's sommelier to pick a bottle, which was then decanted before being brought to the table for blind tasting. The goal of the game was to identify the *Denominazione di Origine Controllata e Garantita* (DOCG). Amusingly, many guesses were wildly off. A bottle of Valpolicella (a wine from the Veneto), for instance, stumped everyone and elicited as many guesses as there were participants.

This game did not ask for valuations. If it had, then the players would have faced a multiconcept, uncertain context. The idea that valence, typicality, and uncertainty affect valuation carries over to this and other more complicated contexts.[7]

On top of those effects, the relevance of multiple concepts raises the possibility of an additional effect—a *penalty*—of conceptual ambiguity. Ambiguous objects inherit less of the valence of the concepts in which they are categorized.

As we see it, the mechanism behind this effect of ambiguity is cognitive fluency. Fluency refers to ease of processing a mental image. Experimental research reveals that people experience positive affect when processing fluently (Alter and Oppenheimer 2008). For instance, Reber et al. (2004) played small samples of music to subjects that varied in how closely the musical structure conforms to widely experienced music. Subjects in this experiment reported great liking for the more familiar patterns that they could arguably process more fluently. Conceptual ambiguity creates an experience of disfluency; people have to work harder to interpret ambiguous objects, decide which concepts apply to them, and decide how to combine the implications of the different categorizations. So ambiguity generally creates disfluency, which gives rise to more negative reactions, including aesthetic valuations.

The multiple categorization setting raises a challenge: how do the valuations under the different single-concept assignments combine? For instance, suppose a winery makes some modern Barolos and some traditional ones. An evaluator who possesses both concepts likely has a valence for each. Does the "hybrid" winery get some average of the two valences? We think this is not generally the case, that combinations get less than would be implied by such an averaging, as we explain below.

5.3   Ambiguity and Interpretability

In laying out an early version of the category spanning problem, Hsu, Hannan, and Koçak (2009) identified two likely sources of lower valuation for organizations that straddle concepts (genres here). They pertain to the different roles in the market. For *producers*, learning to perform in multiple genres is more difficult than doing so for one. This is an issue of specialization and learning. For the members of the *audience*, the issue is ambiguity, the difficulty of making sense of producers that span genres.

Specialization in production, in economic terms, means focusing on only a few tasks rather than many. Specialization generally supports higher productivity and increased quality of output. The productivity of specialists at particular tasks depends on how much knowledge they have (Becker and Murphy 1992). As workers become more adept at a task, they become more efficient and production increases. A worker who does not specialize and performs all the tasks—a jack-of-all-trades—allocates their working time and investments among the tasks. However, it is possible for workers to do better by specializing in fewer tasks or just one and then combining their outputs with that of other workers who specialize in others. The increasing returns from concentrating on a narrower set of tasks raises the productivity of a specialist above that of a spanning jack-of-all-trades.

Growing grapes, vinification, and aging wine entail many tasks. Differences among wine genres means that some of these tasks must be done differently. We have concentrated on differences in aging, but there are many more. Workers in a winery that produces in more than one genre have to learn more; they have to master different ways of doing the same kind of task. Therefore specialization and concentration of the producer on a single genre can lead to greater skill and greater productivity than would be achieved by the same producer spanning several genres. Increased efficiency and productivity is one mechanism through which specialization can increase product quality and appeal to the audience. If this is the case, spanning genres results in relatively lower quality and appeal.

Recent sociological research has concentrated on a second reason why spanning results in lower appeal for producers and their products: the fact that multiple-category memberships make producers/products more ambiguous and therefore less appealing. The core idea is that agents find objects with high focus to be easy to interpret and understand. That is, the cognitive ease in categorizing and understanding an object is high when it is highly typical of one concept (or a set of concepts that lie close to each other) and atypical of the other concepts for an agent.

Hannan et al. (2019) developed this argument in terms of fluency. Fluent experiences (in terms of cognitive ease) give rise to positive emotional response. Conceptual ambiguity generally causes disfluent processing and thus negative affect. In our case, negative affect means lowered valuations, such as scores given to wines in tastings. Given the argument that ambiguity lowers fluency, then we predict that ambiguity lowers evaluations. In other words, *there is a penalty paid for spanning genres.*

5.4   Genre Spanning and Ambiguity

What does spanning mean for producers of Barolo/Barbaresco? Because we focus on the method of aging for wines and we distinguish wines aged at least partly in barriques from those aged only in botti, we end up coding individual wines as either traditional or modern. That is, spanning and ambiguity do not characterize the wines. Instead, in our context, it is the *wineries* that differ in ambiguity. In the usual social sciences language, the unit of analysis in this chapter is the winery.

A winery's portfolio might consist of several wines labeled as Barolo or Barbaresco and therefore potentially of a range of genres. A producer can focus narrowly by producing wines only in one genre. In previous chapters we gave well-known examples of the pure types, such as Altare, Gaja, Bartolo and Mauro Mascarello, and Rinaldi. Other wineries have produced portfolios with a mixture of types. For instance, both Poderi Luigi Einaudi and Cascina Ballarin produced one botti-aged, one barrique-aged, and one barrique-and-botti-aged wine in some vintages, and Marchesi di Barolo has sometimes produced instances of each genre.

Many modern producers started new wineries, but others continued the activities of their parents or grandparents in a different way. The market success of the modern wines induced some traditional producers to straddle by making wines in both genres or by using practices from both genres sequentially for the same wine. In our interview in 2013 with members of the Minuto family from the Moccagatta winery, Anna Minuto described their path to change as primarily market driven:

> The botti grandi were like houses; people renovated them but never changed them . . . We reached a point where these botti were worn-out, did not give anything to the wine, and had defects . . . Instead of replacing old botti we bought barriques . . . When we made that decision, it was also to follow the market.

Alessandra Bovio from Bovio Gianfranco winery gave a similar account:

> Apart from certain producers (for example, Altare who started using barriques of his own choice because he wanted to do something different from the old producers) . . . all the others started because of the demand of the market.

Such spanning reduces the distance between genres. Shifting from traditional to modern is a temporal form of spanning for at least some transition period. Shortly after such a transition, a producer has on the market its wines from previous vintages (in the other genre). Critics and aficionados remember the producer as something different than it now is. This is why we call transitions between genres a temporal form of spanning. In the previous chapter, we claimed that this kind of spanning was seen as problematic by the traditionalists because spanning generally blurs the boundaries between the genres, and the identities of the wineries and their products become less clear. The views expressed by experts provide insights consistent with this idea. Wine critic Franco Ziliani, who has contributed to several national and international publications and published a blog on Italian wines, put it this way:

> You must choose which way is your way. You can't do it all. Some do half-half. It is crazy. I don't like them. They are insipid. You must choose.

The opinions of critics like Ziliani seem to be a direct response to the logic with which some producers made the choice to diversify. For instance, Sergio Germano from Ettore Germano winery told us:

> We use botti and barriques and try to get the best out of each. That's why we also have two labels. One American critic defined us as hesitant [*indeciso*]. Every journalist wants you to identify yourself, to line up. But what is the sense in that?

Ziliani also argued with us in 2008 that the division between the two market identities in Langhe wine production was not a thing of the past:

> The division between traditionalist and modernist is *now*. A large part of the Barolo producers may prefer the real Barolo. But they have been forced to change at least to some extent.

In 2005, the editor of *Civiltà del Bere* commented:

> The result is that there exists a contraposition between traditionalists and innovators; however, many of the classicists [traditionalists] produce modern wines as well because the market expects them to. In the end, classic and new [modern] products coexist even in the historical producing houses, generating a schizophrenic situation.

Straddlers are viewed as displaying a lack of commitment to any one interpretation. Their behavior confuses the audience by reducing the coherence of the genres. We asked Daniel Thomases, a co-editor of the *Vini di Veronelli* (VV) wine guide and contributor to international publications including *Wine Spectator* (WS), what he thought of wineries that switch to different aging methods. He replied:

> Some producers were not too sure about which way to go, what technique to use, and offered two products here and two products there . . . Frankly, when that happens, I find it strange. I think a producer should have one line of products. That line of products should reflect a specific zone as well as that producer's philosophy. A winery is not a supermarket.

Some of the producers with whom we discussed these issues offered views similar to those of Zilliani and Thomases. They insisted that consistency was crucial for building and maintaining a clear identity. Ambiguity can bring a winery's identity into question. For instance, Alfio Cavallotto, who makes Barolo in his family winery Cavollotto Fratelli, told us:

> A winery, more than the wine, has identity. A winery needs to ensure consistency across different wines and different vintages. Using different methods for different wines makes it [consistency] more difficult and less likely.

Valter Fissore, who runs Elvio Cogno with his wife, reflected on his own experience in having experimented with the modernist practices during the 1990s and told us that:

> It is important to preserve identity. To follow the market and change the method of production is dangerous . . . When you change the method of production, you change the cellar, the workers, the philosophy—your identity. Then it is difficult to have the right approach and you arrive at a final situation where you don't know who you are, and your wine is not so clear: Is it modern? Traditional? What is it?

For products like these fine wines, consumers arguably prefer the offerings of more committed producers. If this is so and if audience members perceive a spanning as signaling a lack of commitment, then critics and consumers will find the wines made by focused wineries more appealing. Thus the identity-based argument points in the same direction as the argument based on expertise. Shifts from a clear identity to a more ambiguous category-spanning identity squanders an important resource. Nonetheless many wineries did just that. We will see below that this choice eventually proved to be problematic.

5.5   Ambiguity and Critical Ratings

Now we turn to empirical estimation of the effect of ambiguity on valuation expressed by critical ratings. We want to see whether the prediction that ambiguous objects generally get devalued holds for Barolo and Barbaresco.

We have developed the argument in terms of the evaluator's subjective assessments. However, in archival research of the kind we have pursued, we do not have access to individual cognition. Instead we must make assumptions about how cognition is shaped by the objective conditions that we can measure. We assume the proportion of the wines of each genre—traditional only, modern only, and some mix of the two—matches the subjective categorization probabilities of the audience members. With this assumption, we calculate such probabilities for each winery in each vintage and calculate ambiguity as the evenness of the set of probabilities. For roughly half of the winery–vintage pairs, ambiguity is zero. The 75th percentile of the distribution of ambiguity is 0.56, and the maximum value is 1.1.

In a regression model that predicts ratings as the number of stars assigned by *Vini di Veronelli* (VV)[8] we see in table 5.1 that ambiguity has a negative effect on the critical rating.[9] A one-unit change in ambiguity reduces the expected valuation by about one-third of a star. Given that star ratings range from one to four, this effect looks to be substantively significant. We then estimated a similar equation for numerical scores assigned by *Wine Spectator* (WS). We found again that an increase in ambiguity is associated with lower scores, roughly half a point for each unit of ambiguity. If one considers that the range of the scores for outstanding wines is ten points, the effect is again substantially large. These coefficients are also statistically significant at the conventional 5 percent level. All in all, we find qualitative and quantitative evidence that the ambiguity caused by spanning genres meets with disfavor among the experts in Italy and internationally.

Table 5.1   The effect of ambiguity on critical ratings for vintage years 1980–2014

	Vini di Veronelli (VV) Stars	*Wine Spectator* (WS) Score
Ambiguity	−0.326	−0.463

5.6   Contrast and Critical Ratings

Category Contrast

We also analyze the implications of the fuzziness of categories, the inverse of which we call *contrast*. The intuition is that categories that appear to have relatively sharp boundaries and stand out from the background in a domain have more social power. Membership in such a category provides more information in the sense of sharper priors about feature values. Previous research has shown that this intuition has merit (Negro et al. 2010; Kovács and Hannan 2015; Negro et al. 2015; Kovács et al. 2021). We measure the contrast of a category as the average categorization probability of its members. If most members are, by virtue of their feature values, very likely candidates for inclusion, then the category will be more homogeneous and appear to have sharper boundaries. Its contrast will be higher.

Contrast depends both on the "shape" of the concept and the distribution over the semantic space of the objects perceived. Suppose that two people with the same concept see different samples of objects and that the objects in one case concentrate near the center of the concept and in the other the objects are more broadly dispersed. Then the contrast of the category in the first context will on average be higher than in the second.

Negro et al. (2010) argued that a clear category boundary (high contrast) benefits all members of the category. If genre specialists predominate in some context, then the perceived distinctions among genres are sharp in that context. If positions are changing, but the movement is mainly toward specialism of one type of the other, then contrast rises. Of course, movement toward positions that are likely to be classified in more than one genre lower contrast. When contrast is high, critics and knowledgeable consumers have a reasonable chance of conceptualizing the differences among genres. Such was apparently the case when Gaja, Altare, and others first challenged the status quo in Barolo/Barbaresco production by introducing wines aged partly in barriques and making other related changes such as shortening maceration times and controlling fermentation temperatures. The critics had little difficulty distinguishing these new products, and they reached agreement about the feature values expected of modern wine (soft tannins, fruitiness, high concentration, deep color, etc.).

We think that the clarity of a category's boundary can be understood as the inverse of the level of ambiguity among its members. A category has weak boundaries if its members are conceptually ambiguous. The notion of category contrast captures this idea.[10] We show the temporal variation in the

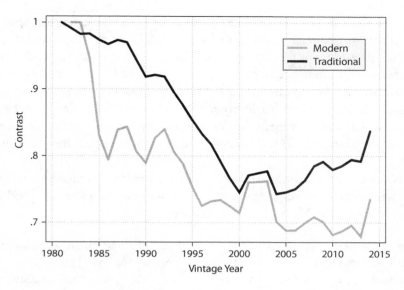

Figure 5.1 Contrast of traditional and modern genres in Barolo/Barbaresco by vintage year.

the contrasts of the traditional and modern categories for Barolo/Barbaresco during 1980–2015 in figure 5.1. The figure shows that contrast decreased throughout the 1990s and early 2000s for both camps. In this period, categorizing these wines became more difficult. This happened because increased spanning of genres clouded the boundaries between them. But toward the end of the period we studied, contrast began to rise, first for the traditionalist category and then for the modern one.

Contrast and Category Ratings

Lowered contrast likely reduces the appeal of all offerings in a category in two ways. One involves the relationships among categories. With increasing fuzziness, clusters of objects become less salient and elicit lower interest.[11] Comparisons become more difficult; audience members have trouble using distinct descriptors and develop attitudes of reserve, strangeness, even aversion or repulsion. In sum, audience members generally react negatively to such a decline in clarity. In situations in which the categories are few and contrast is lowered by common spanning of these categories, we expect lower appeal as measured by ratings for all products.

Second, the penalty for spanning should decline as the categories spanned lose contrast. Reduced contrast implies that audience members find it more difficult to assess the fit of patterns of feature values to their expectations. The reduced prominence of prototypical patterns reduces the consistency of evaluations (McArthur and Post 1977). Blurred boundaries also make transgressions less salient and harder to identify (Geertz 1983; DiMaggio 1987). In particular, category spanning ceases to serve as an identity-discrepant cue for the audience, so it does not bring such strong penalties (Rao et al. 2005).

Producers, critics, and enthusiasts debate about the implications of spanning winemaking genres for the interpretability of a winery and its products. Italian wine expert Esposito (2008) argued:

> It seems like a simple, straightforward question: traditional or modern? But in Piemonte, there are no easy answers where style [genre here] is concerned. While there used to be a very fine line between the two styles, the narrow middle ground has virtually exploded, rendering classification almost impossible.

After a period of increasing ambiguity about the meaning of Barolo and Barbaresco, traditionalist producers mobilized to support their practices and their market identity. In the last decade, the rediscovery of traditionalism resulted in a relative simplification of the cultural boundaries between groups of producers of Barolo and Barbaresco. As spanning decreased, two distinct interpretations of winemaking and two distinct market identities coexisted in the region.

We calculated average stars from *Vini di Veronelli* (VV) and contrast of genres in each vintage. Then we estimated a linear regression of average stars on average contrast.[12] The graph in figure 5.2 illustrates the marginal effect of average contrast on average rating.[13] The figure shows that the average rating increases as contrast increases. In other words, when the boundaries of the categories sharpen, Barolo and Barbaresco wines as a class become more appealing for critics. In the regression model that we estimated, the coefficient of contrast is also statistically significant at the conventional p-value of 0.05. In separate analyses we estimated the same model using the wine scores from WS. In this case we did not find statistically significant associations between critics ratings and contrast. The ratings of the international publication showed significant effects of ambiguity, as we described earlier. It appears these WS raters react more to winery-level than category-level ambiguity.

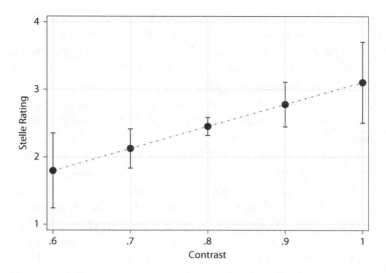

Figure 5.2 Changes in *stelle* (stars) ratings for change in contrast of genres of Barolo and Barbaresco wines, for reviews in VV for vintages 1980–2014.

5.7 Shaping the Cognitive/Cultural Landscape

This chapter and the three that preceded it have ranged widely over issues that have shaped the cognitive/cultural landscape of elite wines in the Langhe. When we refer to a cognitive/cultural landscape, we mean a pattern of related cognitive representations that have gained widespread use.

At its core, the landscape changed from one with a pair of concepts for the fine DOCG wines Barolo and Barbaresco to one in which each of these concepts was divided into modern and traditional genres. As we analyzed the situation, the first move was the creation of a conception of modern subconcepts. The impetus was the rise to wine-world superstardom of Gaja and his modern Barbarescos. But the actions of one winemaker was not enough to create a new concept because there was no way to distinguish Gaja Barbaresco DOCG from modern Barbaresco. It was the collective consensus about the wine's identity based on a cluster of wineries and network of winemakers that made the separation possible. And the Barolo Boys, led by Altare, provided this collective representation.

The second step in reshaping the landscape was a recognition by locals that the nonmodern winemakers were actually traditionalists. Here too a collective movement, led by Mascarello, Rinaldi, and Cappellano, provided the basis for a cultural representation of traditional Barolo/Barbaresco. This representation of the paired concepts was explicitly oppositional.

The motivations of the actors in this story reflected their market identities as closely tied to the modern/traditional distinction. The changing fortunes of the two concepts, with modernism first favored by the market and then traditionalism resurging, strongly affected the dynamics of the Barolo/Barbaresco wine world, as we have shown in analyzing movements of winemakers between the categories.

How audience members judge wines depends on the concepts that the context makes relevant. Once the new conceptual landscape is formed, wineries whose features do not align with one genre are seen as ambiguous. The important point is that a winery with exactly the same practices and products in a context in which there is only one concept (as in the context before the two genres became conceptualized and culturally agreed upon) could be less ambiguous than in the revised cognitive landscape. This matters because ambiguity shapes affective reactions to a winery and its products. As we have shown, wineries with more ambiguous positions received lower ratings from critics, which translates to lower prices in the market. So success and failure for a winery depends not just on its practices in the vineyard and cellar but also on the cognitive landscape.

Once the cultural distinction between modern and traditional wines took hold among journalists, retailers, and consumers, the winemakers lost control of its use. So it does not matter that many Langhe winemakers tell us that the distinction has lost its relevance and importance as long as the audience for their products continues to make the distinction. We have shown that this is the case today.

We gained empirical leverage by treating use of barriques for aging as a marker of membership in the modern genre. This is, of course, a simplification because the modernists also adopted extremely short macerations; more controlled fermentation; use of new technologies such as rotofermentation; and also changed management of the vineyard with green harvests, denser planting of vines, and so forth. Any of these changed practices could have been the basis for distinction. Consider the use of green harvest. We quoted Gaja earlier in recounting the reaction of the village elders of Barbaresco to his first green harvest. They claimed that only a novice could make such a mistake. Similarly, Marco Boschiazzo of Bovio told us that when his father-in-law first saw vineyard workers cutting bunches, he said, "You should be killed for doing what you are doing." Despite the opposition from the older generation, the new practice spread quickly and became established. Indeed

Boschiazzo ended his story by noting that his father-in-law had shifted to green harvest within five or six years.

So why did use of barriques—and not green harvest—become that focus of the persisting distinction? Put differently, why did the difference in size of barrels used for aging wine emerge as such a clear signal of market identity? While it could have been any number of markers, we have already mentioned that the choice of aging vessel is immediately obvious to anyone who visits a cellar or looks at the ubiquitous photos of cellars on winery webpages. Practices in the vineyard are more difficult to observe. A second possible explanation considers the source of the practice. Green harvest spread widely though the world's wineries and does not appear to be associated with any particular source. At least, none of the winemakers and critics that we interviewed mentioned any. Barriques, however, are distinctly French. As we mentioned in an earlier chapter, the fact that the Langhe winemakers use the French term for these barrels instead of the Italian highlights their foreignness. Moreover, barriques were used almost without exception in California, as Bartolo Mascarello highlighted in his public opposition to bringing "French/California" models into Barolo. So the opposition to the Bordeaux barrels was easily tied to a concern that winemaking in the Langhe would lose its local identity as the tides of globalization overwhelmed their historical specificity. Yet, as we will see when we turn to Tuscany, specifically Montalcino, the use of Bordeaux barriques did not become as contentious. So the foreignness per se and the worry about globalization did not spark a general opposition in the case of elite Italian wineries in Montalcino.

When we view our analyses through the lens of social movement theories in chapter 11, we highlight another kind of answer. Altare's notorious destruction of his father's botti grandi with a chainsaw provided an "origin myth" for the modernist movement and forged a strong bond between the use of barriques and modernist winemaking. This story also illustrates the awakening of an oppositional identity, which in turn can clarify boundaries by producing higher contrast among market identities.

CHAPTER SIX

Brunello di Montalcino

WE TURN NEXT TO THE producers of another of Italy's most-esteemed wines: Brunello di Montalcino. The comparison of Brunello with Barolo/Barbaresco is useful because the two wine regions are similar in many important respects. Their *Denominazione di Origine Controllata e Garantita* (DOCG) wines have roughly equally high status and command similar prices on world markets; the rules of production for these wines mandate the use of single grape varietals; the two regions have roughly the same scale of production; and most producers in both regions are organized as family firms that integrate grape farming, vinification, aging, and marketing.

Yet the origins of quality wine production developed very differently in the two regions. We argue that this divergence caused a persisting difference in the social structures of production. Specifically we propose that the weak solidarity of the community of producers of Brunello produced a comparably weak consensus about the meaning of the genre. This chapter concentrates on the community's structure. We take up the effects on conceptual consensus in the next chapter.

As we discussed in chapter 2, the Langhe largely escaped the dominant Italian system of sharecropping. Farms were commonly family-owned and operated. As a result, local social structures were apparently robust. Despite the role played by the House of Savoy in creating the modern conception of Barolo/Barbaresco, the collective project was—and still is—driven by family farmers with long local histories. Family firms have also played an important role in Brunello production. But many did not have local origins. In addition, large firms from outside the region are much more important in Montalcino than in the Langhe. Why?

For one thing, the wineries that produce Barolo/Barbaresco generally have multigenerational local family ownership and differ little in size compared to what we see in other wine regions. As we show below, the situation in Montalcino is different. In particular, the social and geographic origins of the producers in Montalcino were very diverse. The Montalcino area, like all of central Italy, experienced pervasive sharecropping from the Middle Ages to the 1950s. Land was owned by outsiders, often noble families or the Church, and poverty was rampant. It is claimed that Montalcino was the poorest town in the country when the Italian government outlawed sharecropping and redistributed farmland to the agricultural workers in the post–World War II period. Farm workers were dispersed and communication among them was difficult. For all these reasons this sharecropping regime allowed little scope for the development of local institutions.

Moreover, wine production for the market began late in Montalcino compared to the Piedmont and much of Tuscany. Most of the founders of the *Consorzio del Vino Brunello di Montalcino* (Consortium of Brunello di Montalcino Wine) were only beginning production when the original *Denominazione di Origine Controllata* (DOC) for Brunello di Montalcino was instituted in 1966. There was no long-standing tradition of winemaking in Montalcino. In addition to the sons of sharecroppers, other early entrants were noble families from Florence. As Brunello started to gain recognition, there was a flood of new arrivals from elsewhere in Italy (some individual families and some corporate entities) and from other countries. As a result, the community of producers of Brunello has much greater heterogeneity than that of Barolo and Barbaresco producers.

We trace the effects of such heterogeneity on current dissensus in producers' conceptions of the wines. At its core, the difference concerns conceptions of the authentic interpretation of the wines, as we discuss in the next chapter.

6.1   Montalcino and Brunello

The zone of Brunello production lies in southern Tuscany. It centers on the medieval hilltop town of Montalcino, which lies about 35 miles south southeast of Siena. The town sits 1,850 feet above sea level and has a population of roughly 5,000. The climate is hotter and drier than in any other DOCG zone. The production zone for Brunello that was established in the DOC and later DOCG regulations consists of only 3,000 acres surrounding the town. By contrast, the Barolo zone includes 4,285 acres.

Montalcino was controlled by the Republic of Siena in early medieval times. When Siena capitulated to the alliance of the Duchy of Florence and the Spanish Empire in 1555, Montalcino came under Florentine control.

Figure 6.1 Montalcino. *Source:* https://www.cinellicolombini.it/.

This dependency continued until Italian unification in 1861. Due to this history, the largest landholders in the area were noble Florentine and Sienese families, along with the Church, which controlled vast agricultural lands in central Italy at the time.

As we have mentioned previously, the form of agricultural organization adopted by these outsiders was *mezzadria* (sharecropping). The system depended on contracts between owners and tenant sharecroppers. The owners supplied the land and infrastructure, including residences for workers and buildings for farm operations. The tenant families paid half of their output to the owners (the Italian term for the arrangement comes from the Italian word *mezzo* [half]. Owners typically divided their agricultural holdings (*fattorias*) into multiple shareholdings called *poderi*. Those who worked these farms lacked security of tenure. The wide dispersal of the farms and the lack of public gathering places isolated the families and impeded the development of a collective orientation.[1]

With only a few exceptions, commercial wine production in Montalcino began fairly recently. This was not due to farmers being conservative or hostile to the market. Throughout the country, farmers readily adopted market-enhancing practices such as planting diverse seed varieties and using chemical fertilizers to improve yield (Cohen and Federico 2001). Rather, opportunities for market-oriented investment and modernization of agricultural operations were limited. Resource constraints also likely played a role. For instance, in northern Italy, rural credit cooperatives were present and provided some funding to members. Material resources and market institutions were more limited in the center and south of the country. Also, the isolation of the sharecropping families impeded not only the development of a collective orientation but also the exchange of information and know-how.

Few Montalcino families can trace winemaking as commercial activity back over generations. There is a long history of commercial production in Montalcino (the initial codification of Brunello arguably took place in 1888), but only a handful of families took part during the nineteenth and the first half of the twentieth century.

One exception was the Costanti family from Siena, which had owned extensive land in the region since the early sixteenth century. According to the family history presented on the website of the Conti Costanti winery (http://www.costanti.it/en/73/history), Crescenzio Costanti was a "dedicated and esteemed wine grower" around 1700. The family continued to make wine largely for its own consumption until the early 1960s, when commercial production began. Tito Costanti presented a wine called Brunello at the wine exhibition of the Province of Siena in 1970.

A second claimant to pride of place in developing a commercial Brunello was another noble Sienese family, the Colombini, which owned land in Montalcino since 1352. The family acquired a farm, now called Fattoria del Barbi, in 1790 and used it as a base for wine production. The family's first reported Brunello was from the 1892 vintage.

Despite the early activity of the Constanti and Colombini families, the story of Brunello centers mainly on one family: Biondi Santi. The Santi branch of the family were major landowners in Montalcino and other areas of Tuscany. Clemente Santi, a graduate in pharmacy from Pisa University, became focused on agriculture at his mother's farm, Il Greppo, just outside the walls of Montalcino. He improved the enological methods used locally, and one of his wines, a Moscatello, won a prize at the Universal Expo in Paris in 1867. His daughter Caterina married Jacopo Biondi, a physician from Florence. The story of Brunello arguably begins with their son Ferruccio, who took the surname Biondi Santi.[2] In the tumultuous period after phylloxera had devastated vineyards throughout France and Italy, he opted for producing a wine of 100 percent Sangiovese suited for long aging, which became the hallmark of the estate. Ferruccio is widely credited to be the founder of Brunello di Montalcino. His son Tancredi, took over management of the Greppo estate and began the practice of topping up bottles of old Brunello Riserva with wine of the same vintage to preserve them. He started this practice in 1927 with bottles of the 1888 and 1891 Riserva, a process he

Figure 6.2 Franco Biondi Santi. *Source:* Paolo Tenti, licensed under Creative Commons 3.0.

repeated until 1970. This practice, made available to customers, established a link for the wine world between Brunello and age-worthiness. The wines also received widespread acclaim. For instance:

> The Biondi Santi Brunello '55 received international attention when it was selected to be poured at a state dinner in honor of Queen Elizabeth II hosted by Italian President Giuseppe Saragat in 1969. With that the reputation of Brunello was made. (Wasserman 1991, p. 388).

The last of the family to run Il Greppo was Franco Biondi Santi, who became an unofficial world ambassador for Brunello. After his death in 2013, the estate was sold.

In sharp contrast with commercial winemaking in the Langhe, almost no other winery produced Brunello before the establishment of the DOC and the consorzio in 1966. The exceptions that we have identified are Fattoria di Barbi, La Fattoria di Sant'Angelo, Fattoria di Montosoli, and Tenuta di Argiano, which all exhibited Brunellos at wine exhibitions during the 1930s in what O'Keefe (2012, p. 47) calls the Brunello revival. However, Fascist agricultural policies shifted resources to cereal production and made access to resources scarce for wine-grape growers. Then World War II crushed commercial production. Indeed the Allied front passed through Montalcino on its way north.

It was not until the mid-1960s that production revived. At this point, families that had been making wine for family consumption as a sideline to farming cereals, fruit, and vegetables began to move to commercial wine production. The most notable step, as in the Langhe, was the successful application for DOC status for Brunello di Montalcino in 1966 and creation of a consorzio in 1967. Our own analysis of the files concerning the incorporation of the consorzio indicates that all of the twenty-three initial signers were listed as farmers and grape growers, but only ten of them produced and bottled wine. We found that this distinction also held for the members who joined the consorzio during its first five years.

Tancredi Biondi Santi had played a leadership role in the process of gaining DOC status and in organizing the producer's association. However, he objected to the inclusion in the DOC rules of an allowance to "correct" the wines by including must (unfermented juice) or wine made from grapes other than Sangiovese. This rule sought to accommodate new growers whose wines did not yield rich-enough wine. It caused Tancredi to leave the effort to found the DOC and the consorzio. The Biondi Santis operated outside of this formal structure until Tancredi's son Franco finally joined it in 2003.

This split between Biondi Santi and the producers' association making rules for Brunello foreshadowed later conflict between two groups of estates. One hewed to the "classic" interpretation of Brunello—that of the Biondi Santi Il Greppo. The wines produced by this estate come as close to a prototype of a wine genre as we can find in all of wine production. Indeed the construction of the rules for Brunello, which we discuss next, essentially codified the practices of Il Greppo–Biondi Santi. But there was another group that looked for shortcuts of various kinds or sought to copy New World wine styles. Curiously the latter were part of the consorzio, but Biondi Santi was not. In other words, the split left the historical and market leader outside the producer collective, which consisted mainly of those with no expertise. In effect, one could say that the collection of winemakers and their main organization was left rudderless. This initial condition, along with dissensus about the meaning of Brunello, made the collective of producers unstable.

6.2 Codification

As we mentioned above, the effort to acquire DOC and DOCG standing for Brunello was led initially by Tancredi Biondi Santi. And we stated that the Disciplinare that resulted in each case followed closely the practices at Il Greppo. Consider that the Disciplinare for the DOC established in 1966 required that all aspects of vinification and aging follow the "traditional methods of the zone." What was the tradition? Il Greppo–Biondi Santi.

Most notably the aging regime instituted in 1966 was set at four years in botti grandi made of oak. The long aging period (the longest of any DOC or DOCG) was influenced by Tancredi's insistence that Brunello should be a wine made for the long haul. And the explicit restriction that only botti be used reflected the extent to which the practice at Il Greppo was treated as the prototype.

The Disciplinare for Brunello di Montalcino DOCG was in many respects similar to those for Barolo and Barbaresco. It dictated several characteristics of the wine, including color ("intense ruby red, tending to garnet with aging"), taste ("dry, warm, slightly tannic, robust and lively, but harmonious"), and smell ("characteristic perfume and odor"). We reviewed the original documentation for the application of the DOCG for Brunello in the archives of the *Ministero delle Politiche Agricole Alimentari e Forestali* in Rome. The initial application for the Brunello DOCG was presented in 1971. However, in February 1973, the president of the *Comitato Nazionale per la Tutela Dell'Origine dei Vini* (National Committee for the Protection of Prestige Wines), Senator Paolo Desana, returned the application to the local authorities on the grounds that it had not made a compelling case that Brunello was a prestigious wine. Desana invited a revised application that followed the content and form of the application from the producers of Barolo and Barbaresco, which was about to be approved.

When the case for a Brunello DOCG was resubmitted, the application included two reports aimed at establishing a long-standing practice of high-quality winemaking and prestige of the wine. One was a technical analysis of the geological environment of the production area in Montalcino. The other was a memoir by Tancredi Biondi Santi that described the history of Brunello and also the organoleptic characteristics that Brunello should have. Tancredi also mentioned that Brunello "cannot be released for sale before four years of aging." Before that time, he argued, the wine "lacks harmony, is tannic, rough, has a full body, but is not drinkable." In other words, what was coded as "characteristic" for Brunello was the wine produced at Il Greppo. And this estate legitimated the high-quality reputation for the wine. The revised application was accepted and proceeded through the subsequent bureaucratic channels. The DOCG status was finally granted in 1980.

One important difference between the Disciplinari for Brunello and for Barolo and Barbaresco owes to the fact that many of the founders in Montalcino lacked vineyards with mature vines capable of producing rich wine. This deficit was compensated for by the allowance of "correction with must and grapes from other areas" to as much as 10 percent of the volume, as we noted above. In other words, producers were allowed to add juice of other grape varietals from other zones to their wine and still label it as Brunello. This allowance was dropped in the 1980 revision of the Disciplinare that established a DOCG for Brunello di Montalcino.

Crucially the consorzio enacted a voting rule that made the number of votes a linear function of the number of bottles produced.[3] Given that size differences among members eventually became pronounced, this system allowed the largest producers to exercise a high degree of control over decisions, including subsequent changes in the Disciplinare.

A 1980 revision of the DOCG Disciplinare had reduced the required period of aging in botti to three and a half years. A subsequent far-reaching revision of the rules in 1996 reduced the aging requirement to three years. It also eliminated the requirement that the aging be done in botti grandi. Rather, it stated that the producers could use "oak containers of any size." Then, in 1998, the rules were revised yet again to reduce the minimum period of aging in oak from three years to two. O'Keefe (2012, p. 68) calls this change "an obvious concession to the use of barriques, which, although they had been in use for a while, were technically violating the production code." While many smaller producers had opposed the change, Franco Biondi Santi supported it. He later told O'Keefe (2012, p. 69)

> That was a mistake ... My decision was based on the assumption that the overall minimum aging period in estate cellars would remain fixed at over four years after the harvest. But this measure has since set off a series of attempts to shorten the minimum cellaring period from four years to three, and to further reduce wood aging from two years down to one.

One of the few producers who opposed the revisions to the Disciplinare was Gianfranco Soldera. In the documents compiled with the Brunello DOCG application and its revisions in the archives of the Italian Ministry of Agriculture, we found an interesting exchange from 1985 between Soldera and the president of the consorzio. At the time, the later proposal to reduce the aging period for Brunello was already circulating among producers.

Soldera expressed his strong opposition to this proposal and requested evidence from scientific research that would support the reduction in the minimum period of aging. The president replied that the proposal was based on collective learning by "local producers" and views expressed by experts. Also, requiring years of aging resulted in keeping the botti empty for six months in the last year. Soldera wrote back lamenting his exclusion from the group of "local producers" whose learning was used to inform the proposal. He argued that the explanations to justify a shorter aging period were based not on scientific reasons but on practical and economic calculations. In January 1986 the consorzio commissioned a technical report to expert Lamberto Paronetto, which would be instrumental in the later vote to reduce the aging period. Paronetto argued that following the tradition in Montalcino of using large oak botti could produce bitter and astringent taste and other negative organoleptic elements in the wine. He also argued that new barrels of small or medium capacity (barriques) would produce the greatest harmonization of aromas and wines that would be exceptionally pleasant in a shorter time. Paronetto concluded that four years (three in barrels and one in bottle) were sufficient for Brunello to demonstrate its quality and traditional features. This episode is yet another demonstration that a shift to aging in barrique in Montalcino lacked the strong cultural symbolism we saw in the Langhe.

Clearly agreement about what it means for a wine to be Brunello di Montalcino has been tenuous. This lack of strong agreement evidences itself in the increasing frequency of changes in the rule and in attempts to further change them. Similar volatility has marked the efforts to codify the second Sangiovese-based wine: Rosso di Montalcino.

The founders of the consorzio wanted a second wine that could be sold to develop some positive cash flow while the Brunello was aging for four years. According to O'Keefe (2012, p. 52), Tancredi Biondi Santi agreed with the idea and proposed that this second wine be labeled as Rosso di Montalcino. The other producers disagreed and instead voted to call it Vino Rosso dai vigneti di Brunello, or Red Wine from the vineyards of Brunello. Biondi Santi objected strongly to this proposal as well on the grounds that this name would diminish the standing of Brunello, and its passage was one of his reasons for abandoning the consorzio before it officially began.

The Disciplinare for Rosso di Montalcino, which stated that this second wine must be composed only of Sangiovese and aged for one year, was originally approved in 1983. The rules were subsequently revised in 1991, 1996, 2011, 2013, 2014, 2015, and 2019. The frequency of changes testifies to the lack of consensus about this second wine as well. One of the changes altered the name of the second wine to what Biondi Santi had originally proposed.

There is also a second DOC wine from the zone, Rosso Sant'Antimo, that allows blending of any varietal including French varietals such as Merlot and Cabernet Sauvignon with Sangiovese. Such wines are called Super Tuscans, as we discuss in the next chapter.

6.3   Social Structure: Heterogeneous Origins

The mix of producers of Brunello include wineries run by families with long-standing ties to the locality. To give some sense of the heterogeneity, this section sketches a number of illustrative examples. We start with two of the wineries whose owners signed the founding document of the consorzio.

Nello Baricci grew up in a sharecropping family. In 1955, he took advantage of new loan programs designed to allow peasants to purchase land formerly owned by the great estates and purchased the twelve-hectare Colombaio Montosoli farm in a favorable location on the Montosoli hill north of the town of Montalcino. He initially engaged in diversified agriculture and did not concentrate on growing Sangiovese until after he joined in the founding of the consorzio. His first wine, a Rosso di Montalcino, was from the 1967 vintage, and his first Brunello was from the 1971 vintage. He did a major replanting of his vineyards in 1988. The Baricci Colombaio Montosoli farm has remained at its original size, with five hectares (about 12.5 acres) planted to Sangiovese. Its annual production runs about 13,000 bottles of Brunello and 18,000 bottles of Rosso. When he passed away in 2017 at the age of 96, he had become a legendary figure in the region. The winery is now directed by his grandsons, who strive to maintain their grandfather's traditional style.

On the lower slopes of the same hill, one finds the neighboring Valdicava farm, which was purchased in 1953 by Bramante Martini and his spouse. Like Baricci, Martini had grown up in a sharecropper family and was a founder of the consorzio. Before entering wine production, he concentrated on raising cattle and selling hides. He grew grapes, which he sold to Biondi Santi. The estate did not release any wine until his first Brunello from the 1968 vintage. So far the story is similar to Baricci's. However, Bramante's son left the winery and moved to Siena. Bramante then announced his intention to sell the winery in 1987. Instead, his grandson Vincenzo Abbruzzese, who had just finished his university studies in Siena, took over the farm. Abbruzzese began to make wine its main focus. He engaged in a long series of improvements in the vineyard and cellar. Most of his attention is devoted to the vineyards. In 2017, we spent most of our interview at Valdicava in the vineyards discussing organic viticulture. Valdicava has risen to the top tier of producers in terms of critical acclaim. For instance, its 2010 Brunello di Montalcino Riserva Madonna del Piano was the first wine in the denomination to receive a 100-point rating from *Wine Spectator*.

Not all of the consorzio's founders had deep local roots. Consider, for instance, Tenute Silvio Nardi, one of Brunello's largest producers. Nardi, an agricultural-equipment magnate from Umbria, purchased the Casale del Bosco estate and planted vines as a hobby. He produced his first Brunello in 1958, nine years before the creation of the consorzio. The winery's website refers to Nardi as "the first 'foreigner' to invest in the wine business in Montalcino."

His daughter Emilia joined with her brothers in the family estate in 1985 and succeeded her father as the general manager in 1990. Emilia told us that wine production in 1990 was a sideline for the family and that the wine was not good. She led an effort to investigate systematically the geology of the estates's sprawling lands and to replant the vineyards in more suitable locations. Nardi is one of the larger producers of Brunello, but it still produces wheat and other agricultural products.

At nearly the same time as Nardi's entrance, Milanese businessman Walter Ghezzi purchased the Camigliano estate in 1957. The estate, still run by the Ghezzi family, does not receive as much attention as the others discussed in this section, although it is one of the larger producers in Montalcino. Perhaps this is because the vineyards lie at a relatively low altitude, and therefore they experience higher temperatures during the growing season, which makes it hard to produce elegant wines.

All of the other large producers of Brunello also entered Brunello production by acquiring existing wine estates. An important instance involves the paired stories of Col d'Orcia, the fourth largest producer of Brunello, and Il Poggione, another large producer. The story begins when Florentine landowner Lavinio Franceschi purchased an estate called Fattoria di Sant'Angelo in Montalcino in the late nineteenth century and began producing Brunello (one of the earliest producers of Brunello as we mentioned above). When brothers Leopoldo and Stefano inherited the family estate, they decided to divide it. Leopoldo called his portion of the estate Il Poggione. This estate is still owned and managed by members of the Franceschi family. Stefano called his portion Col d'Orcia, which means the "hill above the River Orcia." Stefano died without heirs, and the estate was sold to the Cinzano family from the Piedmont, maker of the eponymous vermouth, among many other brands. The winery today is run today by Count Francesco Marone Cinzano, who also owns wineries in Chile. He has converted his grape production to organics. In 2012 Cinzano told us that he intended this to be a step toward conversion to biodynamic production.

A more radical departure from Montalcino tradition took place with the creation of the Castello Banfi winery. American brothers John and Harry Mariani had become the dominant importer of Italian mass-market wines to the American market, especially Lambrusco bottled under the Reunite label, which sold in the millions of cases per year in the 1970s. The brothers purchased roughly 8,000 hectares (almost 20,000 acres) of land at the far northern edge of the production zone that had been devoted mainly to cereal production in 1978. According to O'Keefe (2012, p. 218):

> Those residents old enough to remember still shudder when they recall how bulldozers were called in to flatten much of the rolling hillside on the Mariani's newly acquired property, allowing them to plant thousands of acres of easy-to-manage vineyards and create what resembled a great swath of California wine country.

The Marianis hired Piedmontese Ezio Rivella as their enologist and set out to produce mass-market sweet sparkling wine, planting mostly the Piedmontese varietal Moscatello. This varietal did not flourish in the heat of the Northern Montalcino, and the vines were eventually grafted with Sangiovese and French varietals. Banfi now produces roughly 10 million bottles yearly, including about 10 percent of the entire Brunello production.

The two Florentine noble families with extensive winery holdings in Tuscany and elsewhere, Antinori and Frescobaldi, also entered the scene. The first mover was the Frescobaldi family, whose ancestors had began producing Tuscan wine in 1308. The family currently owns nine estates in Tuscany. In the case of Montalcino, the Frescobaldis purchased an estate featuring a twelfth-century castle in 1989, and they named their Brunello brand Castel-Giocondo after the castle. Brunello production had begun several years earlier by previous owners. According to O'Keefe (2012), Frescobaldi replanted at higher density and took steps to improve quality. American critic James Suckling chose its 2010 Brunello as the world's top wine of the year in 2015. CastelGiocondo is currently the second largest producer of Brunello, behind only Banfi.

The Frescobaldi family also created a second Montalcino winery in cooperation with Robert Mondavi, a leading Napa Valley producer, in 1995. The joint enterprise, called Tenuta delle Luce—now simply Tenute

Figure 6.3 Gianfranco Soldera Soldera. *Source:* tenzingws.com.

Luce—purchased land that had been owned by French investors and was planted to Merlot, Cabernet Sauvignon, Sauvignon Blanc, and Sangiovese. The new winery produced a Brunello DOCG and two Super Tuscans.

The Antinori family, which claims to be a twentieth-generation wine-maker, owns eight estates in Tuscany and Umbria; two in California's Napa Valley; and one each in Washington State, Hungary, Malta, and Romania. The Antinori family's entry into Montalcino took the form of the purchase of Pian delle Vigne in 1995.

It was not only large enterprises that entered Montalcino and Brunello production. Some newcomers established family wineries. Two estates that have claim to the greatest Brunello followed this pattern. One was Società Argicola Case Basse, created in 1972 by Gianfranco Soldera, who had been an insurance broker in Milan. The second was Cerbaiona, which was created in 1977 by Diego Molinari, a former Alitalia pilot, and his Egyptian-born wife Nora. They were the first to establish a winery in a location that turned out to be superb for growing Sangiovese. Nora told us that "this was a place forgotten by God. It was such misery, really misery. The neighbors bet that we would not last more than six months."

Others include the Venetian Giuseppe Sesti, who directed musical festivals and wrote monographs on the history of astronomy. He purchased the Castello di Argiano estate (now Sesti Castello di Argiano). In our meeting in 2012, he described his early experience in Montalcino:

> I arrived here in the 1970s, I was looking for a place to settle with young children, I was writing books on the history of astrology. In the 1980s, Brunello became a more important wine internationally. People started coming here: winemakers, academics, and more. Lots of farms made wine in the classic style. I was the only one who spoke some English. Everyone called me to help communicate with their customers. I helped without being paid in money. I was paid in knowledge, a lunch, and a bottle of wine in the end. I introduced many estates to one another and to foreign customers. After ten years, I knew which was my favorite Brunello, what kind of technology could produce it, and all of the craft. Eventually, I planted vines because I was sitting on very good land.

6.4   Accelerating Outside Ownership

So far we have concentrated on the inflow of outsiders as founders of wine estates. The representation of outsiders has also grown through sales of ongoing wineries. One case involves the pair of wine estates Tenuta Caparzo and Altesino. Both had local roots. According to Caparzo's website (https://www.caparzo.it), a group of friends purchased a ruined estate with vineyards in the late 1960s to initiate production of Brunello. In 1998, the estate was purchased by Elisabetta Gnudi Angelini. Angelini was originally from Rome; her husband Paolo Angelini was heir to Italy's largest pharmaceutical company. She made the purchase after selling her share of Angelini SPA (her husband died at an early age) and first purchasing the Borgo Scopeto in the Chianti Classico area. A year after she purchased Carparzo, the estate pioneered using barriques for aging Brunello. Next, in 2002 she acquired Altesino. At the time of the purchase, *Wine Spectator* referred to the estate as "one of the greatest names in Tuscan wine" (www.winespectator.com/articles/tuscanys-altesino-estate-sells-for-25-million-21508). Altesino was founded by Guilio Consonno in 1990 with the purchase of land long-owned by the Tricerchi family.

Another of the largest producers, Argiano, developed from an estate that had a series of noble owners over the centuries. It was one of the founders of the Brunello Consorzio. In 1992, ownership of the estate passed to Countess

Noemi Marone Cinzano, the elder sister of Francesco Marone Cinzano, who owns Col d'Orcia. The countess modernized the vineyards and cellars and hired the famed enologist Giacomo Tachis, who moved wine production toward modernism. The estate was sold to a group of Brazilian businesspeople in 2013.

Castiglion del Bosco, whose owner was another signatory to the founding document of the consorzio, was sold in 2003 to Massimo Ferragamo, son of the creator of the fashion empire Salvatore Ferragamo. At the time, this was the fifth largest winery in the area. The new owner renovated the winery and built a luxury hotel and golf course on a UNESCO World Heritage Site.

Some of the other most historic and noteworthy wine estates have recently been sold to outsiders. Most notably, after the death of Franco Biondi Santi, his estate Il Greppo was sold in 2016 to the French luxury goods firm Européenne de Participations Industrielles, which also owns the Charles Heidsieck and Piper-Heidsieck champagne brands. Diego Molinari's La Cerbaiona was sold in 2105 to an American group of investors led by venture capitalist Gary Rieschel. Poderi Salicutti was sold in 2016 to the Eichbauer family, which owns a construction business in Germany. Poggio Antico, one of the largest producers in Montalcino, was sold in 2017 to Belgium's Atlas Invest, an energy holding company.

This sketch of some of the representative producers of Brunello highlights social diversity along several dimensions. The most important dimensions concern place of origin and form of organization. We discuss the importance of the two alternative modes of organization—family domain versus corporation—in the next chapter.

While some producers have deep roots in Montalcino and the area, many more came from outside. Some of the outsiders came early in the history of the DOCG and built family wineries; the flow of entrants of outsiders into the pool of Brunello producers continues unabated and might have accelerated. The most respected producers continue to be family-farm wineries. But the largest producers have corporate forms, outside ownership, and large-scale production. In contrast, the Langhe is extremely homogeneous. We trace some of the implications of this difference in the next chapter.

CHAPTER SEVEN

Tradition, Modernity, and the Scandal

HOW HAS THE FRACTURED SOCIAL structure of the producers of Brunello shaped the genre? This chapter argues that the combination of weak producer solidarity and the market pressure to produce modern wines lowered the consensus about the meaning of the genre. These processes came to light in *Brunellopoli*, the Brunello scandal.

7.1   Tradition and Modernity in Montalcino

As was the case for Barolo/Barbaresco, producers of Brunello came to agree on a distinction between modern and traditional genres. It appears from our interviews that the producers of Brunello borrowed from the Langhe the view that the choice of barrel (barrique/botti) signals a winery's position in this spectrum. The distinction between tradizionale and moderno is used routinely among the community of Montalcino winemakers. However, the issue seems never to have become as sharp and divisive as in the Langhe. We do not see that clear market identities developed around modernism and traditionalism. We discuss first what we learned of the local interpretations of the opposition, and then we speculate about why the division was less sharp than in the North.

Some notable producers proudly claim affiliation with local tradition, especially with sole reliance on aging in botti. For instance, the late Franco Biondi Santi told us in 2005:

> In recent decades, big-structured wines, colored wines, and unnatural wines have emerged due to the action of American producers, including the use of barriques ... There are ridiculous names given to wine colors

and wine flavors: dry leaves, wet leaves, and these flavors can be obtained using barriques. Basically, they use tricks in the cellar.

On the other hand, there are producers like me that use large oak-wood casks from Slovenia. There are two ways of thinking, one influenced by the mass media, and the other one that is linked to tradition, to a solid experience. Mine comes from my family: this is the traditional way of producing.

Guilio Salvioni, a highly regarded producer, put it more succinctly when we asked in 2005 what it means for him to be a traditionalist:

First of all, I don't use barriques—absolutely!

The less you modify the wine process, the better it is. Large producers have to use modern techniques, but for small producers, this is not a good idea. It's like comparing Fiat and Ferrari cars.

The late Gianfranco Soldera, whose Brunellos fetched by far the highest prices in the denomination, characteristically framed the issues in absolute terms.[1] In 2005 and again in 2008, he told us that he did not allow variations in typicality; there is only one way to make wine:

It's wrong to think in terms of traditional or modern wine. There is just wine, which is the one produced as the law says, and then there are other beverages. Among the various transformations of these beverages there is the use of barriques. In my opinion a producer who uses barriques admits that he has poor grapes, with low tannins. That's a newer method, but the finished product is not "wine."

While sole reliance on botti grandi for aging has been dominant in Montalcino, large market-driven producers like Banfi used barriques. Here the goal was to make an unabashedly modern Brunello.

However, some highly regarded producers with local roots rely wholly or partly on the small Bordeaux barrels. Giancarlo Pacenti, son of one of the founders of the consorzio and educated at Bordeaux University, led the way. In 2008, when we asked him about the motivation for this choice, he echoed what we heard from modernists in the Langhe about adapting to the market:

When we approached the market we ran into a problem. Brunello was recognized in the market for its high potential after a long aging in the cellar. But if we participated in international tastings with wines from other countries, one of the problems was that ... the wine was still young. The customers would have problems with the tannins.

If you go to a restaurant and decide to drink a bottle of the latest released harvest, you must have a good wine in the glass. Perhaps not the best is possible, but a good wine. This was our first problem, the necessity to have a wine good to drink when we released it, but also after ten to fifteen years of aging.

Pacenti told us that he prefers to work with barriques:

Why? With barriques we can have a very good wine, which means a good structure, very good tannins, very soft and not hard tannins. A very good wine means also a wine with a very clear personality. A possibility to recognize it, to sell it, to say this wine is from a specific vineyard and a specific terroir.

The pair of elite producers we discussed in the previous chapter, Soldera and Molinari (of Cerbaiona), were outsiders; but they hewed to local traditional practices. They vinified with minimal intervention and used large botti for aging. Soldera released his wines after longer aging than other Brunello producers. On one of our visits to Casse Base, Soldera told us proudly that he thought he was the only winemaker in the world with six vintages still in barrel.

The origins of many Brunello producers from outside the region complicate the picture on tradition. Consider the Cupano winery. In 1994, Lionel Cousin, a French cinematographer from Bordeaux, and his wife Ornella Tondini, a journalist from Rome, settled in Montalcino and created a new winery. In 2012, when we asked Lionel about barriques he responded that he uses nothing else. Ornella quickly added, "He is French, anyway, so it's not new using the barriques. For him it's a tradition."

We have discussed the large firms started by outsiders in the previous chapter. Some of these have opted for use of small barrels. For instance, Col d'Orcia makes a mix of modern and traditional wines, including blends with Cabernet Sauvignon and Syrah. Francesco Marone Cinzano told us that he has a flexible strategy in choosing the size of the barrel for the blends (Super Tuscans), but not for Brunello:

For Brunello, the choice was made before me. I'm all for it because, the more time goes by, the more my very traditional positioning sets me apart from the rest of—or from many of—the 250 producers in Montalcino. I'm pushing my traditional canter in Montalcino to differentiate myself from most. It's a conscious decision.

Giuseppe Sesti told a similar story. When we asked about choice of barrels, he replied:

> When we started we noticed that the wine that we loved the best was made in the old-fashioned way ... For us the use of the barriques for the Sangiovese is nonsense because the wine just needs a home to rest, a good home. It doesn't need anything added.
>
> We have some barriques in the cellar because we have a small production of Merlot-Cabernet without Sangiovese. This is for sentimental reasons because I was brought up with Merlot and Cabernet in the north.

Others small entrants brought a modern interpretation of Brunello. Florence-born visual artist Sandro Chia bought an abandoned castle called Castello Romitorio and its farmland in 1984. He began planting vineyards and constructing a cellar. Winemaking was originally done using traditional practices. However, a new winemaker, Carlo Ferrini, joined the firm and moved its production toward modernism. Its wines are now aged in *tonneaux* (500-liter barrels).

None other than Angelo Gaja, discussed extensively in our account of the modernist movement in the Langhe, purchased former church property Pieve Santa Restituta in 1994 and built a winery with that name. As with his Langhe production, Gaja ages his Brunello Pieve Santa Restituta for one year in barriques and one in botti grandi.

Castiglion del Bosco, under its new owner Massimo Ferragamo, uses only barriques for its Brunellos. As its enologist Cecilia Leoneschi put it, "We want immediately enjoyable wines upon release" (quoted by Monica Larner, *Wine Enthusiast*.[2]

Francesco Leanza, originally from Sicily, founded Podere Salicutti in 1990 after working for twenty years as a chemist in Roma. His production was organic from the beginning, the first in Montalcino. The winery was certified organic by the time of his first harvest in 1996. In 2008, he told us that he sees himself as following a middle style:

> I am in the middle between innovation and tradition ... The use of large botti here in Italy was due more to practical, logistical reasons than anything else ... These logistical factors have become less relevant, and producers started focusing more on understanding the interaction between the wood and the taste of the wine, and experimentation started. The

choice of barrel, depending on which type of Brunello you want to obtain, started to be viewed as flexible.

Filippo Baldassarre Fanti of Tenuta Fanti, one of the historic estates of the region, also emphasizes the desirability of a flexible view. In 2008, he told us that he uses 60 percent barriques and 40 percent botti, vinifies separately, and blends before bottling. When we asked why, he replied:

> We used to make Brunello using only new barriques. However, you have to pay attention to the differences across vintages. Some vintages are more powerful than others, and it is difficult to understand the evolution of the wines in barriques. If the wine tastes of wood, it has a defect. The wine must have a taste of grapes, not wood. We chose an intermediate solution to balance the mass. I think this is the right direction.

So we see a divergence in the choice of barrel for wine aging that closely parallels the choices made in the Langhe. However, the choice does not appear to have generated much contention. Aside from the always polemical Soldera and Biondi Santi, we did not hear major criticisms between camps or sense any tension. And the lack of heat is reflected in the analyses of critics, who rarely focused on the traditional/modern distinction in discussing Brunellos. However, we get the impression from reading critical commentary and marketing that the traditional/modern distinction has become more salient. It is as if the cultural template forged in Barolo/Barbaresco is now being applied by external audiences to Brunello di Montalcino.

The cleavages that emerged in Montalcino were based on ownership structure rather than genre affiliation, as in the case of Barolo/Barbaresco. The shaper division in Montalcino pitted large wine estates, generally with outside ownership, against much smaller family wineries. The two groups diverged in their conceptions of Brunello and therefore in what methods of production to use. The salience of the divergence was sharpened for family producers by the voting rule in the consorzio. As we explained in the previous chapter, the number of votes is proportional to the volume of output. This means that a winery like Banfi has many times more votes than any family winery. According to the figures for roughly 2010 obtained by O'Keefe (2012), Banfi produced more than 700,000 bottles (CastelGiocondo made 280,000). Compare that number with Biondi Santi (50,000–70,000), Cerbaiona (8,000), Il Marrorneto (20,000), Salvioni (15,000), and Soldera (15,000).

7.2   Super Tuscans

It is hard to understand the strategies of the big wineries without considering the phenomenon of Super-Tuscan wines. This is initially the story of two wines against the backdrop of the Denominazione di Origine Controllata (DOC) for Tuscany's iconic red wine: Chianti. The formal rules for Chianti arose in a process exactly parallel to that for Brunello di Montalcino. As Brunello was modeled on the practices of a single winery, Il Greppo–Biondi Santi, the production rules for Chianti followed those laid down in 1872 by a single individual: Baron Bettino Ricasoli (the second prime minister of Italy). The recipe was 70 percent Sangiovese, 20 percent Canaiolo, and 10 percent Malvasia (a sweet white varietal). When the Chianti DOC was first implemented, it kept this basic mix but allowed another white varietal (Trebbiano) to replace Malvasia. Today the thought of mixing these whites with Sangiovese would be unthinkable; this requirement was later dropped, and the addition of these varietals is now forbidden by the current DOC. Note that the initial Disciplinare forbade a wine made only of Sangiovese to be labeled as Chianti. Among other things, this made Biondi Santi's Brunellos much more distinctive in Tuscany than they are now, when wines made only of Sangiovese are commonplace.

In the 1970s and 1980s, some Tuscan winemakers rebelled against the Chianti DOC. One branch went in the direction of Brunello by making Sangiovese-only wines. The most notable of these was Montevertine and its Le Pergole Torte. Given the rules at the time, this and similar wines could declare only the lowest rung on the official hierarchy: *Vino de Tavola* (generic table wine).

The other branch sparked the creation of the label Super Tuscan. The label referred to wines produced in Tuscany that use non-native grapes, principally Cabernet Sauvignon, Cabernet Franc, and Merlot, possibly in combination with Sangiovese.[3] Pride of place goes to Marchese Mario Incisa della Rocchetta, who grew up in the Piedmont. Inspired by his boyhood stays at the Rothschild family's chateau in Bordeaux, he planted Cabernet Sauvignon in his wife's family's estate San Guido in Bolgheri beginning in 1942. Bolgheri, which lies in Toscana's coastal region, had not been a center for producing fine wine. But Rocchetta recognized a similarity of the soil to that of Bordeaux. For several decades he produced wine for his family and friends. His nephew Piero Antinori proposed that he distribute the wine commercially and sent his family's renowned enologist Giacomo Tachis to work at San Guido. The first commercial release of Sassacaia was the 1968 vintage. The critic Luigi Veronelli, whose guide serves as one of our main sources of data, wrote a rave review of a Sassacaia in 1974. More important, it came first among thirty-three cabernets, including those from top Bordeaux chateaux, in a blind tasting organized by *Decanter* in 1978. Robert Parker gave a perfect score of 100 to the 1985 vintage, and James Suckling of *Wine Spectator* (WS) compared it favorably to the top-rank Mouton-Rothschild of the same vintage.

During this rise to global critical acclaim, Sassacaia and its growing cohort, including Piero Antinori's Tignanello and Solaia and Lodovico Antinori's Ornellaia, did not fit any DOC or *Denominazione di Origine Controllata e Garantita* (DOCG). The official classification system relegated them to the class of *Vino da Tavola*. This was a major embarrassment for the authorities who controlled the classification system, and an adjustment was made in 1992 with the introduction of a new class: *Indicazione Geographica Tipica* (typical of the region). Eventually a Bolgheri DOC was created. (Sassacaia even got its own DOC.)

Among those who joined the Super-Tuscan bandwagon were the large wineries in Montalcino. Consider some examples. Castello Banfi produces one Super Tuscan called Excelsus that combines Merlot and Cabernet Sauvignon and another called Summus, which combined Sangiovese, Cabernet Sauvignon, and Syrah. Frescobaldi's two Montalcino estates produce Super Tuscans: CastelGiocondo makes a Syrah called Lamaione, and Tenute Luce makes Luce, a blend of Sangiovese and Merlot, and Lux Vitis, a blend of Cabernet Sauvignon and Sangiovese. Argiano makes Solengo, a blend of Cabernet Sauvignon, Merlot, Petit Verdot, and Sangiovese.

The scandal we analyze next involved the illegal mixing of other varietals with Sangiovese (the Super-Tuscan formula) while fraudulently labeling it as Brunello. The large estates producing Super Tuscans in Montalcino had these other varietals on hand. And many claim that these wineries wanted to expand the international appeal of their "Brunellos" by making them as Super Tuscans.

As with the Nebbiolo-based Barolo and Barbarescos, Sangiovese yields wines with a fairly light ruby color, much lighter than the Merlot-based wines loved by the international critics. The American critics, led by Robert Parker and James Suckling, had (in the view of many commentators and many producers we interviewed) consistently favored dark, heavily extracted, and concentrated wines. In effect, true Sangiovese wines had low typicality in their concept of fine red wine. It is possible to imagine that the decision makers at the large Montalcino wineries were frustrated that their lighter-colored wines were losing in critical acclaim and market success to the Super Tuscans.

7.3　*Brunellopoli*

As in the Barolo Wars, Montalcino witnessed contention over the meaning of Brunello. However, the basis of contention did not concern the size of the barrels used for aging the wine. Instead it concerned a more fundamental issue: compliance with the DOCG regulations about the composition of the wine. As we explained in the previous chapter, by law (the DOCG regulations) Brunello can be made only from Sangiovese grapes.

Virtually all Brunello producers export much of their wine production, and the United States is their most important market. There was divergence among producers in how strongly to attend to the evaluative schemas of Parker and *Wine Spectator*. Some tried to make their wines in a way that would appeal to these critics. As British critic Jancis Robinson wrote:

> In the 1990s, too many producers seemed to be using Napa Valley Cabernet as their model. Their wines were densely purple, aggressively alcoholic, sweet, and oaky—and tasted very unlike the variety from which Brunello is supposed to be made, Sangiovese, the Chianti grape whose attributes are verve and transparency.

Franco Biondi Santi warned us in 2005 that something was amiss in Montalcino:

> Some producers try to challenge nature by making a darker wine . . . I don't want to say that some of them blend different grapes because there is no evidence. One day we will have the DNA of Brunello codified, and we'll have a complete database of all producers. Then we'll be able to collect evidence about it . . . There are many Brunellos on the market. I have doubts about some of them.

Other producers and critics shared this view. Some Brunellos were getting darker—much darker than even new clones of Sangiovese could produce. And rumors abounded that some producers were violating the law by using unauthorized varietals but still labeling their wines as Brunello.

A scandal broke out in 2008 when a court in Siena revealed that it was investigating a number of Montalcino wineries for breaking the law by adding unauthorized varietals such as Merlot to their "Brunellos." The scandal came to be known as *Brunellopoli* in Italy (a reference to the massive bribery scandal called *Tangentopoli* (Bribesville) that shook Italian politics in the 1990s).

The anglophone press referred to the scandal as Brunellogate, with obvious reference to the Nixon Watergate scandal.

The details of the investigation are murky, perhaps due to strong privacy protections granted by Italian law.[4] The identities of the firms being investigated by the Sienna court were published at the time by a small local newspaper in Siena, *Siena Free*. Italian critic and blogger Franco Zilliani reprinted this report in his blog VinoWire. A story based on Zilliani's report was then published in the national daily *la Repubblica*. The producers named were Antinori, Argiano, Castello Banfi, CastelGiocondo, and Col d'Orcia, the largest producers in the area.

O'Keefe (2008) described the immediate local reaction:

A tense silence has fallen like an iron curtain among the majority of Montalcino's growers and winemakers, as well as their governing consorzio. This near-total communication breakdown has not only left Brunello fans in the dark but has also generated controversial media coverage that has confused, exaggerated, or even made up the facts, while at the same time casting doubt as to the fate of Brunello as a varietal wine.

The effort to stonewall shows up in the press release issued by the consorzio on March 29, 2008. The first numbered point states:

Rumors that producers in Montalcino have used wines from Southern Italy in Brunello 2003 vintages: this is a very grave accusation that we find hard to believe and which the consorzio has no evidence of whatsoever.

It seems likely that the whole affair would have remained shrouded in mystery except that the U.S. government got involved. The Bureau of Alcohol, Tobacco, Firearms, and Explosives (ATF), the agency responsible for controlling imports of alcoholic beverages, invoked a law that forbids the import of any item that contains a declaration of authenticity that cannot be justified. It announced on May 9, 2008, that, in light of the investigation in Siena that questioned whether the Disciplinare had been followed and the fact that the seals on all bottles of Brunello certify compliance with it, the agency would block the import of all Brunellos unless it was accompanied by a laboratory certificate that the wine was 100 percent Sangiovese.

Given the importance of the U.S. market for the sales of Brunello, this decision seems to have forced everyone's hand. Some of the producers who had been named in the investigation claimed that the testing by the Siena magistrate had exonerated them. Argiano declassified all of its 2003 Brunello to Indicazione Geografica Tipica (IGT). According to a report posted on VinoWire on October 22, 2008, prosecutors Nico Calabrese and Mario Formisano released a statement that "6,500,000 liters of Brunello di Montalcino and 700,000 liters of Rosso di Montalcino were impounded. Roughly 1,100,000 liters of Brunello di Montalcino were declassified." The statement goes on to say that wine that was shown to be in conformity with the rules by (in part) laboratory tests could be released.

By July, ATF was satisfied by the assurances of the consorzio and the Italian government and allowed Brunello to be imported into the United States once again. We happened to be in Montalcino in July 2008 when the U.S. ambassador came to sign an agreement with the Italian minister of agriculture reauthorizing export. We expected that producers would be willing, even anxious, to clarify what had gone on. This did not occur. The always combative Gianfranco Soldera discussed the situation openly with us. This might have been because it was widely rumored in the town that he had sent damning evidence to the magistrate that had initiated the whole affair. He assured us that he had not. He explained to us:

The worst thing is that the problem has not been treated in the right way. In my opinion the vintners under investigation ought to be suspended by the consorzio. The rulers must provide additional guarantees. Additional controls to safeguard the winemakers who are not under investigation were necessary. This should have been the strong signal we needed to send to the market. The consorzio and the producers denied, denied, and denied. Then, the next thing we know is that hundreds of thousands of bottles of Brunello were confiscated.

When we asked about the number of producers who were being investigated, he replied:

They are not a few. Those who came out in the press were about ten but probably there are others. The lack of clarity was very damaging... It's not the new producers; it is the large producers who are involved.

Francesco Leanza of Podere Salicutti described the situation in these terms:

Some producers... tried to satisfy the demand of the mass market in a furtive way that came in open conflict with the rules of the Disciplinare. The tension was already latent but now is clear and formalized. And as such it must be resolved. How?... One position argues that the wine has to conform to the Disciplinare; the other argues the Disciplinare has to conform to the wine as producers make it, and the market. Obviously, I support the former position . . . I see no compromise in this respect.

Filippo Baldassarre Fanti, proprietor of Tenuta Fanti and former president of the consorzio, expressed a different view one that we heard several times:

It is a difficult moment for Montalcino. A bad newspaper article started the rumor of illegal activities. Brunello producers did not deserve this attack. In fact, producers are working very well here. The illicit is something that needs to be proved. The USA required clearer rules, but I think that it is quite a pedantic necessity.

The legal case ended in obscurity. Only the Italian daily *la Repubblica* in its Florence edition of October 1, 2010, provided any details. (As far as we can determine, these have not been corroborated.) The article states that the director of the consorzio, Stefano Campatelli, was sentenced to sixteen months in prison and Filippo Baldassarre Fanti was given a twelve-month sentence for falsifying public documents. Both sentences were commuted, according to the report. In addition, Lamberto Frescobaldi (from CastelGiocondo) and Niccolò D'Afflitto (CastelGiocondo's lawyer) were given sentences of three months and one month, respectively, for sale of adulterated products. *La Repubblica* reported that both sentences were reduced to monetary fines. The legal representative of Argiano, Giampiero Pazzaglia, was formally indicted for sale of adulterated products, but no conclusion was reported. Finally, the report mentions that eleven others had previously negotiated plea bargains.

What we find striking about *Brunellopoli* is the absence of any organized response from the producers. We mentioned above that the consorzio had interests to keep the affair under wraps. The first thing it did after its press release claiming that there was no basis to the "rumors" was to hire a public relations firm to manage the crisis. Not only did the producers' association not react to defend the collective definition of Brunello as pure Sangiovese, no other informal groups did either. In one of our discussions with Gianfranco Soldera, we mentioned that we had also heard rumors of some producers in the Langhe violating the Disciplinare and asked if he thought it was true.[5] Soldera responded:

[There] the situation has been treated in a better way. The actions of some producers and the consorzio have been decisive. They have warned the "sly" producers and these producers stopped. They told these producers to label their wines differently—as table wines, or else—but not Barolos or Barbarescos. There was a response, and the cheeky ones stepped back.

This contrast between the two regions fits our characterization of the difference in the social structures of production. It seems that the greater heterogeneity among Brunello producers made it impossible for them to act collectively, even when it came to violations of their own Disciplinare.

7.4   Proposals to Make the Rules More "Flexible"

Brunello

It took another attack by the large producers to get an organized response. As *Brunellopoli* unfolded, the director of the consorzio resigned after being implicated and eventually convicted of fraud. He was replaced by Ezio Rivella, a Piedmontese, who was the director of Banfi and its long-standing enologist.

With the support of other large producers, Rivella argued that the Disciplinare should be revised to allow two versions, two labels for Brunello di Montalcino. One, to be called something like "artisanal Brunello," would certify that only Sangiovese was used. The other Brunello would allow some mixing of other varietals.

In November 2008, Angelo Gaja posted an open letter in *Il Sommelier*, the official magazine of Federazione Italiana Sommelier Albergatori e Ristoratori (FISAR), the Italian association of sommeliers, restaurant owners, and hotel owners (Gaja 2008), making a similar argument. It distinguished between two types of producers: (1) small, artisanal producers who made Brunello from vineyards located in a suitable microclimate and (2) large-volume producers who made Brunello from vineyards that lacked the suitable microclimate. For the first group, Gaja advocated the use of a label reflecting the faithfulness to the Sangiovese varietal. For the second group, he advocated "elasticity" in the rules about which varietals with which to make the wine. However both types of product, he argued, should have the right to bear the name Brunello.

This was too much for the majority of the producers. Seven drafted a petition that the consorzio "state once and for all" that Rule 2 of the Disciplinare that mandates that only Sangiovese be used in Brunello not be changed. The proposers of the petition were Il Greppo–Biondi Santi, Il Poggione, Col d'Orcia, Fattoria Barbi, Le Potazzine, Tiezzi Enzo, and Caprili. The petition was signed by representatives of 149 wineries, which represented 59 percent of the membership and 51 percent of the votes. This effectively blocked the proposal.

Why did this proposal, unlike the widespread violation of the Disciplinare, spark a collective response? In chapter 4 we analyzed four abstract scenarios concerning change in collective concepts in markets. We claimed that the most contentious scenario is one in which (1) a change in genre is initiated by insiders and (2) the proponents of the new genre claim the label of the established one. This is what we see here. Insiders, notably the elected director of the collective association of producers and high-status producers like Gaja, support the change. And they argue that the existing label Brunello di Montalcino be used for two wines, one that did not then conform to the rules for Brunello as well as the conforming version.

Rosso di Montalcino

The tension between large and small producers was made clear during the *Brunellopoli* scandal and the attempt to create two Brunellos. It came to a head once again in 2011. At this point, large producers shifted to trying to change the Disciplinare for Rosso di Montalcino to allow 10 percent or perhaps even 20 percent of grapes other than Sangiovese. Many viewed this tactic as a step toward the main goal of changing the rules for Brunello. In his 2008 letter, Angelo Gaja himself wrote that the Disciplinare for Rosso was "presumptuous" because it assumed that all producers legally authorized to make the wine also had vineyards located in zones suitable to make a high-quality wine. This is the same argument he made to motivate change of the legal rules for Brunello.

Resistance to the proposed change was initiated by outsiders. Widely respected American wine writer Nicholas Belfrage posted an open letter to the producers on August 11, 2011 and then asked Zilliani to post it on VinoWire. It reads in part:

> I would urge you in the strongest terms not to support this change. Rosso di Montalcino, like Brunello di Montalcino, has created for itself a strong personality on international wine markets based largely on the fact that it is a pure varietal wine.
>
> In these days, when more and more countries are climbing on the wine production bandwagon, it is more important than ever to have a distinctive identity, to make wine in a way which no one else on earth can emulate. It is my belief that the strongest factor in the identity of Rosso di Montalcino

(and, of course, Brunello di Montalcino) is the fact that it is 100 percent Sangiovese.

Our interviews revealed strong opposition to this proposal. On the eve of the vote, Rivella weakened his proposal to allow 3 to 5 percent of non-Sangiovese in the Rosso. The vote of the consorzio membership decisively rejected the proposal.

Implications

It is hard to discern the consequences of the scandal. Many producers told us that there were losses, especially in foreign markets, in the short term but that conditions were returning to normal within a few years. In our view, there was an opportunity cost. The demand for Barolo and Barbaresco rose steadily over the decade following 2006. Indeed, Aldo Vacca of the Produtorri del Barbaresco told us in 2017 that Barolo and Barbaresco were so hot that, "I feel weird because my job in the last two years is trying to sell less wine, which is kind of strange." The prices of the highly regarded wines soared. This did not happen with Brunello. It is difficult to compare average prices meaningfully for these wines because the production zone for Brunello was expanded to parts of the region that independent experts regarded as unsuitable for growing Sangiovese. Nonetheless, it appears that the producers of Brunello missed an important opportunity and that the scandal was at least part of the reason.

Some of our informants opined that the scandal had at least two positive results: the Disciplinare started to be taken more seriously and consumers might have learned its significance. When we asked Stella di Campalto about the scandal, she told us:

> For me, what happened was good . . . people want to know more. It's more effort for me because now people want to go to visit the vineyard, they want to go deeper into things. But it's more interesting as well because I can show them what I do. Now they want to know more, it's positive.

For us the most interesting question is why it took so long for the family wineries to organize a response to the challenges posed by the large producers. One would think that the scandal was sufficiently damaging to their collective interests that they would have mobilized. Our answer is the one we suggested in chapter 1: the local social structure was weakened by the great heterogeneity among the members of the consorzio. This heterogeneity undercut agreement about the meaning of their wine. Lack of a strong consensus diminished the possibility of mobilizing on the basis of solidarity and shared meanings.

It is interesting to compare Montalcino and the Langhe. The Barolo Wars certainly entailed considerable contention as the name suggests. Nonetheless, the contention did not rupture the strong local social structure. This episode resembles a family fight in which members can dispute bitterly and then hug and make up. Consider the following vignette. At the end of a meeting with Elio Altare in 2005, he asked whom we were meeting next. When we replied that it was Giuseppe (Beppe) Rinaldi, Altare said, "I will lead you there—I haven't spoken with Beppe in a while." When we arrived at Rinaldi's, the two chatted amiably for a while, seeming like old friends. When Rinaldi died in 2019, Angelo Gaja spoke warmly of him at the funeral. We do not sense any such solidarity in Montalcino, especially among the principals at the large and small wineries. We contend that the absence of such solidarity explains why conceptual consensus and the institution supporting Brunello proved to be so fragile.

CHAPTER EIGHT

Alsace

WE NOW TURN TO A French wine region: Alsace. We chose this site because it posed an interesting sociological puzzle. Many of the region's highest-status wineries follow a very unconventional approach to winemaking called biodynamics. This approach implements the prescriptions given by one man—the Austrian polymath Rudolph Steiner. In a series of lectures in 1924, Steiner proposed a holistic approach to farming based on principles involving unmeasurable cosmic forces; for example, "gnomes, undines, sylphs and fire spirits are actively involved in plant growth" (Steiner 2003 [1924], 158) give an idea of this approach. Given the oddness of biodynamics, we wondered why prominent winemakers were attracted to these practices and why affiliation with the biodynamic genre has gained a favorable reception from critics and consumer audiences.

The answer that we propose has to do with the fact that use of the biodynamic approach sends a strong signal to market audiences about difficult-to-observe features of the producers and their products as well. Biodynamics has become a collective, categorical signal in the wine market. Understanding how this unconventional approach has evolved in Alsace can shed light on some questions about the role of genres in markets.

In analyzing two communities of winemakers in Italy, we developed the argument that one key difference between the Langhe and Montalcino had to do with differences in the social structures among the producers. The community of producers of Barolo/Barbaresco showed stronger cohesion than the community of producers of Brunello di Montalcino, and we argue that this difference also influenced the emergence of wine genres and the development of collective market identities. This is a plausible argument, but we did not account for many other differences between these two communities. Now, as we turn to Alsace, we get to make a different kind of comparison within the same region. The most interesting comparisons in Alsace are among communities of producers who follow different philosophies of farming. The social structures in these communities also differ, with one being more cohesive than the others. Again we find a stronger collective identity arose around the more cohesive producer group (biodynamic farmers) and weaker identities emerged from a less cohesive set of producers who followed classic organic farming and sustainable farming. The fact that the differences between producer groups emerged in the same region helps to support our argument in more general terms because we can hold constant many of the unobserved factors that are specific to one of the two Italian regions.

8.1   Winemaking in Alsace

The region of Alsace is a narrow strip located between the Rhine's west bank and the Vosges mountains to the West. It is roughly an hour's drive from top to bottom, from the northerly town of Marlenheim to Thann in the south is a distance of 120 km, roughly 75 miles. Along this axis, there is an almost continuous swath of vineyards. The width (east to west distance) of the fine wine region varies from 1.5 to 3 km (about 0.9 to 1.9 miles).

The Vosges mountains to the west provide considerable protection for the region from the winter storms from the Atlantic. Alsace has a microclimate with cold winters and hot summers, both with relative low humidity. Indeed, the city of Colmar has the second lowest annual rainfall of any city in France.

This geographical configuration creates three main kinds of vineyard: steep slopes at the base of the mountains, moderate slopes in the foothills, and the plain between the river and the foothills. Varied soil, bedrock, and exposures can be found across sites in this area and even within a narrow bandwidth of 200 meters (about 650 feet) of elevation. Yields tend to be higher and quality lower in the plains. Extensive planting in the alluvial plain is geared toward the production of so-called supermarket wines, often selling for €2. Our focus is on *Appellation d'Origine Contrôlée* (AOC) ("controlled designation of origin"). AOC represents the classification system developed to certify geographical indications for wine in France. This leads us to concentrate on wineries with vineyards in the foothills. Figure 8.1 shows an example of the steep vineyard Rangen de Thann.

Alsatian winemaking represents 2,000 years of tradition. First planted about 60 BC, the vineyards are some of the oldest in the world. Although the tradition of growing Riesling dates to the sixteenth century, a succession

Figure 8.1 View from the Rangen de Thann vineyards to the village of Thann. *Source:* Thann_vue_depuis_le_Rangen.jpg by Florival.fr, used under license CC BY 2.0.

of wars fostered viticultural mediocrity for most of this history. The French Revolution led to redistribution of land that did not improve the situation. Surface dedicated to good but low-yielding varieties declined. Cooling climate made things worse. And so did the transfer of Alsace from France to Germany in 1870 until 1918, when Alsatian wines were denied access to the French market and Germany used Alsace to produce base grapes for cheap sparkling wine. As was the case for the other regions we studied, a strong push to improve quality set in during the 1960s.

According to data compiled by Alsace Crus and Terroirs (backinalsace. com/stories/act-alsace-crus-and-terroirs/), the total surface area of wine growing was 15,621 hectares (38,583 acres) in 2017, up from 9,441 (23,319 acres) in 1969. Of this, AOC vineyards constitute 70 percent and AOC Grand Cru vineyards, 6.3 percent. The remainder are vineyards dedicated to production of AOC Crémants, the local sparkling wines.

As is the case for other French wine regions, including Champagne, the Loire Valley, and Chateauneuf du Pape, Alsatian wine producers work with many grape varietals. These include the following, with figures in parentheses indicating the percentage of total production in 2017, according to the records summarized by the website lostinalsace.com. The so-called noble grapes, Gerwürztraminer (11.8 percent), Muscat (2.4 percent), Pinot Gris (17.4 percent), and Riesling (20.1 percent), are the only grapes allowed to be given the highest-quality label Grand Cru. Other grapes commonly grown in the region are Pinot Blanc (25 percent), Pinot Noir (11.6 percent), and Sylvaner (7.6 percent).

When we asked winemakers why they work with so many varietals, some told us that this was the tradition of the region. Most claimed that the composition of the soil varies greatly even within named vineyards and that different varietals are suited to the different soil types.

Codification

In chapter 1 we sketched the outlines of the French hierarchical system of classification. The three top levels are AOC (now AOP) village wines. Next comes Premier Cru and finally Grand Cru. The structure is intended to be hierarchical. Burgundy provides a prototypical illustration. The classification system for Burgundy identifies 585 Premier Cru vineyards, which constitute 5 percent of the AOC territory. It also identifies thirty-three Grand Cru sites, which comprise less than 1 percent of the land designated as AOC.

In contrast, the Alsatian system has only two distinctions above the table wine level: AOC and Grand Cru. That is, the system does not contain the Premier Cru designation.[1] As we explain below, the Grand Cru designation is used much more liberally in Alsace than in the rest of France. Regulators have approved fifty-one sites as Grand Cru in Alsace. They collectively constitute 4 percent of the AOC vineyards.

The Alsace AOC rules also codify two levels of sweet wine: Vendage Tardive ("late harvest") and Sélection des Grains Noble ("selection of noble berries") wine made from a selection of berries affected by noble rot (Botrytis). The difference between them is the minimal sugar content in the must (grape juice prior to fermentation). These designations apply to various grape varietals so that a wine will be labeled with the varietal name, vineyard (in the case of Grand Cru), and Vendage Tardive or Sélection des Grains Nobles.

8.2   Structure of Production

Production in the region is divided among three kinds of entities: long-standing family domaines, firms that combine family domaines and activity as merchants or négociants, and producer-owned cooperatives.

Family Domaines

Family domaines integrate grape growing, production exclusively from their own grapes, and bottling the wine under their own names. In Alsace many of the family domaines can trace a long family history of wine production in the area. Consider a few prototypical examples.

Domaine Zind-Humbrecht was created in 1959 as a merger of two family domaines, Humbrecht and Zind, when heirs of each married. The Humbrecht family can trace its history of wine production to 1620. However, it did not bottle its own wines until 1947. The domaine is currently owned and managed by Olivier and Margaret Humbrecht.

This domaine is the most highly regarded winery in Alsace, the equivalent of Giacomo Conterno in the Langhe and Soldera in Montalcino. American critic Robert Parker remarked: "I don't know what is more mind-boggling, the quality of Domaine Zind-Humbrecht's wines or Olivier Humbrecht's complete dedication to quality. This tall, powerful, and intellectual man may well be the finest winemaker in the world."

Like many other producers in the region, Humbrecht produces a dizzying array of wines: twenty-five wines for the 2017 vintage including one Pinot Noir, one Chardonnay-Auxerrois, two Muscat (one Grand Cru), eight Riesling (two Grand Crus), seven Pinot Gris (one Grand Cru), five Gerwürztraminer (Grand Crus), one VT Pinot Gris, and one SGN Pinot Gris. Production at the domain averages roughly 16,000 cases (190,000 bottles) per year.

As we discuss in the next chapter, Humbrecht has been a leader in promoting the use of biodynamics in Alsatian wine production. Since 2002 he has been president of Biodyvin, a union of biodynamic wine producers in France, Germany, Italy, Portugal, Spain, and Switzerland. He was also France's first master of wine.

Domaine Ostertag is a much younger domain, having been founded in 1966. The domain now owns fourteen hectares of vineyards composed of seventy-five plots in five villages. Its annual production is roughly 85,000 bottles. It produces the usual Alsatian copious menu of Riesling, Gerwürztraminer, Pinot Gris, and Pinot Noir.

The current winemaker and "maître de scene," André Ostertag, took the reins from his father in 1980, after completing studies in enology in Burgundy. Ostertag immediately set out to challenge the winemaking conventions of the region. Due to his training, he reasoned that Pinot Gris and Pinot Blanc, as close relatives of Pinot Noir, would benefit from Burgundian-style aging in barriques. His 1983 Pinot Gris from the Grand Cru Muenchberg

Figure 8.2 Olivier Humbrecht plowing in the Rangen de Thann vineyard. *Source:* kobrandwineandspirits.com.

was rejected by the AOC commission and therefore could not be labeled as such. However, he persisted over vintages and eventually overcame the official opposition. And, as he told us in 2009, about the use of barriques for aging Pinot Gris, "It's no longer experimental; it's part of the style."

Like Feiring (2017), we were struck that Ostertag is a very philosophical winemaker.[2] Consider the view he expressed to us about terroir:

> I think that terroir is all about humans ... What you find in the wine, of course, is a result of a vintage, a climate, a specific soil—of course ... There is a misunderstanding about terroir, at least in France. Terroir is always related to the climate and the geology. And this misunderstands the key to terroir. The key to terroir is the people. It's man. Because without man, there is shadow, night, no light. Man brings the light. He enlightens the entire process. So, if you think about that, you have the key to the system. And what the man is, is what his wine is.

Figure 8.3 André Ostertag with his barriques. *Source:* lavinia.fr.

Ostertag's domaine was converted to biodynamic farming in 1997, as we explain in the next chapter.

Domaines Viticoles Schlumberger, the largest domaine in Alsace, is located in the far south of the region in the town of Guebwiller. This bleak postindustrial town could not be more different from the wine villages. It was the location of the Schlumberger family's textile equipment factory created in 1810 by Nicolàs Schlumberger. Nicolàs also purchased a twenty-hectare plot of land with vineyards on very steep terrain. Family heirs gradually purchased additional adjoining land, bringing the winery to its current size of forty hectares (98.8 acres) in a single holding. The domaine includes major portions of four Grand Crus: Kessler, Kitterlé, Saering, and Spiegel. These four vineyards make up half of the total vineyard area of the domaine. They are planted on slopes with as much as 50 percent grade, much too steep to use tractors. Consequently these vineyards are worked with horses.

Current production is roughly 80,000 cases (960,000 bottles) per year. The domain bottles all of the common varietals of the region. Seventy percent of sales are export, and the United States and Canada are the second and third largest, after Belgium.

Thirty-eight percent of the vineyards are farmed organically and 30 percent biodynamically. Thomas Schlumberger told us that they were moving toward biodynamics in the Grand Cru vineyards but that the steep slopes have hampered their efforts so far. They have gone so far as to use helicopters to spray the required preparations (discussed in the next chapter) over the vines on the steepest slopes.

Domaines/Négociants

A handful of famous old family firms combine grape growing and wine production for their own grapes as well as from grapes purchased from others. The two most important examples are Hugel and Trimbach. Wines from these two firms have long been the most visible Alsatian wines in American retail outlets.

Hugel et Fils traces its origin as a wine producer/merchant to 1639 when Hans Ulrich Hugel settled in the village of Riquewihr, was made a freeman of the city, and took control of the Corporation of Winegrowers. The family have been winegrowers since that time. The period of their fame begins in 1918 after the vineyards of the region had been devastated by the Franco-Prussian War, World War I, and the infestation of phylloxera. Frédérick Emile Hugel replanted with only the noble grape varietals and generally upgraded quality. His son Jean (Johnny) Hugel became a legendary leader of wine-making in the region and the face of Alsatian winemaking in international markets.

Today the family owns thirty hectares (74.1 acres) of vineyards in Riquewihr, the region's most picturesque village. These vineyards are all farmed organically. Nearly half are vineyards classified as Grand Cru. The négociant business involves purchase from growers under long-term contract who farm more than 110 hectares (271.1 acres) in more than a dozen villages. Total production is roughly 110,000 cases (1,320,000 bottles). Roughly 90 percent of their sales are exports, with the United States being their largest market.

Maison F.E. Trimbach, founded in 1626, is quite similar. Its headquarters and production facilities are location in Ribeauvillé, which is about a five-minute drive from Riquewihr. The domain consists of forty hectares (98.8 acres) in six villages, and they are farmed sustainably. The négotiant business vinifies grapes from farms constituting sixty hectares (148.2 acres). Total production is roughly 80,000 cases (960,000 bottles), of which 85 percent is exported. The United States is Trimbach's biggest market.

Trimbach produces the region's most famous wine, Riesling Clos Ste. Hune, from a 1.67-hectare site in the center of Rosacker Grand Cru. This wine is also the most expensive (non-late-harvest) wine produced in Alsace.

Cooperatives

Most wine villages in Alsace had cooperative cellars along the lines of the Produttori del Barbaresco in the Langhe. Individual owners grew grapes and submitted them for winemaking and sale by the cooperative. Many cooperatives have merged or been acquired, and there are now fifteen. Most estimates say that cooperatives are responsible for roughly 40 percent of the region's wine production. Historically much of this production has been sold in bulk, for example, to supermarket chains who bottle under their own names. However, most of the cooperatives have members who own parcels in Grand Cru vineyards. This allows the cooperative to produce and market wines labeled Grand Cru.

Bestheim and *Wolfberger* are the region's largest producer-owned wine cooperatives. Bestheim was created as a merger of village cooperatives in Bennwihr, Obernai, Sigolsheim, and Kientzheim-Kaysersberg. It combines the production of 428 members, who farm a total of 1,366 hectares. Wolfberger, which began as the village cooperative in Eguisheim, also grew by acquisition. Today it has 450 members who farm 1,200 hectares, including forty-eight hectares in fifteen Grand Crus. Both cooperatives have extensive production of sparkling wine (Crémant d'Alsace) as well as still wines made from all of the common varietals and blends.

8.3   Confused Identity

If we take the perspective of the producers, the market identities of the producers are clear. They are based on the long history of wine production in the region. For many—perhaps most—the choice of grape varietals and the styles of production are justified in terms of that tradition.

But from the perspective of outside audiences, critics, retailers, sommeliers, and consumers, the picture looks quite different: the Alsace wine region has a confusing identity. These outside audiences recognize that the region has a favorable climate and geology for wine growing and that it contains many skillful winemakers backed by a long history. Nonetheless, outside audiences have difficulty making sense of the scene, as we explain below. The result is that the wines have difficulty penetrating external markets, especially in the Anglophone world. With only a few exceptions, the wines do not seem to garner prices commensurate with their quality.

Franco-German Hybrid

We discuss several sources of this identity problem. One is that the region is neither clearly French nor German. While it has been part of the French state since the end of World War II, it had been part of Germany off and on as Franco-Prussian wars raged. The local dialect is Germanic, as are the family names, as we shall see. Two of the four noble grapes allowed in Grand Cru production are also those historically associated with Germany: Riesling and Gerwürztraminer. Moreover a third, Pinot Gris, was called Tokay d'Alsace until a 1993 European Union (EU) agreement to limit the term *Tokay* to wines produced in Hungary. Consumers naturally wonder whether they should expect the wines to be French or German or something in between.

Indeed, the Alsatian manner of labeling wines is a Franco-German hybrid. As Rémy Gresser, proprietor of the eponymous domain, explained to us:

> We are in the center of Europe, between two main wine conceptions, the French and the German. In the 1920s, after the phylloxera hit in the south of France, the winemakers of Languedoc ... asked the government for a law to control the wine production. When a winemaker asked the government for protection, they believed that they owned the best places and asked the government to recognize and to classify these places.
>
> German authorities decided to create a system of labeling based on the name of the grape. This classification depends on the level of sugar in the grape. When you produce a grape that is less than 10.5 percent alcohol, you have a table wine, and so forth. When the Alsatian winegrowers wanted a little bit more of the French conception, they had to accept that the merchants wanted a little more of the German conception. For this reason ... we have a blend between the two conceptions.

Sweetness

A second vexing issue concerns sweetness. Wines made from the same grape and labeled identically can range from bone dry to quite sweet. Jane Anson, writing in *Decanter* in June 2016, discussed a tasting of multiple wines vinified from production in the Grand Cru Brand vineyard.

> Brand ... is split between thirteen producers, including many of the biggest names of the region such as Zind-Humbrecht, Josmeyer, Charles Baur and Albert Boxler. Tasting through the wines was a fascinating exercise, with

many displaying the stunning potential of Riesling in this most northerly of French wine regions. And yet they did little to show a family signature of Brand, even though all were from the Riesling grape, partly because the residual sugar within the wines on display ranged from totally dry (Josmeyer, with less than 2 grams per liter) to 9 grams per liter (François Baur) and everything in between.

Only consumers with detailed knowledge know what to expect from a given bottle. Many sommeliers are reluctant to list Alsace wines on their menus. Eric Asimov, wine writer for the *New York Times*, expressed this view in an October 2008 column entitled "The Sweet and the Dry: Decoding Alsace Wine":

> With excitement and some trepidation, I prepared to open a bottle from Zind-Humbrecht, one of the world's great wine producers and certainly one of the best in Alsace. It was a 2001 pinot gris from Clos Windsbuhl, a legendary terraced vineyard, and I was thrilled to have the opportunity to drink this wine.
>
> But I was concerned as well. Many wines from Alsace that consumers might legitimately assume to be dry are in fact sweet, and in my experience this had especially been true with Zind-Humbrecht. Sure enough, the pinot gris was by any standard an exceptional wine—complex and structured with lovely mineral, herbal and fruit flavors—but confoundedly sweet.
>
> In the right circumstances it could have been a beautiful wine, but the dinner I had prepared … would not have been a good match. I recorked the wine, with a vague thought that I should get some blue cheese or foie gras to go with it very soon.
>
> It's become a familiar predicament with Alsatian wines, happening often enough so that it has become an obstacle to opening a bottle unless I know the producer well.

Since 2001, Zind-Humbrecht has provided a 5-point sweetness scale on its labels. Some other producers followed with variations on the scale. Wine critics complain that the scales are subjective and difficult to compare across wineries. In any case, the practice does not seem to have proliferated broadly among the community of producers. The consumer's confusion persists.

There was an organized but unsuccessful attempt to deal with the problem in 2015. The membership of the Association des Viticulteurs d'Alsace (Association of Alsatian Wine Growers) voted to require that wines be labeled as *sec* ("dry") that meet the EU standard for "dry wine" (less than 4 grams of residual sugar per liter up to less than 7 grams if the acidity meets a minimum standard). However, the ruling was never adopted by the national regulator and thus did not come into force. Séverine Schlumberger told Phoebe French of *The Drinks Business* (April 9, 2019):

> We are pushing to have them [labeling regulations] imposed by law. The co-ops are against it as they often make sweet Riesling and they don't like people knowing how sweet it is.

Moreover, critics like James Suckling complain that the wines overall have become sweeter and less food-friendly. Measured levels of residual sugar have indeed increased over time. This rise has also blurred the boundary of the concept of Alsatian wine. During the 1970s and 1980s, Alsace produced mostly dry wines. At that time, the German system of classification encouraged sweetness. So the two styles were quite distinct. In recent decades, German producers have gradually shifted toward a drier style, while the Alsatians moved in the opposite direction.

Overproliferation of Grand Crus

A third source of confusion stems from the rules of the AOC for Alsace. Unlike the rest of France, the community of producers opted to promote in every village one or more vineyards to the status of Grand Cru. (As we noted above, the Alsatian producers collectively decided that the classification system would not designate Premier Cru vineyards.) As a result, the region has an odd status structure with an elaborate high and low end and no middle. As we describe below, the proliferation of Grand Crus undermined the status associated with this distinction.

Finally, the industry structure contributes to the confusion. Large cooperatives produce roughly 30 percent of the AOC wine in Alsace, and their production overlaps considerably with those of the family domaines. The existence of a large number (fifty-one) of Grand Crus, some of which are also very large in size, has resulted in members of the cooperatives owning portions of Grand Cru vineyards. This allows the cooperatives to produce wines labeled as Grand Cru that, according to the regulations, are equivalent to those of the domaines. This results in the "same" wines being sold at very different price points and in different distribution channels.

Each village in the parts of Alsace most propitious for making great wine mobilized to make sure that one or more of its vineyards was included in the list of the Grand Crus. There is still grumbling among critics and among the producers that the decisions were more political than practical. The region appears to have created a version of Garrison Keiler's fictional town of Lake Woebegon where "all the children are above average."

Expert committees came up with the original proposals for the classification. These were then subject to a consultative and representative process. The result was that the Grand Cru sites were many times larger than the size imagined at the outset. For instance, the original proposal for the Grand Cru Sporen specified two hectares (4.94 acres) of land; the eventual outcome was a plot of 23.7 hectares. Not only are the growable areas of individual Grand Crus large, they are divided among many owners in most cases. It is difficult to pin down the exact numbers, but as far as we can tell, Hengst is divided among twenty-eight owners and Schlossberg among more than sixty. Each owner, of course, can bottle wines with the Grand Cru label.

Another complaint about the classification system is that it forced Alsace into the world of strict varietal purity (the Burgundian tradition). Whereas varietal blends were a popular tradition in the old days, they are now the exception. Aside from a few producers (such as Marcel Deiss) who are trying to revive the tradition, most of the blended wine in Alsace today is cheap bulk wine marketed locally as Edelzwicker. Even if it is a great wine from a Grand Cru site, a varietal blend cannot be labeled as such.

Three famous domaines/négociants, Hugel, Trimbach, and Léon Beyer, opted out of the scheme, refusing to use the Grand Cru designation at all. The late Étienne Hugel, then the head of the family firm Hugel et Fils, told us in 2009 why they did not subscribe to this classification system:

> Although we have more than 50 percent of our vines in Grands Cru designations, we have never used the name Grand Cru on the label, although all of our customers know that our Jubilee wines are 100 percent from the best part of the Grand Cru [Schlossberg].
>
> My uncle was president of the Grand Cru committee. He wanted to do a thing that would last forever, which means small Grand Crus . . . Unfortunately, he was the only one with a long-term perspective, and he was kicked out. All the others said "if it's three times bigger, we get more money."
>
> How can you maintain prestige when someone sells Grand Cru wines for 5, 6, 7 euros, and wine from the other area of the same Grand Cru is 10 or 20 times the price? Apparently, nobody was aware about this danger thirty years ago.

Jean Trimbach gave us a similar explanation:

> By now too many Grands Crus are too large. So why should I be a driving force for Grand Cru Osterberg? It's 23 or 25 hectares. But then I see it sold in my supermarket at five euros!

While Hugel and Léon Beyer still do not use the Grand Cru designations on their labels, Trimbach recently relented in its opposition to it. It rebranded its Cuvée M as Mandelberg Grand Cru Riesling. So what prompted this change of heart? Anne Trimbach told *Wine Searcher* (posted on February 2, 2020):

> I think we've reached a decisive point in our firm's history. Modern consumers aren't interested in buying wines with nondescript labels like Cuvée M. Terroir in Alsace is increasingly important, both for us and our customers. People want to learn about the vineyard differences and, therefore, referencing Mandelberg now makes commercial sense.

Trimbach has also begun marketing a Riesling Grand Cru Geisberg and a Schlossberg Grand Cru Riesling produced from newly acquired plots. However, it has not (yet) designated its flagship Clos Ste. Hune as a Rossacker Grand Cru.

Supermarket Grand Crus

There is a related, fourth source of identity confusion: high overlap of the production of Grand Cru wines of famous domaines with that of cooperatives and marginal domaines that own portions of Grand Cru vineyards. Consider the case of Grand Cru Schlossberg, the largest of the Grand Crus. A search for prices of Riesling Grand Cru Schlossberg in Europe for the years 2016–2018 reveals an enormous price range. The cheapest was a 2016 vintage offered by the discount German supermarket chain Lidl: €9.49 (At this time, the euro/dollar exchange rate was roughly 1.2.). This is a store brand, a bottling of wine from the Grand Cru site.[3] At the high end, wines from Albert Mann, Trimbach, and Weinbach were offered at roughly €55. This is an extreme case, but other Grand Crus reveal a similar pattern. For instance, the lowest price during this period for Riesling Grand Cru Brand was offered by the cooperative Cave de Turckheim: €15.75. At the other end of the continuum, Zind-Humbrecht's wine was offered at €56.84.

Of course, aficionados know the difference between Zind-Humbrecht and the cooperative Cave de Turckheim, or between Albert Mann and Lidl's house brand. But consumers generally will find this situation difficult to interpret. The category "Grand Cru producer" is not very informative with respect to price and quality. Likely this will lower the probability of choosing an expensive wine from Alsace.

Uncertainty about how to distinguish higher from lower quality and identity confusion for external audiences creates conditions in which signals of quality can be especially powerful. We develop this argument in the following chapters.

CHAPTER NINE

Biodynamic and Organic Winemaking

BEFORE WE ANALYZE THE COMMUNITIES of producers that engage in the various forms of farming, we need to provide background about these alternative forms.

9.1 Conventional and Alternative Agriculture

Conventional agriculture refers to industrial farming methods that include the use of synthetic chemical fertilizers, pesticides, herbicides, genetically modified organisms (GMOs), heavy irrigation, intensive tillage, or concentrated monoculture production. Conventional farming brings some clear benefits, particularly cheaper production costs and larger crops that can meet the growing demand for food supply. It does not surprise that conventional farming makes up the dominant share of farmland overall. According to Pew Research Center data from 2019, there were only about 5 million acres of farmland in 2016 in the United States that were certified organic, the main alternative to conventional farming. This value represents less than 1 percent of the 911 million acres of total farmland nationwide.

But conventional farming also produces health and environmental hazards, for example, by introducing pollutants to the environment. In recent decades, alternatives to conventional farming have emerged internationally. They propose cultural, biological, and mechanical practices that foster cycling of resources, promote ecological balance, and conserve biodiversity. One such alternative is organic farming. Rather than using synthetic fertilizers, pesticides, growth regulators, and livestock feed additives, organic farming relies on crop rotation, animal and plant manures/composts as fertilizers, some hand weeding, and biological pest control.

Alternative methods to conventional have also developed in wine production. Biodynamics and organics feature as the more prominent alternatives to conventional farming. What are these methods? The biodynamic and organic genres are based on sets of practices and rules of conduct, or codes. The codes for both genres proscribe the use of fertilizers and pesticides. However, the biodynamic code subsumes the organic and goes further.

Organic Farming

Compared with conventional farming, organic agriculture uses ecologically-based pest controls and biological fertilizers derived largely from animal and plant wastes, thus decreasing health and environmental hazards associated with nitrate contamination of groundwater and surface water. Using biological fertilizers also recycles livestock wastes to make materials such as compost, which then can be put back into the earth for growing crops, plants, and vegetables. These benefits are counterbalanced by generally lower yields and higher food costs for consumers. Biodynamic expert Monty Waldin reports that yields drop about 21 percent for organics and 30 percent for biodynamics compared to high-input conventional farming.[1]

The concepts of organic agriculture were developed in the early 1900s by botanists Albert and Gabrielle Howard. The Howards worked in India as agricultural researchers and were inspired to integrate agricultural science with ancient Indian techniques of sustainable farming practices, including the traditional aerobic method of composting. It was not until 1940, when English agriculturalist Walter James, fourth Baron Northbourne, published *Look to the Land*, that the term organic farming was coined. This book described the deleterious "chemicalization" of the food chain and laid the ideological and philosophical foundation for contrasting organic farming with conventional farming. A central idea was that of the farm as an organism that must have a biological completeness. The farm must be a living entity, a unit with a balanced organic life.

Organic farming is defined by the use of fertilizers solely of organic origin, such as compost manure and green manure, to improve the humus content of soils. It also emphasizes techniques such as crop rotation and companion planting. Biological pest control, mixed cropping, and the fostering of insect predators are encouraged. Legal standards regulate production methods for organic agriculture. The production and labelling of organic products within the European Union or the United States follows a strict certification process. Farmers must first register with an authorized inspection body or authority in their country and, according to an agreed conversion plan, undergo a conversion period (in the European Union, a minimum of two years) before they can begin producing agricultural field crops that can be marketed as organic. During this time, the farm is said to be in conversion. Farms must be subject to inspections by acknowledged inspection bodies or authorities to ensure compliance with organic legislation. Successful operators are then granted organic certification and are allowed to have their goods labeled as organic.

The European regulation on organic agriculture (Reg. 2092/91 and 834/07) defined the rules of organic grape growing but did not specify any requirements for organic *vinification*. Based on existing provisions, in Europe the only lawful denomination is "wine obtained from grapes from organic agriculture," while the denomination "organic wine" has no judicial basis, although it is commonly used in trades and in economic and marketing literature.

Biodynamic Farming

Biodynamics proposes a unified approach to agriculture that relates the ecology of the farm to planetary and cosmic rhythms. It sets itself apart from other agricultural systems, including organic farming, by its association with the precepts of anthroposophy proposed by Rudolph Steiner in the 1920s. Steiner is considered the father of anthroposophy, a philosophy rooted in German idealism and mysticism that aims to apply rational thought to phenomena of spiritual experience. Anthroposophy has a complicated intellectual reputation, supported by influential cultural figures that include Nobel Laureates but also criticized by many who dismiss it as a dangerous quasi-religious movement that is antirational and antiscientific. Steiner is also credited as the founder of biodynamic agriculture, which developed with a series of lectures he gave in Silesia (then Germany, now Poland) held in response to invitations from farmers who noticed deterioration in soil conditions and the health and quality of crops and livestock.[2] Steiner's teachings propose that the farm is a living organism, similar to the organics idea, but has a connection to other forces in the universe.

Biodynamic farming prescribes the use of certain practices, including use of a set of preparations to promote healthy soil and plant growth (Steiner 2003 [1924]), which are listed in table 9.1.

While organic agriculture has become fairly mainstream, biodynamic farming remains more esoteric. Its colorful and mystical practices mark a very strong turn from the scientific winemaking of Bordeaux and the New World. Especially conspicuous is the use of several fermented "preparations" as field

Table 9.1   Codes of biodynamic and organic farming

Biodynamic and *Organic*
Exclude chemical fertilizers
Exclude growth regulators
Excludes GMOs
Avoid risk of pesticide drifts from neighboring farms
Long-term plan for maintaining soil fertility
Monitor suitable cleaning measures

Biodynamic Only
Philosophical motivation
Observation of lunar and other cosmic rhythms for crop cultivation
Create biodiversity in the field
Moderate or no use of sulfur dioxide (SO_2)
Manual harvesting
Manual selection
Preparations:
500 Cow manure buried in cow horns in the soil over winter
501 Ground quartz buried in cow horns in the soil over summer
502 Yarrow flowers buried sheathed in a stag's bladder
503 German chamomile flowers sheathed in a cow intestine
504 Stinging nettles buried in the soil in summer
505 Oak bark buried sheathed in the skull of a farm animal
506 Dandelion flowers buried sheathed in a cow mesentery
507 Valerian flower juice sprayed over or inserted in the compost
508 Common horsetail made either as a fresh tea or fermented liquid manure applied to the vines or to the soil

sprays and compost inoculants. These preparations consist of plant parts or extracts stored in animal tissues that have been buried in the soil. For instance, the iconic Preparation 500 is made by filling cow horns with manure from lactating cows fed with biodynamic grains, burying them in the vineyard on the autumn equinox, and digging them up on the spring equinox. Steiner proposed the application of homeopathic doses of the preparations. Most of the current recommendations we have found propose, for instance, that 10 grams (about 0.35 ounces) of Preparation 500 be applied per hectare.

Farmers then make very diluted liquids by combining about 5 ml (one teaspoon) of the cured manure with about 40-60 liters (10.5-16 gallons) of water and stirring for one hour in a pattern that "dynamizes" it.

The preparation is then sprayed on the vines in the descending phase of the moon. Reliance on astral and lunar calendars for timing actions in the vineyard and the cellar is a hallmark of this approach. Adherents believe

Figure 9.1 Making Preparation 500: cow manure is buried in cow horns in the soil over winter (left) and in the spring the cow manure has decomposed (right). *Source:* Craig Camp, used by permission.

that these preparations stimulate soil cycling, promote healthy plant growth and optimal compost development, and have myriad other beneficial effects. Maurice Barthelmé from Domaine Albert Mann described well how producers think about the alternatives:

> With conventional farming, you feed the plant and you try to fight against the diseases. With organic, you feed the soil and the plant gives what it can give; it's not fed artificially. And when you work in biodynamics, it's the same system, but you consider that the plant is a terrestrial being in the solar system. We have a mechanical conception of life as it relates to other life. I cannot explain exactly, but there is energy coming from the cosmos, energy coming from the earth; and what we try to do is to accumulate as much energy as possible in the plant.

Demeter International, a German-based association, owns the trademark for "biodynamic." Demeter is a nonprofit organization consisting of a network of individual certification bodies in forty-five countries—including France. Only those companies that consistently meet these standards are permitted to display the Demeter certification logo. Registered in 1927, Demeter certifies products coming from biodynamic agriculture and their processing and packaging methods with its own logo. In the case of wine and beer, provided that they have an alcoholic grade, the allowed labels should indicate that the inputs respect the Demeter quality. This happens only if following requirements are satisfied: (a) conformity to Demeter processing standards; (b) at least 95 percent of the ingredients must possess the organic certification, according to regulations; and (c) between 50 and 90 percent of the total ingredients must respect the Demeter quality norms. As with the

Figure 9.2 Making Preparation 500 continued: a very small amount of decomposed manure is put into water and dynamized (stirred in a specified pattern for one hour). This is then sprayed on the soil to prepare it for sowing and planting.

general organic wine production, we are not aware of rules regulating the process of biodynamic vinification.

In 1995, a group of European winemakers created an alternative certification body called Syndicat International des Vignerons en Culture Biodynamique (Biodyvin for short) that deals only with wine. The founders believed that the broad scope of Demeter (and a continuing legacy of Steiner's opposition to the consumption of alcohol) did not fit well with viticulture. Most of the leading biodynamic wineries in Alsace are members of Biodyvin (and not certified by Demeter). These include Albert Mann, Barmès-Buecher, Bott-Geyl, Dirler-Cadé, Josmeyer, Kreydenweiss, Zind-Humbrecht, and Zusslin. This association delegates the inspection process to Ecocert SAS France, a global company in organic farming certification. All the members of Biodyvin are therefore certified organic as well.

Lutte Raisonnée

The unique—esoteric for some—preparations are one reason why biodynamic practices stand out more relative to conventional and organic farming. Another reason is the lack of consistent interpretation of what is organic.
Survey studies among European consumers at the time on which our analysis
focuses suggested that unconventional farming, particularly organic, is perceived as having benefits related to a series of values focused around health,
safety, and ethical soundness (Torjusen et al. 2004). An international review
that covered North America in addition to Europe draws similar conclusions (Yirode et al. 2005). However, the definition of *organic* recalled different labels including "green," "ecological," "environmental," "natural," and
"sustainable" (Hutchins and Greenhalgh 1995). This can lead consumers to
choose products that do not in fact have the attributes implied by the label
and, as a consequence, it can lead to skepticism.

In particular, in Alsace the contrast of the organic category is lowered
by its perceived overlap with the producers following *lutte raisonnée* (rough
translation: "reasoned struggle"), which might be called sustainable farming.
This competing code specifies "minimal" use of herbicides and pesticides. In
Alsace, this alternative is promulgated by an association called Tyflo, which
encourages "production of economically-viable high-quality grapes, giving
priority to ecologically sound methods . . . in order to preserve the environment and human health" (Tyflo 2011).

In agriculture, there is no unique model of sustainable economic activity that would be applicable to all geographic, economic, and social envi-
ronments. The Organisation for Economic Co-operation and Development
(OECD), an international organization that coordinates domestic and international economic policies of high-income countries, states that there "can
be a co-existence of more-intensive farming systems with more-extensive systems that overall provide environmental benefits, while meeting demands for
food" (OECD 2001). The OECD recognizes that "all farming systems, from
intensive conventional farming to organic farming, have the potential to be
locally sustainable" (OECD 2001).

Lutte raisonnée incites strong reactions for its ambiguity. This theme
emerged often in our interviews particularly with biodynamic winemakers.
For instance, André Ostertag objected:

> Lutte raisonnée—it's a big lie. It's an invention from the classic agriculture
> to give a smoke screen about the real practices and to produce confusion

with real organic practices. If it brings people to move from high use of herbicides and chemistry to organic, it can be a good thing. But I'm not sure it's made for that. It's made to bring confusion in the consumer's mind because consumers are not always used to all the names and the labels.

Catherine Faller of Domaine Weinbach argued:

> Lutte raisonnée means you pay attention, but how much attention do you pay? It is expected from anybody to adapt your spraying to what is needed. Whatever you do, you try to adjust to the diseases or whatever. If you are a doctor, you will not kill a fly with a gun. I think it's like . . . bullshit.

The related claim of being "nearly organic" also triggers negative reactions towards lutte raisonnée. Jean-Pierre Frick objected:

> We should call it "pollution raisonnée." The solution was to say we do lutte raisonnée—they are organic but we are reasonable; it's almost like organic farming. That's not true! It has nothing to do with organic farming.

According to Etienne Hugel, then the director of the large organic family winery Hugel et Fils in Riquewihr:

> Lutte raisonnée is . . . a big bag, because "raisonnée" means that you think. So if you are not lutte raisonnée, you don't think. I've never met somebody who's not at least raisonnée. Because if you are not, you are really a dirty bastard!

Marc Kreydenweiss argues that lutte raisonnée should not even exist: "It's confusing. Many consumers see the name and they think it's organic, and therefore good."

Winemakers working in sustainable farming tend to elide the difference between lutte raisonnée and organic, emphasizing instead the pragmatic aspect of sustainability. Éric Kientzler, who runs the family winery with his brother Thierry, told us that the gap between lutte raisonnée and organic is not so significant:

> For instance, we use herbicides so we don't have grass—but just between the plants, not between the rows of plants. So you think it's two different approaches, but it's the same, so just a few products, of course, that make the difference. The way of doing the work, for me, is not so different. If

the weather conditions allow, we get really close to organic. But if we need to use a product that is good for the vineyard, we don't hesitate.

Kientzler added that they chose lutte raisonnée because "with time, history showed that some techniques are good one day and not the other day and then good again."

9.2   Who Adopts Biodynamic and Organic Farming?

Analysis of Winery Quality Data

Biodynamic and organic practices have spread rapidly in Alsace. In 1980, only one winery in the region was biodynamic and one was organic. By 2010, roughly half of the wineries in our data had joined one of these categories (about 21 percent biodynamic and 26 percent organic). As we mentioned in the previous chapter, one reason why this development is interesting is that many of the most prominent wineries in the region have adopted these unconventional practices. Moreover, adhering to biodynamics and organics increases production costs considerably. It was not clear that the market would pay a premium for these wines or indeed if they would have more than a fringe market.

Does the quality of a winery affect the choice to become biodynamic or organic? We collected data to answer this question. First, we tried to measure winery quality by relying on Robert Parker's *Wine Buyer's Guide* (Parker 1988–2011). During the period we studied, Parker was widely regarded as the world's most influential wine critic (Hadj Ali et al. 2008). The guide compiles scores for wineries on a five-star scale, where five stars indicate the highest rating, producers that "make the greatest wine of their viticultural region, and they are remarkably consistent and reliable even in mediocre and poor vintages" (Parker, 1993, p. 8). We constructed a time series of ratings from the seven editions of the guide.[3]

We combined the data on winery quality with information about wineries becoming organic or biodynamic. For this information, we relied on multiple sources. The first is *Le Guide des Vins de France*, curated by *Gault et Millau* (GM), a sister publication to the well-known review of restaurants in France.[4] Beginning with the 2007 edition, GM tells about the viticultural practices of interest. The second source is the U.S. publication *Wine Spectator* (WS), arguably the most influential wine guide internationally. Its online database contains tasting notes for Alsatian wines from the issues of February 1987 through August 2010. WS sometimes provides information about viticultural practices, and we used it when available. In general, we lacked such data for earlier periods. For this reason, we conducted a telephone survey in 2010 with informants from all the wineries with wine ratings in the wine guide. We asked about viticultural practice, particularly biodynamics and organics.[5]

We wanted to know whether high-quality wineries were more likely to adopt biodynamic and organic methods (and certification) overall and also whether they did so more quickly. In other words, we wanted to estimate whether the speed of movement toward these two categories varied with a winery's status.[6] We examined the period ranging from 1981, the first year of available winery scores from Parker, through 2010.[7]

The strong and consistent finding is that the the speed of movement toward biodynamics significantly increased with winery quality. In contrast, winery quality was not significantly associated with the speed of initiating organic farming.[8] In particular, the speed of adopting biodynamics at the highest value of winery quality was about 30 percent higher than when quality is at its lowest. So on average, wineries had high quality when they joined biodynamics, but this was not the case for those using organic-only farming.

We also examined whether joining biodynamics became more prevalent as the practice proliferated.[9] We think these results reinforce our interpretation of the reputational basis for efficient category signaling. In markets where both high- and low-quality producers operate, if high-quality producers join a category early on and the information conveyed by the track record of numerous high-quality producers is consistent, the signalers will succeed at having their quality signaled (Levin 2009).

The Producers Explain Their Choices

The producers we interviewed point to three types of reasons for why unconventional farming practices have succeeded in Alsace, where now more than 6 percent of the cultivated land is argued to be cultivated biodynamically and more than 10 percent organically. The first reason is the region's location and climate. Etienne Hugel told us:

> Alsace is the most continental area in France. We are the furthest area from the sea. This means the area is dry, protected by the Vosges mountains. It's a sound area ... So, you can have more flexibility in experimenting.

Olivier Humbrecht also mentioned that Alsace is a small region in France by size but one with a high population density (the second highest) per square kilometer. "I guess more people on top of each other means that either everything collapses or you pay more attention to what you have and try not to pollute."

Other producers cited the proximity to Germany and the influence that German writer Goethe had on Rudolf Steiner with his ideas about the power of imagination to synthesize the perceptions of things in the world with their conceptualization. More generally, social and cultural factors associated with environmental movements that opposed France's nuclear policy in the past few decades might have been important. The small Alsatian community of Fessenheim has hosted France's oldest nuclear power plant next to the Grand Canal d'Alsace. Construction at Fessenheim began in 1970, and the plant was commissioned in 1977, making it the oldest in service in France. In the 1990s and 2000s, several safety failures were reported at Fessenheim, including an electrical fault, cracks in a reactor cover, a chemistry error, water pollution, a fuel leak, and nonlethal radioactive contamination of workers. The plant was decommissioned in 2020.

Finally, we frequently heard from producers that they considered moving away from conventional winemaking practices after perceiving a change in the taste, smell, and quality of their wines. This recalls the historical anecdote about the development of biodynamics in Germany, when farmers requested Steiner to help them find solutions for their crops that were getting worse. Olivier Humbrecht provided an interesting and detailed account:

My father was a classic grower in Alsace. He knew how to cultivate a vineyard with a horse. He expanded the estate in the 1960s and 1970s. Then, people came and told him "Oh! You're so stupid to waste so much energy, time, and money." They said, "Take this bottle of chemical fertilizer, put it on the ground and you'll see." These products and technology were a real miracle. They helped a lot of growers in reducing the amount of heavy duty, physical work.

People said, "This is new, it's modern, it works, it doesn't pollute, it's clean," all the stuff you want to hear. Eventually, after ten, fifteen, twenty years, some growers realized that what was supposed to help them was causing more and more problems. The soil had lost its fertility. If we used natural manure or compost, it would not decompose in the soil. This increased the need for more and quicker fertilizers. But gradually people started to ask the questions: "What is happening? Why is my soil losing fertility? Is it possible to go back to another system of cultivation?"

Other producers told us that they started to notice off-aromas in the wine, increasing heaviness, less minerality, and the loss of the ability of the wines to age properly. Jean-Christophe Bott of Domaine Bott-Geyl noticed that "the soil was becoming dead, with lots of moss; it was also becoming harder to work." The wines he was producing sold nicely; they had good reviews even by Parker. But he found that he liked them less and less. "They were becoming too heavy, and I wanted to have more minerality."

We learned that the initial turn to biodynamic and organic production stemmed from a mix of intertwined reasons. Shifting to unconventional practices of growing wine grapes seemed to be a way to improve "objective," technical quality in the wines, for example, whether a wine has off-aromas due to mold. We also learned that unconventional practices might allow the wine to better reflect the terroir of the region and protect the environment.

This argument concerns quality, as came through strongly in our interviews, especially with biodynamic winemakers. For instance, Christophe Erhart, then the winemaker at Domaine Josmeyer, said:

My objective is not to be biodynamic . . .[but] to make the best wine from the place, from our soils, from our terroir. And the icing on the cake is that it's biodynamic . . .because [this is] the more natural way to reach this goal.

André Ostertag insisted to us:

Terroir is the key for great wines. There is no great wine without *terroir* . . .that is why you move to biodynamics, because you are convinced, because you have an environmental consciousness, but also you can come to biodynamics without any environmental consciousness because biodynamics increases *terroir* in taste.

Microbiologists and biochemists report mixed evidence about the impact of biodynamic and organic methods. A study comparing organic and biodynamic vineyard treatments found that both improve soil quality over conventional cultivation, but soil parameters or tissue nutrients of the two unconventional approaches do not differ significantly (Reeve et al. 2005). More recently, a comparison of chemical profiles finds that the three methods do not directly influence the biochemical characteristics of grapes and wines (Tassoni et al. 2013).

Laurence Faller of Domaine Weinbach (a biodynamic winery) offered a winemaker's perspective on this evidence:

I think that if the wines were not good before, they're not going to be miraculously better. If they were bad before, they're not just going to be good because of biodynamics. But we noticed a better focus in the wine, more precision in the aromas, more purity, and maybe higher levels of acidity, which means more balance.

And Jean Boxler of Domaine Albert Boxler, an organic producer, said that when a producer has a great terroir, "to find the difference between that producer and an organic or a biodynamic producer, to tell them apart when tasting, it's difficult." He added:

I adapt my work to what I observe. To do biodynamics, I would have to feel it. Maybe in a few years I will. Right now, the more biodynamic wines I taste, the more I wonder. Biodynamic does not automatically mean higher quality.

These last two comments dovetail with the empirical evidence provided earlier in the chapter. There, we showed that wineries that became biodynamic were considered to be of higher quality *before* their conversion. Also, working with unconventional methods implies spending more time and effort in the vineyard, given that producers cannot rely on chemical products. Then, the quality increase attributed to the unconventional methods might be something of a self-fulfilling prophecy.

We learned that in response to the perceived deterioration of the grapes and wines, producers started to experiment with new practices to improve that situation. André Ostertag described how, in 1997, after having converted to organic farming, he decided to divide his vineyard into two parts and grow half organic and the other half biodynamic. He found that the plants in the biodynamic half "changed behavior" and that the difference (with organic) was stunning. Even though he did not understand what was behind it, he "felt it" and was convinced he had to do biodynamics. The next year he converted the entire estate to biodynamics.

Olivier Humbrecht did similar kinds of experiments and agreed that choosing unconventional farming practices, particularly biodynamics, involved work that combined observation, intuition, feeling, and personal interpretation. He explained that at least the early movers into biodynamics did not do it for commercial reasons but to preserve their vineyards' potential, keep the soil alive, and make sure that the vines would feed from the transformation of the organic matter into humus and not just "from the stuff you dump on the soil."

Humbrecht provided some insights about relationships within the community of biodynamic producers. He told us that he had made significant investments in searching for new suppliers and learning about their methods. When he found suitable partners, he developed long-term relationships with them to ensure reliable quality of inputs and processes. He experimented with new techniques in the vineyard and learned that communicating with other producers about them was important. He told us that he had attended a two-day workshop by François Bouchet, a winegrower from the Loire who had become a biodynamic consultant. In Humbrecht's words:

> It was crazy, but also fascinating and interesting. I bought a small dynamizer [stirring machine]. There were ten or twelve of us at the workshop. In 1997, we each started to experiment with biodynamics in the vineyard to see how it worked, what you had to do. Bouchet would visit us every few weeks to discuss which preparations to use and when. I didn't understand what it meant. But I did what he said.

Twenty years later, Humbrecht still sees many other growers who work in biodynamics on a regular basis and shares information with them. Marc Kreydenweiss told us of similar informal relations. Specifically during his early experiments with biodynamics, he gathered with vintners from seven other domaines, and they started discussing what each of them was doing and why. Together these producers created what he called "an emulsion," a joint solution of parts that are otherwise dispersed. Martin Schaetzel brought together a team of microbiologists, geologists, and biodynamicists to organize training sessions for other winemakers to study, experiment, analyze, and better understand the relationships between terroir and biodynamics. He said, "I thought about those things for myself and also for others."

The highly systemic approach followed by biodynamic producers and their intense interaction contrasts with those following other unconventional methods. Producers seeking certification in organic farming follow a European Union (EU) regulatory regime that details the rules of production, processing, distribution, importation, and labeling of food and agricultural products. This legislation is completed with additional rules of implementation. Biodynamics rules instead are primarily maintained by farmers. For example, the Demeter trademark is held by a farmer's association, and the association believes that all the different producers in biodynamics—winegrowers but also farmers of other agricultural products—should stay together. Organic rules are primarily maintained by the government. Certification is overseen by a public agency, but inspection and certification is actually done by private associations, notably Ecocert. This top-down system of regulation reduces the need for collective work. To illustrate this point, Marc Kreydenweiss remarked, "Organic farmers are not members of a group that has created a chart, a code of conduct, that forbids the use of certain molecules."

Producers can be uncomfortable about communicating their membership in the organic category because this can be misinterpreted as meaning just sustainable. Etienne Hugel hinted at this in discussing the use of copper in the vineyard. Copper is used in many types of agriculture, and particularly in organic farming, to control a variety of fungal and bacterial diseases, most importantly in vineyards. Copper appears on the list of substances approved by organic (and also biodynamic) farming rules because it is not synthetic. Hugel argued that highlighting his firm's membership in the organic category might suggest that it too uses copper:

> The problem is that the organic method uses copper but copper destroys the life in the soil, and organic is oriented to the life of the soil. It's contradictory. And honestly this is why we don't want to advertise too much that we are organic.

The wine region of Alsace has been perceived among consumers and critics as having a confusing identity. In the previous chapter, we described some factors that contributed to such confusion, including the large number of Grand Cru designations that are also shared by producers with varying quality—some sell the wines from the same Grand Cru at low prices in supermarkets and others at high prices at specialized high-end retail stores. In recent years multiple genres of wine emerged as alternatives to conventional farming, biodynamic, organic, and sustainable ("raisonnée"). In a way, these genres are opposed to conventional farming, but they are not explicitly opposed to one another. The relation between biodynamics and organic can be confusing. The organic code is a subset of the biodynamic code. In other words, in a formal, logical sense, biodynamic farming is a subconcept of organic farming. However, research on concepts shows that people do not always follow logic in deciding subconcept relations.[10] When it comes to biodynamic and organic wine growing, most with whom we have discussed the matter treat the two as alternative approaches, as potential rivals.

These genres also vary in their collective identities. Biodynamic farming has a very clear identity. The biodynamic producers in Alsace and elsewhere created a community with sustained, repeated, and strong relationships in which they experiment, learn together, and share knowledge. This seems to be less the case for organic wine growing, a genre whose rules are codified top-down by the government and for which collective action is perhaps less useful. The organic genre has a less clear identity. Producers working in sustainable farming (*lutte raisonée*) appear to be even less involved in collective action, and this genre has an decidedly ambiguous identity. Although not explicitly defined in opposition to lutte raisonée, producers practicing biodynamic or organic farming share negative views of the sustainable approach. Producers following organic also risk being confused as sustainable because the proponents of lutte raisonnée claim to be nearly organic. This association between the two genres is problematic because lutte raisonnée allows the use of chemical products while organic does not.

Unconventional farming proposed an alternative to the dominant industrial farming approach designed for the mass market. Multiple genres developed within unconventional farming, with complex relations between each other. One of these genres, biodynamics, shows more social cohesion among producers, and it has a stronger market identity. Why is that the case? The next chapter addresses this question.

CHAPTER TEN

Why Biodynamics? Category Signals and Audience Response

MANY HIGHLY REGARDED WINEMAKERS IN Alsace broke ranks with the highly technicized modern approach to winemaking and adopted the seemingly irrational practices of biodynamics without receiving a negative reaction in the market. Because critics and consumers see high-quality producers move to biodynamic production in the first place, the subsequent higher quality of biodynamic producers can operate as a "self-confirming belief" (Spence 1973a). One benefit of the systematic association between high quality and biodynamics in Alsace is to help reduce the problem of confusing identity (discussed in chapter 8) for at least some Alsatian wines.

Trying to explain the pattern of the move to biodynamics led us to think of category memberships operating as market signals. This chapter documents evidence of the signaling mechanism in the marketplace, particularly critical ratings of quality and retail prices. The differences in the critics' tasting methods allow us to isolate the role of the signal from confounding influences. We will show that biodynamic wines receive better ratings than organic wines when the evaluator knows the producer's identity and therefore the farming methods used to make the wine. This conceptualization requires attention both to costs of membership and to category boundaries.

10.1 Market Signals

Theories of market signals emphasize that signals provide information about quality (in equilibrium) when the costs of producing the signal are lower for the producers with high quality. When the signal comes from membership in a social category, the strength of the signal increases with the contrast of the category. Of course, whether the signal is positive or negative still depends on the average quality of the members.

The conditions for category signaling appear to hold for Alsatian wine-making. Biodynamic and organic methods are costly, but they are more costly (and more risky) for less capable wineries. However, the biodynamic category has higher contrast than the organic one due both to its many strange practices and lack of overlap with the "nearly organic" lutte raison-née. So biodynamics, because it has a crisper boundary, can send a stronger positive signal of quality than organic wine growing.

Producers and their goods generally differ in quality. Information about quality tends to be asymmetric: the producer—a job applicant, a loan seeker, or a used-car seller—knows more than the audience—an employer, lender, or buyer. According to theories of market signaling, some producers can signal their otherwise hard-to-observe quality and the audience can use the signal as a screening mechanism (Spence 1973a, 1974). For an action to be an effective signal, the cost of producing the signal must be lower for producers with higher quality. If this condition holds, then a separating equilibrium can result in which those who provide the signal have higher average quality.

In general, both high-quality producers and audience members benefit from transmission of reliable information about quality. The benefits for producers consist of material advantages such as higher prices to reward higher quality. This is difficult to achieve when the audience cannot observe the producer's quality because the audience is willing to pay lower prices than what high-quality producers expect, and this induces high-quality producers to leave the market. Other kinds of motivations for valuing reliable information also matter. For example, some producers simply take personal pride in the recognition of their goods as having high quality.

Those possessing high quality face a problem: how can they communicate their capability to the audience? This is where market signals come in. The signaling mechanism can address information asymmetry by yielding an equilibrium in which only high-quality producers find it worthwhile to invest in the signal. In Spence's best-known analysis of signaling, prospective employees can demonstrate their potential productivity by investing in education (Spence, 1973a, 1973b, 1974). Individuals with lower capability find it more costly to invest in education, in the sense that it requires more effort for them to obtain a degree. Individuals with high capability instead find it less costly to do so.[1]

The condition that producing the signal costs less for highly capable producers defines the key mechanism of market signaling.[2] For a signal to be effective, it has to meet a second condition: the audience must be able to detect and decode the signal. Many markets populated by a mix of high- and low-quality producers (such as consumer goods like food and clothing) pose challenges to interpreting market signals. Similarly, market labels that communicate the investment in the signal can only provide summary information about a product or producer, making quality difficult to ascertain. Identifying quality also becomes complicated when names and labels of producers of different quality can resemble one another. In these cases, individual signals can lose their diagnostic power, and the resulting equilibrium will be a pooling equilibrium (with mixes of high- and low-quality producers lumped together) rather than a separating one that clearly distinguishes producers of high and low quality.

10.2 Category Signals

Noise can affect the observability and interpretability of individual signals, particularly in markets with large numbers of producers and labels. In these cases, *category* signals—collective signals of category membership—can solve the problem of information asymmetry when individual signals are difficult to observe and decode. One advantage of category signals comes from the fact that multiple producers display the same signal, which increases the visibility of the signal to the audience.[3] Because multiple producers use it, a collective signal also enhances interpretability. The audience likely trusts conformity to a category more than idiosyncratic individual observables. For example, collective enforcement has more credibility than individual monitoring over one's own actions.[4] Social scientists have long maintained that costly signs of group membership are correlated with intra-group cooperation and reduced free-riding behavior.

Category signals can, under specified conditions, identify otherwise unobservable differences in quality and operate as markers of collective identities in the interface between producers and the audience. The two main conditions under which category signals are effective require that (1) low-quality producers find it more costly to gain category membership, as we described above, and (2) the category has a relatively sharp boundary, that is, high contrast.

Signaling theories do not explicitly address why specific actions come to be interpreted as signals. The general point is that a reliable signal, however chosen, separates high- and low-quality producers in equilibrium. A focus on categories provides some analytic leverage on this issue. It seems likely that audience members take category memberships as a signal of superior capability when a category's members have a history of high average quality. In other words, category membership emerges as a signal similarly to how groups develop reputations (Tirole 1996; Levin 2009). In the previous chapter we showed that high-quality domaines were more likely to shift to biodynamics in Alsace and that the biodynamic category had higher contrast than the alternatives. So there is reason to expect that biodynamics might operate as a category signal in this wine region.

In the next section we provide some details about the inverse cost–quality relationship that is key to the signaling mechanism. Then we discuss how the audience views producers who adopt unconventional farming methods. The biodynamic category has higher contrast than organic winemaking for two reasons. First, its unique required practices, for example, using cow horns and red-deer bladders to cure manure and yarrow blossoms in sprays for vineyards and compost, and the additional commitment these practices represent make biodynamicists stand out. Producers remain convinced that the impact of biodynamics is real, even if they cannot exactly pinpoint how.

The organic category also has a fuzzier boundary due to the perceived overlap with another protocategory, "sustainable," which in France is labeled *lutte raisonnée* and whose adherents claim to be "nearly organic." This confusion lowers the contrast of the organic—but not the biodynamic—category. We surmise that membership in biodynamics sends a stronger market signal because of its high categorical contrast.

10.3   Biodynamics as a Market Identity in Alsace

We contend that use of biodynamic agriculture sends a positive category signal in the context of Alsatian wine production. In this sense, membership in the category of biodynamic producers creates a positively valued market identity. The argument has several steps.

Winemaking Practices and Quality

Whether viticultural science has demonstrated that the unconventional modes of farming lead to improvements in quality or that the alternative modes differ in average quality is hotly debated. It is possible that the answer to both questions is no. What, then, is the value of using them? It is plausible that unconventional winemaking methods do not produce "objective" improvements but that the unique imagery of these practices, particularly biodynamics and its apparatus of precepts, could still serve as the basis for a very distinctive positive identity in the market.

Although quality depends on many actions and decisions that cannot be fully observed by outsiders, audience members look for signals. Indeed the value of the signal increases with the opacity of the practices that yield high quality. Wine critics are actively engaged in this role: they visit wineries and consultants, attend wine fairs and conferences, contact industry associations, and communicate with one another. Through these mechanisms, critics learn about producers and their category memberships. Wine customers learn about wine in similar ways. However, they tend to have less knowledge than critics. For this reason, in wine like other mediated industries (film, music, art, stocks, etc.), the assessments provided by critics represent an important source of information for the choices of final consumers

Costs of Biodynamic and Organic Practices

Organic and biodynamic practices impose higher costs than sustainable or conventional wine growing. Adhering to either organic or biodynamic codes rules out the use of some labor-saving practices (e.g., the use of herbicides as a substitute for plowing). And biodynamic farming also imposes costs above and beyond those of organic farming, such as spraying with the preparations and elaborate procedures of composting.[5]

The producers we interviewed provided some information about costs. Biodynamic producer Valentin Zusslin estimated that there are, on average, two workers for each 10 hectares of cultivated land in Alsace but that his domaine has eight workers for thirteen hectares: "It's different. So there are many winemakers who would like to go into biodynamics but they can't do it. Or some do not want to do it because it is too much work." Christophe and Chantal Braun of Domaine Camille Braun said that "conventional producers sell the grapes by the pound; the more kilos they have on the plant the better it is. When you go biodynamic, your goal is not to maximize quantity." Christophe Erhart was more specific:

> We earn less money than a conventional winery because we have 20 percent lower yields. We have 30 percent more hand work. In France, this costs a lot of money. So for me, producing a bottle of wine costs at least 50 percent more. But we cannot charge 50 percent more. But it's a choice. I prefer doing that and also bringing a kind of message of quality.

Olivier Humbrecht also told us:

> It's not the organic and biodynamic estates that make the higher profits because we have higher costs but the price of the bottle is not that much more expensive. An organic or biodynamic wine doesn't sell at 40 percent or 50 percent more than a conventional wine at the same quality level, from the same area, and in the same style. We might be less profitable... I employ about seven more people per hectare than the average in the area... For a bottle of wine my labor cost is several times higher.

As we mentioned above, a central issue for signaling is whether the cost of producing the signal is lower for higher-quality producers. There are good reasons for thinking that this is the case here. Both organic and biodynamic codes bring viticulture closer to the traditional craft of farming but impose discipline. Eschewing chemical pesticides requires great attention to the vineyard and skill in reacting to the appearance of pests. Writer Kramer (2010, 117) argues the case for biodynamics, which requires elaborate manual procedures and organizing by multiple natural cycles:

> Biodynamic cultivation signals a willingness to pay extreme attention to vines and wines. Like driving a race car, if you take your eyes off the road— or in this case, a highly vulnerable vineyard—an irremediable disaster can result. Ask any farmer: attentiveness is always a good thing... Biodynamic processes are a form of discipline, some of which may actually work, while other practices may be more emotionally and psychologically sustaining to the practitioner than practical to the plant or wine.

The costs of acquiring the signal of biodynamics might be too high for some producers. Vincent Stoeffler, an organic producer when we interviewed him in 2010, confirmed that working with the lunar calendar as biodynamics mandates was too difficult for him.

In his argument about biodynamics and the human factor in terroir, André Ostertag also added that biodynamics requires intense observation of the vines, "being very close to what's going on, but being able to leave the processes alone. This is the opposite of modern winemaking. In modern winemaking you use prevention for everything." According to Christophe Erhart, "95 percent of biodynamic work is farmer's common sense because if you are making everything, step-by-step, correctly with regard to the natural rhythms, you have fewer problems."

In sum, part of the supposed effect of biodynamics might be due less to the direct effect of the preparations and more to the constant attention to the process of grape growing and winemaking in the absence of preventative treatments. Jean-Christophe Bott of Bott Geyl said that what he appreciated about unconventional farming methods is that one has to "watch, observe, and adapt to the conditions outside." Jean-Marie Winter and Thomas Schlumberger of Domaine Schlumberger, who in 2010 were in conversion from organic to biodynamic production, told us that their wine-maker spent more time in the vineyards than in the cellar and that he had completed about 350 check-ins for ripeness of the grapes the previous year.

Contrasts of Biodynamic and Organic Categories

Many consider the practices of biodynamic viticulture esoteric and unique, which makes them highly visible. Biodynamic farming is also highly visible to outsiders because its adherents promote the growth of plants among the vines. According to Valentin Zusslin, who joined biodynamics in 1996, many scoffed at these methods: "Early on, everyone was laughing at us. They were only waiting for us to have problems, to lose a harvest. These were hard times. But I knew what I was doing. I was sure." Christophe Erhart, then at Domaine Josmeyer, had a similar story: "A neighbor . . . told me, in Alsatian dialect, "At your place, you really have grass for the rabbits." I mean, for him it was dirty because you had plants, herbs, and flowers in the vineyard."

In the previous chapter we mentioned the conspicuous preparations that are used in biodynamics, such as field sprays and compost inoculants and the ideas that cosmic influences from the sun, moon, planets, and stars are important factors to consider in decisions about farming. It is precisely the unusual quality of these practices and principles that makes this category stand out, that gives it high contrast. Adhering to the biodynamic category demands use of peculiar practices and incurs ridicule, in addition to greater amounts of time investment, and plausibly signals a commitment to quality.

Organic production is sometimes seen as a step along the way to becoming biodynamic. Indeed biodynamic certification required an initial (audited) conversion to organic farming. As a result, the movement of higher-quality producers to biodynamic from organic further lowers the contrast of the organic category as biodynamic production becomes regarded as the end goal.

Of course low-quality producers have an incentive to imitate market signals. Lutte raisonnée appears to us as an effort to imitate the categorical signal of adherence to the code of organic farming. This is a problem for the organic signal. The practitioners of lutte raisonnée claim to be "nearly organic." Indeed organic and sustainable are often used interchangeably (Ministère de l'Agriculture 2011; European Commission 2012). The result, we think, is lowered contrast for the organic category.

Higher cost and contrast establish biodynamics as a stronger candidate for category signal. Biodynamics also stands out as a stronger signal in that it is linked to charismatic authority. Sociologist Max Weber described charisma as a certain quality by virtue of which an individual is set apart from others and treated as if endowed with supernatural, exceptional powers or qualities. The construction of charisma involves communication that invokes values, symbols, and emotions. In the case of biodynamics, Rudolf Steiner's strange and esoteric ideas, coupled with the use of cultural symbols (e.g., cosmic forces, the farm as a living organism) and rituals (e.g., the preparations, the lunar calendar) fit with this picture.

Charisma is effective as a mechanism for recruiting followers who develop a strong attraction to a leader and feel inspired by her or his vision. This source of authority is particularly powerful. Consistent with this idea, evolutionary psychologists who conduct research on charisma and human behavior argue that signals from charismatic leaders can better attract the attention of others and align their behaviors (Grabo and van Vugt 2016). Something we heard from Olivier Humbrecht illustrates this point for biodynamics:

> I don't know that Jupiter has any action on earth like this. But the biodynamic concept is that, as life started to form on earth, life took the energy from both the earth and the cosmos and took in its memory all these different influences, all the planets, constellations, whatever. When we cultivate vines today in biodynamics, you bring back to the cultivated plants all these initial sparkles of life by using plants or animal organs that have the signature of these planets. It sounds completely weird in a way. There's a lot of symbolism in it; but, again, one can see it working.

As a signal, organic farming does not depend on charismatic authority but on another source of authority: legal rules. Many countries have introduced laws that define organic farming. Many producers conform to this method and believe in its effectiveness. We have not heard any organic producer, however, speak with the same fervor about organic as did Humbrecht, Erhart, and others for biodynamics.

Certification and Labeling for Biodynamic and Organic Categories

Producers can work using biodynamic and organic methods without being certified, but many choose a certification. Both biodynamic and organic methods are regulated by certification processes that guarantee that certain farm production criteria have been met. Organic certification is overseen by the government, and commercial use of the term *organic* is legally restricted in Europe. Biodynamic certification is controlled by private organizations, primarily Demeter and Biodyvin. Certification procedures include filling out preinspection questionnaires, paying for visits of inspectors and for laboratory analyses, receiving announced and unannounced visits for evaluation, and annual follow-ups. The required forms are highly detailed. Cole (2011), writing about biodynamic certification in Oregon, pointed out:

> Biodynamic spraying forms say not only what you put on, but also when you put it on, what the lunar phase was, what the time of the day was, what were your thoughts and feelings as you were stirring, what were your thoughts and feelings as you were spraying, and what did you notice.

Both organic and biodynamic certification systems are costly, but they are higher for biodynamics. Yearly cost of biodynamic certification by Demeter includes a royalty for the use of the Demeter trademark equal to 2 percent of revenues by selling products with the Demeter trademark, a membership fee, and the cost of an inspection. These costs are too high for small firms, who often prefer to certify grapes as organic. Therefore, to the extent that the Demeter trademark is an important requisite to work with large supermarket chains, certification costs might be a barrier to entry in that channel and to the growth of smaller firms.

Rémy Gresser indicated that he started using a certification logo for biodynamics starting with the 2009 vintage:

> I changed my labels, and it was a very good experience because the art designer made me look at this from the the side of the consumer, what does the consumer want? Also, if you don't give information, then the sommelier has nothing to say to the consumer.

Christophe Erhart also explained that certifying and labeling of the use of unconventional methods allow Josmeyer to communicate its strategy in other, related contexts:

We are not only certified by Demeter and Biodyvin in the vineyards. We are also, I would say, *certified* in the cellar. We don't add yeasts, enzymes, acids, or sugar. The aim is really to have the best, balanced grapes and to bring this balance into the bottle in a natural way.

Alsatian wineries practicing unconventional methods, and biodynamics especially, often seek to avoid confusion with wineries practicing conventional and generically sustainable methods. Christophe Erhart told us:

It is important to ask producers to prove that they are really doing biodynamics because it's becoming fashionable. Some people say they are "working in biodynamics," but they are not. And this is not positive. So it's very important for us that you really are doing what you say you are doing.

It can't be an easy certification. It can't be like a competition for medals where everybody wins, and you give 300 gold medals, 800 silver medals, and 2,000 bronzes. The fight we will have to do is to preserve the seriousness of organics and biodynamics.

Labeling wines as biodynamic or organic appears to strengthen the collective identity of the category as well as communicate clearly with the audience. Jean-Pierre Frick told us that he has always communicated that he is biodynamic because he thinks that, when an idea is good for people and the environment,

I want to spread the news. If producers get certified, they have to renounce using fertilizers, weed killers, and that's positive. They can do it for ethical or marketing reasons, but what I care about is that there are less pesticides on earth and in the water.

Our fieldwork indicated that using unconventional farming can operate as a signaling mechanism whereby some producers that invest in the signal can be identified—separated, in the language of signaling theory—from the others. Here, membership in the biodynamic or organic category sends a signal of quality about producers who can observe and attend to more carefully the many activities in the natural process of grape growing and winemaking.

10.4   Audience Response

In addition to the fieldwork described above, we conducted a statistical analysis of the audience response to the use of unconventional farming among wineries in Alsace. We characterize such response in terms of (1) ratings assigned by specialized critics and (2) prices in retail markets.

Ratings

We collected data from multiple archival sources. The first is the *Wine Spectator* (WS) online database, which contains tasting notes and ratings for Alsatian wines from the issues of February 1987 through August 2010. WS conducts blind tasting: its tasters and editors do not know who made the wine or how much it costs when they assign a score, but they do know some of the context, including the vintage, appellation, and grape variety. Each editor generally covers the same wine regions from year to year, allowing lead tasters to develop expertise in a region. Other tasters might participate in blind tastings to help confirm impressions. However, the lead taster always has the final say. The second source is *Le Guide des Vins de France*, curated by *Gault et Millau* (GM), which we described in previous chapters. We coded label-level information in yearly editions through 2010. The GM guide has considerable influence in France. Wineries often highlight the ratings received from the guide under the Pressroom tab on their websites.

Finally, we located another influential French wine critic, the *Revue du Vin de France* (RVF) (www.larvf.com), which adopts a mixed tasting method. RVF publishes an annual guide with ratings obtained from open (nonblind) tastings, but it also conducts special tastings and publishes a monthly magazine and a second guide of lower-priced wines with ratings from blind tastings. Using their online archive, we identified 385 white wines from Alsace that were tasted twice, once nonblind and once blind. This allows us to address the counterfactual that the differences in ratings reflect differences between tasting methods rather than between critics.

The difference in the method of evaluation used by these sources allow us to address two questions. First, is membership in the categories productive? That is, do category members receive different evaluations on average from those who practice conventional winemaking when the evaluator does not know either the identity of the producer or its categorical membership? Second, do the results of nonblind tastings and blind tastings diverge as our argument suggests, such that the returns in ratings are substantially higher for biodynamics than for organics in nonblind tastings compared with blind tastings?

In all analyses of critical ratings we control for persistent differences stemming from endowments and winemakers' skills in analyzing ratings by examining only *within-winery* variation over vintages.[6]

Table 10.1 Effects of biodynamic or organic-only categories on critical evaluations from blind tasting

	Blind Tasting		Nonblind Tasting	
	WS	RVF	GM	RVF
Biodynamic	0.706*	0.204	1.30*	1.35*
Organic only	0.860*	0.519	−2.08*	0.436
Number of observations	3,775	385	4,715	385

* indicates that the effect is significant at the 0.05 level.
Note: WSF, *Wine Spectator*; RVF, *Revue de France* or unblind tasting; GM, Gault et Millau; RVD, Revue du Vins de France)

We explore the productivity question by analyzing the blind WS and RVF ratings. We compare a producer's ratings after shifting to biodynamics or organics to its ratings before. Table 10.1 gives the key results. The entries are the (adjusted) average changes in ratings when a winery shifts to biodynamic or organic methods. The first column contains the estimated effects using the WS ratings. We see that the ratings increase by almost one point for both categories, and the increases are statistically significant. The difference between the biodynamic and organic effects is not statistically significant.[7] In theory the WS ratings range from 0 to 100 points, but in practice, ratings below 75 are rarely observed. In our data, less than 1 percent of the wines receive a rating of 74 or lower. Similarly, less than 1 percent of the wines receive more than 94 points. Overall, the assigned scores concentrate in 20 points, and a change in almost one point as seen in the table is significant.

The second column in table 10.1 reports the effect of changes in category membership on the ratings—measured on a 20-point scale—of the wines using the RVF data.[8] Here, changes to the organic and biodynamic categories have smaller positive effects on ratings.[9] Unsurprisingly given the low statistical power from the small number of observations, these effects are not statistically significant.

We turn now to our second hypothesis: does category membership convey a signal of quality? We explore this question by comparing effects of the category memberships on the open (nonblind) and the blind evaluations. The third column in table 10.1 gives the results for the (open) GM ratings.[10] We see that the effect of biodynamic production is again positive and significant; indeed the magnitude of this effect is nearly double that estimated from the WS ratings from blind tastings.[11] Ninety-five percent of the GM ratings fall in the range between 65 and 95—a range of 30 points compared to 20 for WS—so overall the effect of biodynamics on nonblind ratings is about 50 percent larger than in the blind ratings. Moreover, the effect of changing from conventional to organic production is *negative* for the open (GM) ratings.

In nonblind tastings by RVF (fourth column), shifting to biodynamic production increases ratings by 1.35 points, and this effect is statistically significant. The coefficient associated with the shift to organic also has a positive sign, but it does not reach statistical significance.

These analyses confirm that producers receive higher ratings after they switch than when they followed conventional agriculture in open tastings, while wines made by organic producers do not. Each critic might have a different taste, but the effects of the biodynamic category signal are consistently positive.

It is natural to wonder whether the effect on ratings of converting to either organic or biodynamic farming remains stable over time. We addressed this issue by estimating dynamic models for ratings. These analyses find that ratings of biodynamic and organic wines continue to diverge after the switch from conventional farming and that the difference becomes greater with the continued use of the two farming methods. Moreover, the positive effect of the use of biodynamics on the change in ratings is much larger in open (nonblind) tastings (GM) than in blind ones (WS). In other words, the strength of the category signal increases with the duration of the period of membership in the category. This seems plausible because the confusion effect of the sustainable category has likely intensified as the size of its membership has grown. The association of wine producers that practice lutte raisonnée, Tyflo, began in 1997 with twenty members; the membership had grown to seventy-one in 2012 (Tyflo 2011).

One might also wonder if the observed patterns are driven by cultural differences between American and French critics; for example, the Americans like organics, and the French like biodynamics and/or dislike organics because the Americans like it. Our analysis so far used blind ratings from a U.S. critic, and open (nonblind) ratings from a French critic. We collected additional ratings on Alsatian white wines from two additional sources, but this time the French critic conducts blind tastings and the U.S. critic conducts open tastings: the *Hachette* guide in France and the *Wine Advocate* (WA) in the United States. *Hachette* uses blind ratings. On WA's website (erobertparker.com/info/legend.asp), founder Robert Parker states: "When possible all of my tastings are done in peer-group, single-blind conditions." Although this claim has been questioned, Parker explicitly describes two exceptions to tasting blind: "all specific appellation tastings where at least 25

Table 10.2 Effects of biodynamic or organic category only on critical evaluations from blind tasting (*Hachette*) or nonblind tasting (WA)

	Hachette	WA
Biodynamic	0.174	0.814*
Organic only	0.039	−0.382
Number of observations	2,996	564

* indicates that the effect is significant at the 0.05 level.

of the best estates will not submit samples for group tastings," and "all wines under $25." While the first condition is difficult to control for using the review data, the second is more tractable, and we coded the ratings for wines priced less $25.

We modeled the wine ratings of the *Hachette* and WA data in a similar way to what we described for WS, GM, and RVF. The point estimates for this analysis are reported in table 10.2.[12] For *Hachette*, changing from conventional farming to biodynamic and organic categories does not have significant effects on the ratings. For WA, the ratings are higher when producers change to biodynamic farming, but not so for changes to organic farming.[13] These findings confirm the pattern of the previous analyses. National differences between French and U.S. critics do not seem to confound the effects of category signaling.

Retail Prices

We also examine retail prices using WS data for the U.S. market. Categorical signals can affect prices in two ways: directly via audiences' interpretations of the categories and indirectly via the effect of critics' ratings. Consumers typically have less knowledge in this context than specialized critics. In the wine world, hundreds of thousands of labels compete in the marketplace. Unlike the critics, the consumer audience might not be aware of the actual practices used by the producers, but they can easily learn about certification from widely posted lists of membership; from wine labels; and from experts such as GM, WS and others. So certification might matter more to American consumers. Including this analysis on retail prices allows us to understand the effect of biodynamic and organic practices in the supply and demand dynamics of the consumer market.

WS reports price information collected from retailers and producers. The approach to the analysis followed closely that used to examine critical ratings.[14] Our main finding is that biodynamic and organic wines garnered higher prices than conventional wines. The effects of the two memberships are nearly equal.[15]

Our estimates indicate that the retail price of a wine rises about 8 percent after biodynamic conversion. Taking account of the indirect effect on prices through the ratings, the combined effect implies an increase of roughly 11 percent due to conversion to biodynamic farming. The evidence from our fieldwork suggests that biodynamic methods increase a winery's operational costs by at least 20 percent. The increase in prices barely goes to repay the associated higher costs of producing the categorical signal. Consistent with what our informants said, biodynamic methods likely reduce profits at least in the short run.[16] We suggested that winemakers value long-term gains in productivity, sustainability, and/or emotional benefits that are not reflected in current prices. These final results also support our interpretation of the situation. The stronger signal comes from membership in the category with higher contrast.

Implications

Ratings by international critics tasting blind (who do not know the identity of the producer or its categorical affiliations) are more positive for wineries after they join either the biodynamic or organic category than before. A parallel analysis finds that ratings by prominent French critics who do know the producer's identity favor biodynamic over conventional wines but not so for organic wines. A final analysis of the American retail market similarly indicates price advantages for wineries using unconventional practices. These effects do not seem strong enough, however, also to increase profitability.

The difference in reactions to organic wines in blind and open tastings seems striking. This difference in blind and nonblind reviews for these two unconventional methods is interesting precisely because it suggests that the signaling power of the high-contrast biodynamic category matters more to reviewers than that of its organic counterpart.

In some analyses of blind tastings, we found a negative effect of organic membership. Why? One explanation for the divergence in the effects of organic viticulture on estimates of quality from open and blind tastings points to a category-reputation effect. But this would not have an obvious basis from our research. In the previous chapter, we described that the hazard of adopting biodynamics was significantly higher for higher-quality wineries, and we did not find that the hazard of adopting organic production was significantly lower for the higher-quality wineries. If the pattern of findings about membership and critical ratings reflects only a reputation effect, then we would expect to find that the wineries that became organic were substantially lower in initial quality, which we do not.

Another explanation for the negative effect of organic methods involves a negative valuation in wine markets (see, for example, Asimov [2012]). In fact, organic tends to be regarded with favor in the wine world. Consumer research shows that organic food is perceived as healthy and safe (Torjusen et al. 2004; Yirode et al. 2005). An online survey indicates that the majority of American respondents who had tasted organic wines had a positive opinion of their quality (Delmas and Grant 2014). The French government and the European Commission also explicitly favor the use of organic practices and define them as "good for nature and good for consumers" (European Commission 2010). The *Gault et Millau* publication, from which we culled some of our data, champions wines that are as close to natural as possible and put organic in this group of "real" wines (in 2010 the editors published a guide focused on organic wineries).

Nonetheless, organic winemaking, which emerged before biodynamics, might have gained an initial poor standing in the French market. Several organic and biodynamic winemakers told us that they did not indicate their category membership on labels and did not want their wines to be sold in wineshops that specialized in organic wines because they regarded some of the wines on offer in those shops as inferior in quality. The winemakers worried about spillover effects of reputation.

What does this mean for the interpretation of the greater positive effect of biodynamic in open tastings compared to blind tastings? Is this evidence of a simple category reputation effect that does not depend on market signaling (the costs of membership being inverse to quality)? If organic and biodynamic viticulture are roughly nonproductive or equally productive, then the initial differences in category reputations would tend to weaken over time. In dynamic analyses that examine the effects of shifting to biodynamic or organic over time, the gap between the two categories as judged from blind tastings is actually growing over time. Biodynamic wines—but not organic wines—improve significantly in ratings over vintages. This suggests that the strength of the market signal of biodynamic wines relative to organic ones is not fading; it is increasing. We view this pattern as one that suggests that market signaling at the category level has been at work.

The surprising devaluation of organic wines by GM does not find a parallel in prices in the U.S. retail market. Consumers can, of course, learn which wines are organic and biodynamic. Some list their category certifications on labels, others indicate their practices on their webpages, and the American wine press has extensive coverage of the move toward "natural" wines. And importers and distributors can take these views into account in setting retail prices. If organic wines have a poor reputation globally, then prices on the American market ought to reflect this. But they do not.

The analyses described in this chapter capitalize on the difference in method of evaluation of different critics. We attribute differences in patterns of association from the two critical sources as reflecting mainly the difference in method. In other words, we rely on the counterfactual assumption that the two sets of critics would produce the same pattern of association if they both used blind tastings. Data from the RVF on a smaller sample of wines allowed a comparison of blind and nonblind ratings from the same source and established two findings. In blind tastings, organic and biodynamic wines received ratings like those of conventional wines; in open tastings, biodynamic wines received higher ratings, similar to those we found in analyzing the GM data, while the penalty for organic wines disappears. These results reinforce the signaling interpretation, but they also underscore that the critics can diverge in their evaluations.

Some treatments of signaling stress intentionality: producers want to signal their quality and take actions accordingly. Like the theory's original account, which argues that signals operate "by design or accident" (Spence 1974, p. 1) we do not rely so strongly on intentions. What matters is that audience members come to associate quality with a practice that is hard to imitate for low-quality producers.

In chapter 2 we discussed how the genres of traditional and modern wine in Italy, and particularly in Piedmont reflected collective concepts supported by high social cohesion among producers and that audiences viewed as sharply separated (as having high contrast in our language). These genres were also in opposition to one another. Does the impact on categorization and evaluation depend on the "tension" between genres and identities? In Roger Gould's analysis of collective action, collective identities only emerge when social conflict exists between groups, and the salience of the boundary that separates them intensifies. What happens if one genre has more cohesion and higher contrast than the other, and the genres are not strongly oppositional? Alsace offers a unique opportunity to explore this question.

Our analysis of unconventional winemaking in Alsace suggests that the biodynamic and organic genres emerged in opposition to conventional winemaking. Yet the two genres do not appear to be oppositional. A third genre, lutte raisonnée or sustainable, also emerged, and its proponents claim it to be similar to organic. This situation has spurred negative reactions among producers who appear worried about confusion with what they consider a diluted, half-hearted form of unconventional farming. We would expect a much weaker defense in communities of producers with less solidarity (as in Montalcino).

Overall, our analysis of unconventional winemaking in Alsace is consistent with our application of Gould's argument (discussed in Chapter 1) to explain that oppositional identities contribute to the development of genres (organics and biodynamics as alternatives to conventional). But opposition also does not seem necessary to maintaining collective identities (organics and biodynamics coexist without being oppositional). What we see, and perhaps expect more generally, is a collective reaction when certain actions or events question the social consensus about a genre among its adherents. Communities of producers in which such consensus is stronger, for example, when social cohesion among its members is also strong, as we observed among biodynamic producers in Alsace, produce symbolic defense of genre distinctions.

10.5   Biodynamics in Other Regions

The Langhe and Montalcino

Biodynamics has so far had little impact in the Langhe. As far as we can determine, there are only three biodynamic estates: Eugenio Bocchino, Ceretto, and Rivetto dal 1902. Eugenio Bocchino and his wife Cinzia Pelazza inherited her grandfather's small vineyard and made a single barrel of wine the following year. They have grown their vineyards to about 5.3 hectares (thirteen acres) and make 20,000 to 25,000 bottles per year. Their farming was at first conventional, but they gradually shifted first to organic and then to biodynamic, influenced by Cinzia's studies in agronomy. More than the other two biodynamic producers of Barolo, Bocchino and Pelazza reflect the activist wing of biodynamics. They have joined ViniVeri, the group begun by Cappellano and Rinaldi (among others) and the Renaissance des Appellations (discussed below).

Due no doubt to the paucity of biodynamic producers in the Langhe, we did not hear discussions by other producers, critics, and sommeliers about biodynamics in this region. There is no apparent buzz, as in the other regions.

There has been more activity in the community of producers of Brunello di Montalcino. The first biodynamic winegrower in Montalcino was Stella di Campalto, originally from Rome. Her husband's family gave Stella and her

Figure 10.1 Stella di Campalto. *Source:* sagerandwilde.com.

husband a gift of the San Giuseppe farm in 1992. This former sharecropping estate had been abandoned in the 1930s and was unused since. The farm lies on the southern edge of the Brunello production zone with few neighbors. Stella began with olive oil production. When at the age of twenty-three she learned of the availability of European Union (EU) funds to subsidize women's entry into wine production, she applied for the funds and won. This funding allowed her to plant six vineyards on the estate. Stella had no prior experience in wine growing or winemaking. She relied on advice from local farmers, including Gianfranco Soldera.

Di Campalto told us that her farming was organic from the start. An important motivation was her concern for the health of her children then aged six and three:

When I started organic, the first importer did not want ... organic. It meant bad wine ... Everyone was laughing; nobody believed it.

[Biodynamics] was a natural evolution. Organic, for me, is the same as the traditional chemical way. The way how you treat is the same. I thought we could do something different. I went to a seminar, and it turned my head upside down... I was afraid when I was trying it... I didn't care if I lost money, I just wanted to do something that's healthy. So I started that way, and then something incredible came out.

Pian dell'Orino, which lies adjacent to the Biondi Santi estate, was purchased in 1996 by Caroline Probitzer, who grew up in the South Tyrol area of the Alto Adige region. She recruited Jan Hendrick Erbach, from Karlsruhe in Germany, to be a consulting winemaker, and the two eventually married. They instituted biodynamic farming in all of their vineyards from the start.

In the case of the San Polino winery, Luigi (Gigi) Fabbro, a chemist from Friuli who conducts research on biodiversity in the Amazon, and his British wife Katia Nussbaum purchased in 1990 a former sharecropping farm that had long been out of production. Although it lies fairly close to the town of Montalcino, the farm is quite isolated and has no close neighbors. Along with their agronomist, Albanian-born Alberto Gjilaska, Gigi and Katia planted vineyards and received certification as organic and biodynamic.

Francesco Illy, an heir to the eponymous Trieste-based espresso coffee company, in 1998 purchased Podere Le Ripi, which then was sheep-grazing land. He set out immediately to establish biodynamic wine growing and planted vineyards, including some at insanely high plant density to experiment with the effects of density on the depth of root development. The domaine now contains a cellar built with ancient construction techniques. The winery's webpage (podereleripi.com) proudly announces itself as a "Biodynamic Winery in Montalcino."

The Corte Pavone estate, owned by a local family named Martini (it is not clear whether this was the same as the family discussed next), was sold in 1988 to a Swiss-owned firm called Bindella, which owned a winery in nearby Montepulciano. Bindella in turn sold the farm in 1996 to the Loacker family of South Tyrol. The Loackers currently own and operate wineries in Bolzano (South Tyrol), Maremma (Tuscan coast), and Corte Pavone in Montalcino. All the properties are farmed using biodynamic principles. The Loacker group joined Renaissance des Appellations in 2019.

Finally, Il Paradiso di Manfredi has apparently been using biodynamic farming for some time. It joined the biodynamic association Renaissance des Appellations (see below) in 2019. Manfredi Martini, who once worked for Biondi Santi, and his wife Fortunata, purchased the estate Il Paradiso in the early 1950s. Martini was one of the founding members of the Brunello consortium. After Manfredi's death in 1982, his son-in-law, Florio Guerrini, took over management of the estate. It has remained small, producing roughly 7,000 bottles of Brunello and 2,500 of Rosso. O'Keefe (2012, p. 150) calls these wines "the most soulful Brunellos in the entire denomination."

We already pointed out that the community of winemakers in Montalcino contains great diversity in backgrounds. This small group aptly illustrates our point. It consists of a young woman from Rome, a couple from South Tyrol and Kalsruhe, a biologist working in the Amazonian rainforests and the English wife he met in Kathmandu, a local family involved in the founding of the Brunello denomination, another South-Tyrol winemaker, and a coffee baron from Trieste.

This brief overview of wineries practicing unconventional farming in the two Italian regions that we studied earlier in the book begs the question: why has biodynamics emerged as a collective signal in Alsace but not among producers of Barolo/Barbaresco and Brunello di Montalcino? Based on our main arguments, we can propose a couple of conjectures. First, with the end of the Barolo Wars, proponents of the traditional and modern genres stopped their public disputes. The market identities that emerged are stable; and critics and consumers do not perceive their coexistence to be confusing. Critics and consumers agree that traditional and modern producers can make high-quality wine. Audience members can sort themselves into the genre that fits with their tastes based on the existing identities.

In this situation, there seems to be a sustainable partition of the market on this genre dimension. Some producers can also practice biodynamic farming; but collective action to promote this approach might not produce the same benefits to separate groups of producers as it does in Alsace: benefits in the sense of helping the producers to activate enough resources to build collective action and a market identity and of helping the audience to distinguish different types of producers and wines. The combination of traditional/modern and conventional/unconventional categories might generate groups too small to activate or to be recognized.

Second, in Montalcino we did not find the same relevance for the wine genres that are so visible for Barolo/Barbaresco. We explained that the lack of a cohesive social structure among producers of Brunello di Montalcino might have been an important reason why collective identities did not develop around traditional and modern wine genres in this production zone. The same factor might be responsible for the limited mobilization in support of unconventional farming in Montalcino. To be sure, some wineries follow biodynamics. But this approach has not emerged as a collective signal that distinguishes producers with clear quality differences.

France

The huge Loire wine region appears to have the most biodynamic domaines of any region in France—probably the world. As a percentage of domaines it appears to come second to Alsace. The proliferation of biodynamics in the Loire likely reflects the evangelizing of winemaker Nicholas Joly (see below). Joly, whose family domaine, La Coulée de Serrant, is itself a monopole Appellation d'Origine Contrôlée (AOC), converted his top vineyard Clos de La Coulée de Serrant to biodynamics in 1981 and the rest of his vineyards in 1984. So this is likely the oldest biodynamic winery in France.

Burgundy has also become a hotbed, and it shows a pattern similar to what we observed in Alsace: biodynamics tends to be embraced by the highest-status domaines. Prominent examples include the elite domaines Marquis d'Angerville, Leflaive, Leroy, Pierre Morey, Trapet, and Domaine de la Vougeraie. Most striking is the case of Domaine de La Romanée-Conti (widely referred to as DRC). The general consensus holds that DRC is the greatest winery in the world. Its wines are surely among the most—if not the most—expensive in the world.[17] The fact that this winery adopted biodynamic farming in all its vineyards in 2008 after using it in test plots appears to have had a broad impact on the image of biodynamic wine. It surely has made a strong local impact. When we conducted interviews in Burgundy and asked winemakers whether they were considering adopting biodynamics, they generally interjected, "DRC!" and shook their heads in some combination of amazement and trepidation at the thought that they risked falling further behind.

For DRC, biodynamics is all about quality. Its long-time codirector, Aubert de Villaine, was asked by Rebecca Gibb (in an interview posted on wine-searcher.com on February 4, 2014) how Steiner's philosophy had influenced him. He replied:

> I'm not really interested in the philosophy of Steiner. I am interested in what Steiner has installed for agriculture, but the philosophy—anthroposophy—it's a kind of religion...
>
> What I look for are the best ways to make the greatest possible wines. We have been organic since 1985, and then I experimented with biodynamics for some time. I realized it was the best way to be as close to the vineyard as possible, and for the vines to be most in harmony with nature.

Renaissance des Appellations (Return to Terroir)

In 2001 Nicholas Joly created an association of biodynamic winegrowers called La Renaissance des Appellations, which the association translates as Return to Terroir. The association has an elaborate charter, which specifies a rating system with three levels. The charter introduces it as follows (renaissance-des-appellations.com/fr/):

> This system encourages the winegrower to act better and informs the customer about the impact of agricultural or cellar actions on the expression of appellations. Our spirit is not to prioritize each according to the acts that each has been able to accomplish, but on the contrary to bring together those who share the same agricultural philosophy, whether they are producers, distributors or consumers. Our goal is also to give back to AOCs their full significance, in France and abroad, and therefore to free themselves from competition that technology has considerably amplified despite the atypicity it implies.

The notion of typicality invoked here is interesting. It assumes that each terroir can be characterized by a certain taste/aroma profile. Wines are then typical of a terroir to the degree that their tastes/aromas fit what is prototypical of the terroir. Who specifies the prototype? In this case it is the members. La Renaissance des Appellations appoints expert tasting committees for each region. Olivier Humbrecht, for example, chairs the committee for Alsace. Acceptance into the association requires a positive judgment by "the unanimity (and not the majority) of the tasting committee."

In addition to passing the typicality hurdle, gaining membership requires certification as organic for at least three years and as biodynamic for at least two years and satisfaction of a standard of noninterventionist winemaking (exclusive use of indigenous yeast, no addition of oak chips, no reverse osmosis, no addition of potassium sulfate or ascorbic acid, no "200 percent" new wood [wines aged for a period in new oak and then racked into other unused new oak for the remainder of the aging], no addition of products resulting from synthetic chemistry).[18] To progress to the second stage of membership, the grower must rely on massale selection[19] for new planting, eschew irrigation (for European producers) and chaptalization,[20] harvest manually, never use acidification or deacidification, and never add gum arabic. The third level requires longer periods of certification, manual harvest in several passages, and no sterile filtration of centrifuge. At this final level, producers in the "New World" are also required to dry farm (no irrigation).

The association's membership now consists of 230 farms from thirteen countries. The bulk of the membership comes from France (142) and Italy (48). Reading the list of members makes clear that La Renaissance des Appellations includes the leading edge of the movement. For instance, the Alsatian grower/producers members include Barmès-Buecher, Deiss, Frick, Josmeyer, Kreydenweiss, Ostertag, Tempé, Zind-Humbrecht, and Zusslin.

So we have seen a tremendous difference in the vitality of biodynamic farming in France and Italy. How can we make sense of this difference? We think that it reflects differences in the social structure of producers. In France, networks of farmers and wine producers developed within regions and then across regions. Knowledge that spread over these networks provided encouragement to experiment and technical support for such experimentation. We have not seen evidence of similar networks spanning regions in Italian wine production, with the exception of the one behind ViniVeri. Perhaps more important, in France associations developed from these networks. These associations accelerated the diffusion of ideas and techniques over the country. Because these were bottom-up associations (as contrasted with government agencies), grower-producers were able to imprint their genre understanding on the practices of the associations. This appears to have resulted in maintaining high-contrast of the biodynamic category by restricting membership to those who share the same understanding of the biodynamic genre. In the next chapter we explore further the general importance of producer associations.

CHAPTER ELEVEN

Community Structure, Social Movements, and Market Identities

OUR ANALYSIS OF THE DYNAMICS of conceptions of winemaking and of the categorization of winemakers emphasizes two interrelated sociological processes. Both concern the emergence of collective market identities as a consequence of community solidarity and collective action. In this chapter we cast these ideas in a broader intellectual context. By doing so, we hope to show that the processes that we have documented for several wine regions have general significance for other markets, identities, and industries.

In chapter 1 we argued that solidary producer communities likely develop collective agreement about the meaning of their products. Such consensus enables a collective to define and defend its conception of its products and to demarcate its boundary. Subsequent chapters concentrated on the consequences of variation in solidarity.

How communities of producers establish consensus about the meaning of their wines entails processes that are common to all kinds of social movements. Gaining consensus is more likely if the members of a collective (1) come to agree that they share an identity, (2) agree on a label, and (3) develop a language that expresses the conventions that underlie their collective identity. Social movement researchers refer to these actions as framing (Snow 2004). In addition, creation of a collective market identity is more likely if the members agree on categorization, on deciding what producers and products "belong" to it. Finally, success in building the collective identity is most likely if the collective creates an organization to represent and defend its interests.

This book considers only a single domain: winemaking. But we believe that the processes analyzed are general—they presumably apply to communities and organizations in different domains in both market and nonmarket settings. Here we want to emphasize this generality by relating our claims and findings to general sociological research on identities and social movements.

We have analyzed three successful cases of an emergence of collective market identities and one failure. The first success was the creation of a modern genre for Barolo/Barbaresco. The second success was a reactive countermovement against modernism and the creation of a traditional genre and associated market identity. The third success was the formation of a biodynamic genre and market identity in Alsace. The failure was the inability or disinterest of producers of Brunello di Montalcino to define a clear collective identity.

Social movement research offers insights for understanding such collective dynamics. By drawing parallels with research on insurgent social movements, we gain insights on how newly established collectivities construct new ways of thinking about their products. Insurgent movements (by definition) convey an oppositional identity that helps clarify the membership boundary of the movement and sets it apart from others. As social movement theorists have emphasized, developing a distinct, contrasting, and oppositional collective identity increases the chances that a movement's goals and tactics will be adopted by other movements (Taylor et al. 2009; Wang et al. 2018, 2019). This research illustrates how the mobilization of social movement actors benefits from an emphasis on contrasting identities.

As we described the social structures of the communities of wine producers in Alsace, Barolo/Barbaresco, and Montalcino, we noted commonality and difference. To a large extent the communities in Alsace and the Langhe had dense structures of interaction. In sharp contrast, the interaction within the producers' community in Montalcino was increasing bifurcated by the partition separating family firms and large corporate entities (often with outside ownership). The weaker solidarity of the community in Montalcino impeded collective action in response to any kind of event, even those that challenged the foundational rules, the Disciplinare of the Denominazione di Origine Controllata e Garantita (DOCG), that benefited all. In the other two sites, higher solidarity supported collective action at the community level. Recall that Gianfranco Soldera told us that the producers in the Langhe had successfully policed the rule that *Barolo* and Barbaresco contain only Nebbiolo but that those in his community of Brunello producers failed to enforce their parallel rule about Sangiovese. Yet the same solidary structures also supported subcommunity mobilization, as in the case of the rise of the modernist and biodynamic movements. Roger Gould's perspective, sketched in chapter 1, explains the seeming paradox: the collective actions at the community and subcommunity levels responded to different events or trends, and the strong solidarity in the relevant communities in Alsace and the Langhe increased the likelihood of collective action.

11.1   Social Movement Processes

The structural conditions just discussed set the stage for the emergence of collective market identities based on new conceptual distinctions. The spark for such emergence is the creation of social movements. As we have argued, solidary communities likely generate collective identities that can form the basis of recruitment to collective action. Solidarity thereby increases the likelihood of collective action. The processes that we have described within the communities of winemakers bear a strong resemblance to how social scientists describe social movements. McCarthy and Zald (1977, p. 1217–18) define social movements in terms of preferences and beliefs:

> A social movement is a set of opinions and beliefs in a population which represents preferences for changing some elements of the social structure and/or reward distribution of a society. A countermovement is a set of opinions and beliefs in a population opposed to a social movement. As is clear, we view social movements as nothing more than preference structures directed toward social change, very similar to what political sociologists would term issue cleavages.

Social movements can create and sustain identities, and, in doing so, they can shape normative expectations about a community's values and practices. In the context of this book, this means that social movements within solidary producer communities are better situated to create and sustain collective market identities. When they adopt a confrontational stand, movements assert what belief systems they reject at the same time as they tell what goals and beliefs they accept. Put differently, a movement's identity demarcates the line between "us" and "them." A group or community benefits when its identity is well-understood by both insiders and outsiders. As we discussed in chapters 1 and 5, having a clear identity to an audience means that this identity will be readily recognized and understood with little cognitive effort. Greater fluency in turn increases the chances that the evaluation of the products of a community will be positive.

Social movements are inherently oppositional. They draw their energy from building and sustaining tension between existing conditions and the desired alternative. The depiction of the present and its alternative are two contrasting collective mental representations. Building energy requires forming these representations (telling what are the relevant features and which values of these features characterize the two contrasting representations) and gaining agreement about them. Contentious behavior makes the identity of an emergent movement more salient (Taylor and Whittier 1992; Polletta and Jasper 2001; Hannan et al. 2019; Negro and Olzak 2019).

Establishing and maintaining an oppositional stance is more likely when the boundary between members and outsiders is sharp. Successful movements attempt to create sharp distinctions by pointing to emblematic or exemplary members on each side of the boundary. They also monitor the behavior of members to ensure that their membership has high contrast. This means that the orientations and behavior of members fit the template of the movement. The relevant categorizations are by members and interested outsiders. As we have seen, critics play a central role in making and disseminating such categorizations.

Especially in the case of the Barolo Wars, we have emphasized the oppositional character of the modernist and traditionalist movements. Oppositional identities do not necessarily breed enmity. The rift between modern and traditional winemaking philosophies might imply that there was high personal enmity between members of the opposing camps. Granted the rhetoric sometimes became heated, but we do not see any evidence of personal dislike. Our first inkling that this was the case came on our first visit to the Langhe in 2006, as we discussed earlier when we saw the leaders of the opposing camps chatting amiably for a few minutes like old friends.

Sociological research on framing clarifies how collective action produces and expands shared meanings and valuations of goals, tactics, and classes of actors (Snow 2004). *Framing* refers to actions by movement leaders and activists who are "signifying agents actively engaged in the production and maintenance of meaning" (Benford and Snow 2000, p. 613). To the extent that these meanings resonate, a movement can expand its base by signaling its messages to like-minded community members. Frame-alignment perspectives thus emphasize how activists and organizations use ideological frames instrumentally as a basis for negotiating meanings and how these frames influence a movement's acceptance by others.

Social movements commonly depend on organizations that provide collective benefits to members. Such social movement organizations generally play key roles in sustaining and reinforcing boundaries. According to the perspective called resource mobilization (McCarthy and Zald 1977), a movement's momentum can be sustained by constructing organizations that produce social cohesion that connects insiders and reaffirms group identity. The existence of such social movement organizations increases the chances that outsiders will recognize a group's boundary (Negro and Olzak 2019). An organization's ability to draw a recognizable boundary around it in the social space will aid in further resource acquisition, which helps social movements to flourish.

We did not see any major participation by social movement organizations in the disputes over the meanings of Barolo/Barbaresco and Brunello di Montalcino. The issues and the contention were highly localized to the villages that produce these wines, building on networks of social ties among producers. However, when it comes to contention over forms of wine growing, the issues take a more global form. Pollution and environmental degradation are not local issues. Neither is the claim that industrial farming has led to standardization at the cost of quality. So, unsurprisingly, contention about alternative modes of farming became embedded in organizations, which sprung up to certify adherence to codes of organic and biodynamic farming and to argue for the superiority of these alternatives for the quality of wine. These organizations include ViniVeri, Demeter, Biodyvin, and Renaissance des Appellations.

11.2   Movements and Collective Market Identities

Earlier chapters have argued that social movement processes aided in establishing and stabilizing collective market identities. We now revisit this claim using more explicitly the lens of social movement theory and research.

Successful social movements are conventionally seen as proponents of novel, progressive, or innovative tactics that explicitly reject old practices and outdated identities (McAdam 1983). Reactionary movements (less frequently studied) are those that advocate for changing the status quo and replacing it with institutions or practices from the past (Cunningham 2013; McVeigh 2009; Van Dyke and Soule 2002).

The modernist movement in the Langhe reveals characteristics reminiscent of classic social movements that challenge the practices, beliefs, and rules about behavior that characterize the status quo. Organizational networks provide vehicles for sharing information, practices, and methods that become synonymous with an emerging movement's identity. In this situation, adopting a modernist identity meant hewing to a different conception of Barolo/Barbaresco, one that emphasized immediate drinkability and the development of characteristics in the wine that would appeal to critics and the world market. Producing in this new genre was achieved by changing practices in the vineyard (especially adopting green harvest) and, in the cellar, using very short periods of maceration, aging in barriques as opposed to the conventional large barrel production that had long been established in the Langhe, and utilizing modern tools such as rotofermenters. These decisions put these producers at odds with those who became the defenders of the status quo.

In contrast, the movements endorsing traditionalism and the adoption of biodynamic practices can be viewed as a pair that reject modernism and oppose forces of globalization (Almeida and Chase-Dunn 2018). The traditionalist winemakers embrace an interpretation of the wine rooted in artisan/craft practices with a long local history. The adherents of biodynamics accept a broad range of esoteric beliefs and practices, as we have described in earlier chapters. Both movements reflect a distinctly local mentality that oppose adopting practices solely in response to market demand.

These unconventional winemakers who choose to adopt either a traditionalist or biodynamic identity see this decision as involving trade-offs between what consumers want and what producers consider to be authentic wine that reflects a region's fundamental nature. They argue that only local and historically traditional winemaking practices will yield high quality wine. This dynamic helps explain the emergence and possibly also the increasing appeal of each of these two insurgent movements within the wine industry.

As explained in detail in chapter 3, the label "Barolo Boys" was applied to the collective of modernist wine producers that served to reify the concept of modernist techniques in the cellar. Differentiation from the rest of the market turned out to be useful. This label captured the imagination of both critics and consumers. In other words, the notion of a producer having a modernist identity had achieved some market recognition.

Similarly, the collective nature of the "Barolo Boys" (and followers) facilitated sharing and disseminating information, and processes of self-criticism within the group that identified with a new modernist identity. As Elio Altare explained to us, the development of a modernist identity was encouraged by the formation of a network of social relations that forged an agreement about making modern Barolo/Barbaresco:

I offered my experience to fifty to 100 people because this new philosophy is not taught in schools . . . Now we have contributed to modifying the old interpretation of the wine. And we created a new philosophy. . . . It's because it is a team game. Now, if we work together, I can't speak badly about my neighbor because we have the same philosophy. You can imagine how big this effect can be on the market! And this was the right answer, the winning solution, working in a group.

As the quote from Altare suggests, a successful insurgent movement fundamentally depends upon the clarity of actors' identities as valid members of the insurgent group (Taylor and Whittier 1992; Wang et al. 2018). Theories of concepts and categories add that identities that are easily understood (more fluent) will be more favorably evaluated. Seen from these two theoretical perspectives, the modernist split with traditional techniques in winemaking can be understood as the process by which modernists attempted to establish an identity that explicitly rejects what had been the default genre. The modernist insurgency was also characterized by experimentation with unorthodox methods and techniques, which further added to the differentiation of their identity from the prevailing model. As recounted in chapter 3, experimentation by modernists included the adoption of barriques, which provided a visible display of affiliation with newer techniques. The motivation to experiment was also reinforced by the collective nature of the Barolo boys.

Market identities with sharply delineated boundaries have a high profile that can be converted into social power and favorable evaluations. Those turning to modernist practices established a distinct identity, which, at least initially, yielded economic rewards as well as critical acclaim. Following the spectacular rise in the financial success of modernist wines in global markets (and the high scores from wine critics), it might have seemed natural to assume that the modernist wave of the 1980s could become the dominant template for winemaking in the Langhe. And, for awhile, this seemed a probable outcome. In an ironic twist that we analyzed in chapter 4, the modernist drive to differentiate their identity served as a spur for traditionalists who reacted to the modernists' success by collectively reconstructing their identity as the sole authentic winemakers in the Langhe. Beyond maintaining clear boundaries as authentic members, movements "borrow" tactics and ideologies from other movements that are seen as trailblazers (the American civil rights movement is a prototype). By this argument, authenticity spills over from one existing movement and the adopter gains credibility as a result, although perhaps not as much as the prototype (Wang et al. 2019).

The movement expressing its identity in traditional winemaking genres borrowed from two exemplary movements: the Slow Food movement and the environmental movement. Both express opposition to existing models and practices, and both movements seek fundamental changes. Slow Food is an international organization that seeks to promote the production of local foods and local and regional cuisines as an alternative to fast food. Its origin was an organization called *Arcigola*, founded in 1986 by Carlo Petrini (a political activist from the Langhe) to protest the planned opening of a McDonald's near the Spanish Steps in Rome. Three years later a manifesto for Slow Food was signed in Paris by delegates from fifteen countries. The strong connection of Slow Food and the Langhe was exemplified by the founding of the organization's University of Gastronomic Sciences in Pollenzo, in the Langhe. Given the ideological orientation of the movement, we find it ironic that Slow Food's wine journal, *Gambero Rosso*, was, for the most part, a leading proponent of modernism in Italian winemaking.

Some believe that GR/Slow Food's activities contributed to the emergence of the Langhe's wines on the international scene. For instance, Alex Sanchez of Bovio said to us:

> In the eighties, Barolo was . . . unknown in the world. Only a few people in this region [locally] . . . knew it, and perhaps in Rome . . . no exaggeration. When Slow Food was born, . . . it began to make these wines better known around the world.

The environmental movement played a pivotal role in the spread of organic and biodynamic wine growing, as we discussed in the context of Alsace (chapter 8). Of course, similar influence has taken place in the world wine industry. During the late 1980s, industrial farming came under attack throughout agricultural sectors in Europe and elsewhere. Until that time, the use of insecticides was taken for granted, even celebrated as an instrument to free growers from the uncertainties of weather, infestations, and plant diseases. Alfio Cavallotto of Cavallotto Fratelli remembers that the use of chemicals was ubiquitous throughout the Barolo area:

> In the seventies, no one spoke of biodynamics. We used heavy doses of chemical products just like at the end of the fifties. Everybody did that. In that period, chemicals weren't an enemy. People cheered for preservatives and colorants and said, "It's a good thing, and it kills insects." Products began to be sold that go inside the plants, so it was fantastic for a farmer, for a grape grower. Even if it rained, no problem.

The collective identity of the biodynamic winegrowers evolved successfully in Alsace in part due to the region's openness to the environmental movement. For some, environmental concerns sparked a commitment to organic or sustainable agriculture practices. But advocates of biodynamic farming draw a sharp distinction between its philosophy and practices and those of all of the alternative approaches. These distinctive practices include, of course, use of the Preparations but it also disavows the goal of producing "international wines." Jean-Christophe Bott of Bott-Geyl in Alsace told us why he decided to convert to biodynamic farming:

> Working in organic farming we try to protect the identity of a region, but we cannot also forget our history and unfortunately in some regions of Italy people started planting Cabernet Sauvignon, Merlot and trying to make international wines. For me it's just as insane as using weed killers because in the end you question the whole historical and empirical past that allowed one to choose the best grape variety in the first place. And that's not taken into account; you change everything only for commercial reasons, to satisfy a few customers. I'm sorry but it really saddens me to see these kinds of things.

By referring to the fact that biodynamic winegrowers follow tradition, adhere closely to biodynamic philosophies, pay attention to the movement of the moon and other celestial bodies, and often rely on horses for plowing, this collection of wine producers has created an identity that is juxtaposed to organizations more concerned with commercial expansion. In making these distinctions, the certification process (which differs across countries) also ensures that the category of biodynamic winegrower will be seen as distinct (have high contrast).

Oppositional Identities

The formation of a movement's identity involves drawing distinctions with existing practices and offering a set of alternative normative beliefs. The same process of differentiation occurs with the emergence of a novel market identity. Modernists were defined by their rejection of local conventional concepts and techniques in favor of French/Californian models of wine growing and winemaking. They were also much more attuned to consumer tastes, market demands, and critics' evaluations, making them open to adaptation and change. In contrast, the traditionalist responded by emphasizing the rules they formulated as reflecting the natural methods, cultural history, and techniques of their forefathers.

The traditionalist winemakers (especially, but not exclusively, in the Langhe) emphasize two practices that indicate a winemaker has a traditional identity: (a) techniques that reflect an earlier, less complicated, and less market-driven mentality, and (b) production of wine that is unique and distinctive to the particular conditions and features that are typical of the local region (terroir). By invoking the concept of terroir, winemakers are consciously asserting a market identity that embodies the indigenous origins of the product. The extent to which a wine reflects its unique terroir (which includes the land, soil, rock formations, and cultural traditions and history) divides the traditional and modern winemaking genres. The claim that a winemaker's product expresses terroir is not an objective one because both modern and traditional winemakers voice their belief that their wines express the terroir of the region. Each side also claimed that the other was misguided in this belief. In particular, traditional winemakers claimed that modern winemaking genres cannot realistically reflect terroir.

Many winemakers remained unconvinced that modernist techniques can produce quality wine. As we discussed in earlier chapters, many traditionalists refer to these global-oriented wines with disdain by calling them Coca-Cola wines, in the sense that they always match consumers' desire to experience a known quantity. The reference to the iconic American soft drink is not accidental because it also connotes the fact that this product has had unprecedented global reach and, as a result, is one of the most recognized brand names in the world. Both of these qualities are rejected by traditional winemakers according to major leaders in this camp.

This point underscores that one way social movement actors distinguish themselves from others is by mobilizing an *oppositional* identity—where the opposition can be government authorities, existing policies, or simply practices that maintain the status quo. In doing so, social movements highlight the differences between existing and emergent identity groups. This focus allows the distinctions to be conveyed more clearly to an audience—which includes distributors, local wine-tasting associations, wine critics (such as Robert Parker and James Suckling), and ordinary consumers. Emphasizing that the market identity of traditional winemakers rejects goals and practices of modernist winemaking makes clear the opposition between the two camps. Many of the producers we interviewed see the local terroir identity as expressed in their own wine as coterminous with their own identity as winemakers.

The oppositional identity of a traditional winemaker involves a rejection of practices that change the color and flavor of the wine. Traditionalists claim to produce wines that better reflect a region's authentic identity or terroir. In this way, traditionalists claim an identity that is *not modernist*. For example, Bartolo Mascarello's "No Barriques" label (shown in chapter 1) characterizes the rejection of modernist practices. Traditional wines and winemaking practices are described mainly as contrasted with—or in opposition to—modern wines and practices. In this sense, the traditional/modern split pairs oppositional identities that reflect social movement processes that convey membership on one or the other side of a movement boundary.

Espousing a traditional identity frequently involves expressing a belief in the spiritual aspect of nature (and natural practices). In Alsace, Jean-Pierre Frick described the beginning of this movement as being "spiritual." The emphasis put on the concept of terroir by traditional winemakers cannot be overstated. Marcel Deiss reflected on terroir in traditionalist terms that resonate with the kinds of demands made by social movements for unquestioned loyalty:

> What is the concept of terroir? It is a mystical concept. It's a concept where you agree to lose some of your individual freedom because you believe that collective freedom, that following collective rules, is what really gives you freedom and above all it gives you an identity.

A key sign that a social movement is emerging is when it begins to offer new concepts and linguistic categories that become accepted (Tarrow 2013). The language of social movement becomes recognized by its distinct set of "codes": new concepts, categories, and practices become validated through collective action, spread by informal networks, associations and social movement organizations. Using the vehicles familiar to movement activists, biodynamic winegrowers formed reading and study groups that adopted and absorbed the principles that became part of the cultural lexicon.

The process of identity formation in social movements usually includes construction of a type of *origin myth* that recounts either a signifying event or an activity by a leader that signals a sharp, discontinuous break with the past. Ethnic social movements typically refer to the origins of the group as indicating its authentic claim to an identity and its link to the past. Rosa Park's refusal to sit in the "colored" section of the bus, Mao's long march, Castro's hideout in the jungle, and the events surrounding Wounded Knee all qualify as examples. The infamous chainsaw event that culminated in a break between Elio Altare and his father resembles a type of origin myth that marks the beginning of the modernist movement in winemaking. It also suggests the significance of a generational shift in preferences. The modernist producers were, on the whole, younger and perhaps more open to innovation than the older generation.

As a result of this innovation, a new market identity became recognized as a viable alternative to traditional winemaking in Barolo. The juxtaposition of modernist versus traditionalist assisted in the creation of this identity. Theories of concepts and categories suggest that, to the extent that a social movement's identity emerges as crisp and clearly formulated, it becomes more easily recognized and accepted, according to Hannan et al. (2019). In social movements and in organizations, having a specialist identity that occupies a narrow but clearly delineated niche improves their chances of tactical performance and survival (Negro and Olzak 2019; Olzak 2020). For market organizations, clearly delineated product identities receive higher evaluations by critics and external reviewers.

Since both modern and traditional genres of winemaking have coexisted for at least four decades, an argument might be made that the market for wine has bifurcated into "localist" and "international/modern" market identities that are positively valued but by different (or non-overlapping) customer bases. The fact that two wine menus list traditional and modern wines separately in local Piedmont restaurants supports this view.

Critics and Identity Confirmation

Outside audiences engaged in ranking or evaluating goods (e.g., critics) play a strong role in determining the shape of the boundary between oppositional market identities. An audience can reinforce (or reject) the claim that a winemaker belongs to a particular category. That the audience plays a crucial role in legitimating winemakers' identity leads winemakers to declare their allegiance to one side or the other. Thus, each wine will be fairly evaluated against its peers. Another important turning point, recounted by Gianni Fabrizio, editor of the wine guide *Gambero Rosso* (GR), is that this guide eventually separated its tastings into flights of either traditional or modern wines. In his view, this separation was the only way to obtain a truly "fair" evaluation.

A parallel process differentiating insiders from outsiders occurs in social movements. When movement mobilization increases, the boundary between movement supporters and bystanders becomes increasingly salient. This pressure forces those not yet committed to the movement to make a choice (Negro and Olzak 2019). In winemaking, critics can and do raise the salience of the boundary between traditional and modern winemaking. Critics thus force producers to either deny that the two sides of winemaking are mutually exclusive or to make a choice to join one side or the other. As Anna Sottimano put it.

We use barriques, but there are other producers using the large botti who make excellent wines. The critics use these words *traditional, innovator,* and other words. We do not. For us it's simpler: you either make an excellent wine or you do not, with the tools that we find suitable.

Social movement theorists also propose that commitment, loyalty, and authenticity of claims of belonging to a social movement continuously get contested: Who is a "real" feminist? Can a man be a feminist? Who is an authentic civil rights activist? These disputes about who belongs to one group or another has the potential benefits (in terms of building a focused identity) and costs (when one's membership is disputed). Critics and wine guides who map the boundary distinctions help reinforce the view that modern and traditional genres of winemaking in the Langhe are in opposition.

Like all other upstart social movements, biodynamic winemaking has its critics. At least some adherents claim that their practices are inherently less harmful to the environment than even organic farming techniques. These claims of moral superiority provoke some winemakers to judge them more harshly. Some refer to its practitioners' insistence to adhere to all of the rules as being overly rigid. Invoking a comparison to other cult-like philosophies, other winemakers openly question some of the more mystical aspects of biodynamic winemaking: "I had some training in biodynamics. I did four days but it was too much for me. When you are lying in the grass just to be connected with the earth, for me, it's too much," says Jean-Christophe Bott in Alsace.

Moreover, the central biodynamicist claim that their techniques are inherently natural and traditional is hotly contested by the nonbelievers. In response to claims of authenticity of biodynamic practices, conventional wine-growers seek to disavow and disdain the purist techniques of biodynamics. We asked Mateo Ascheri of Cantine Ascheri Giacomo in Bra if he considered using natural winemaking techniques, and he answered:

The debate is huge. Organic approach, okay a lot you can respect, but this means that in certain years you are not able to produce grapes. Or the quality of your grape is very low. If your grapes are not great—full of mold, rot and all those kinds of things,—you need more sulphites. Then, the quality of the wine is also lower. From my point of view, it is like when you are sick you take medication, and when you are not sick you don't. For the vineyard it is the same. Then there is biodynamic. It is much more, you know, a religion. You have to be a believer. I am not a believer in these kinds of things, I believe in more pragmatic things. So, *natural* is a word that is difficult to understand because everything is natural—there is nothing that is not natural at the end of the day.

The contested identity of biodynamics provokes criticism that includes comments that ridicule requirements such as scheduling each task according to lunar phases, filling cow horns with dung, and other practices that seem unscientific and mystical. Nonbelievers also claim that biodynamic wine must be low quality. Giacomo Conterno's criticism suggests that biodynamics is a fad that deserves some scorn: "Today it is fashionable to go biodynamic, to have your grapes listen to music, to be walking on the moon."

Pierre Trimbach in Alsace goes one step further to claim that "natural" wine is not wine at all:[1]

> More and more winemakers make wines without sulfur, using nothing... They do nothing in the vineyard, they have low crops because everything is eaten by the mildew or the odium. And then in the cellar, they do nothing... nothing, nothing. At the end they make a wine that, for me, is not wine. For me, it's not drinkable.

Christophe Braun (of the Domaine Camille Braun in Oschwhir) sees biodynamic winemaking as more philosophical but points out that it has a practical side because it conveys a winemaker's focused identity. Such an identity is facilitated when a winemaker also has been Agriculture Biologique (AB)) certified "because one can see what you are doing. And you must think of our children... anyway... You must not do organic to make more money. It's a philosophy."

Organizations and Legitimation

The organizational component of the organic and biodynamic movements sets them apart from other trade associations in that it specifically limits membership to those actively using organic/biodynamic practices and philosophies. Jean-Pierre Frick described to us the differences among three major groups of biodynamic winemakers that have solidarity-building features akin to social movement organizations:

> There really are three complementary aspects with these three organizations. Biodyvin is very professional; they care about the preparations, but they also care to show what kinds of results they can get with the wines. They have also training sessions. Renaissance des Appellations, they seek to

reach the outside more, to introduce the concept [to outside constituents]. They are more about communication, and maybe helping out with sales. Demeter is more about training, not wine-growing training but agronomical training, and certification.

As discussed in chapter 9, movements with strong charismatic leaders stand out in part because the leaders define clearly bounded goals or purposes that motivate members of the movement. Charismatic leaders are often viewed as having magical qualities that inspire loyalty. As is the case with social movements, more cohesive groups promote an even stronger sense of purpose for their followers. According to Jean-Pierre Frick, an early group of biodynamic winemakers in Alsace spent their winters carefully studying the original Steiner writings:

> Today, the world of viticulture is the leader in biodynamics but in the 1980s, there were very few winegrowers using these methods in Alsace. Thirty years ago, on Sunday morning, when the breeders were done taking care of the animals, we would all meet and study the agriculture book— Steiner's—all winter long.

Frick now organizes biodynamics conferences and has helped organize an organic fair (now held in Colmar) to discuss and display products produced by biodynamic and organic farmers across France and elsewhere. The goal is to produce a clear, focused identity that is distinct from those associated with other types of farming practices and philosophies.

The practices embedded in biodynamic farming demarcate the boundary around a biodynamic winegrower's identity. Some of these practices specify that planting must be done at certain phases of the moon (descending moon) and the use of dung, but other, more debated practices are allowed, such as adding copper to the soil. The use of copper is especially contested by nonbiodynamic farmers, who claim that its use contradicts the biodynamic claims to be more healthy and natural. The use of copper seems to incite both criticism and defensiveness among winemakers in general.

One measure of success in building these identities can be measured by whether the category of winemaking has been institutionalized. Biodynamic certification involves a lengthy process that takes place over a number of years. Investment in this certification process is also costly, both in terms of a learning curve and in terms of opportunity cost to shifting production techniques.

11.3   Globalization

As we explained in section 1.4, solidary communities often take action in opposition to the outside world. Studies of social movements have highlighted such reactions to forces of globalization. Globalization processes that link knowledge, practices, and trade flows across national boundaries commonly create a backlash based in local beliefs that reject external pressures from global markets and worldwide demand that expects uniformity within a product label.

Forces of modernism have paradoxically generated a number of reactive social movements that seek a return to values and goals of a past worldview that was once held sacred. This chapter suggests that the distinction between classical and reactive movements helps explain some of the antagonism that has been directed toward producers identified by modernists. Reactive movements are those that reject modernism and seek to replace it with an (often idealized) nostalgic sense of tradition and history. Such movements range broadly and include ethnic, terrorist, populist, right-wing racist, and nationalist movements (Tarrow 2013). The traditionalist and biodynamic winemakers make strikingly similar claims opposing global forces driven by increasing homogeneity of consumer tastes. Why have these antiglobal forces produced so many oppositional movements and identities?

One possible answer lies in recasting the argument as a dynamic in which globalization triggers powerful opposition to globalization. In this view, globalization poses a threat that can only be countered by returning to local traditions, histories, and identities. Globalization processes are those that increase geographic, cultural, and organizational ties across regions, making them more alike. As a result, the increasing scope of globalization threatens to penetrate and replace local culture and local identities with products like Coca-Cola and McDonald's hamburgers. Reactive movements adopt the view that globalization and modernization threaten local traditions and must be resisted at all costs.

Reactive movements uniquely emphasize localism over global/international identities and associations. Examples include "buying local," "farm-to-table," and "handmade" and "artisan" labels that associate this ideology with products that are not "industrial." Reactive movements are also often depicted as movements of the dispossessed, who have been cast aside by global processes that privilege only a select few. Increasing inequality is often depicted as an inevitable consequence of globalization.

Antiglobalization movements share a strong desire to preserve authenticity, which is seen to oppose forces of modernization that penetrate and erode the importance of local traditions and distinctiveness. The term *authenticity* is associated with concepts such as "core, essence, spirit, character, soul, terroir, secret, mystery, mysterious, unobservable" (Verhaal and Carroll 2019). Such concepts are emblematic of traditional winemaking and biodynamic producers as they seek to clarify an identity apart from global pressures to produce international wines. In this sense, the emergent market identities in the wine industry can trace their roots to other social movements rejecting globalization.

Expansion of a customer base requires having a product that appeals to a wider audience. As discussed in previous chapters, the choice to become biodynamic involves an inherent trade-off because of the higher costs involved (lower grape yields, more labor-intensive cutting of the vines, adherence to strict calendar dates for planting, etc.). It also carries the promise of being able to create a more distinctive identity, apart from organic or sustainable agriculture. In this sense, biodynamic winemaking disavows more industrial winemaking practices that produce higher profits. Yet this claim has not gone uncontested, as the critic Gianni Fabrizio of GR remarked:

> Or take the fact that (as a reaction) there are lots of these "biodynamic" producers for whom all the other winemakers are too "industrialized." For them, if a producer makes any use of a machine, he is accused of being industrialized.

It should be pointed out that use of modern techniques for winemaking are not always rejected by traditionalist or biodynamic winemakers. For example, the new practice of dense planting in vineyards has won wide acceptance. Instead, the disagreement with globalization revolves around a philosophy that values authenticity. Globalization of the wine industry is believed to produce a uniformity in the taste of wines and eradicates any sense that the wine has a unique character or structure. Teobaldo Cappellano, one of the leaders of the traditionalist resurgence in Barolo, distinguished globalization from forces of modernization in this way. In reacting to the statement that "sometimes some wine does taste like wood, including Barolo," he replied:

> Oh yeah, that is called modernity. But some people confuse modernity with globalization. Globalization is terrible. I love internationalism but not globalization. There is a big difference. Like I love to go to Austria and I don't need to show my passport, and this is great! But they have to preserve their history and we have to preserve ours!

When asked if globalization has had an influence on winemaking and law-making designations in Barolo, Giuseppe Rinaldi took a defensive posture:

> Yes, because instead of defending Barolo, a wine that can be produced only in eleven villages and should be considered as a national resource, they are destroying it. The value of Barolo is in the difference and not in the homologation or the standardization.

Opposition to strategies designed to maximize appeal across different national and cultural markets is emblematic of many reactive movements. For producers operating in market domains, insurgencies against globalization emphasize craft/artisan identity in opposition to market-driven identities or organizations motivated solely by consumer prices or preferences. The frequently encountered disdain of international wines draws on two antiglobalization mantras: the first is antihomogenization—the opposite from a McDonald's hamburger, which is expected to taste the same (and look the same) in Uganda, France, or China. The second dimension is its appeal to the lowest common denominator of taste—appealing to everyone, offending no one. The fact that Coca-Cola and McDonald's aim at appealing to highly generalized audiences and sell products that have a highly uniform content is viewed as antithetical to local traditions, culture, and historical uniqueness.

Maria Teresa Mascarello remembers her father's insurgent stand against global market forces, which was embodied in the famous label:

> My father designed a label saying "No barriques, no Berlusconi." This was a sort of philosophy of production and of a lifestyle. The ideal that Berlusconi embodies is to not remain small, as we are, but to grow bigger and bigger.

Forces of globalization are often described by reference to wine producers that are believed to have a ruthless market orientation. In the view of traditional winemakers, devotion to market demand for more uniform tasting wine ignores or actually depletes the quality of their products. In chasing profit, winemakers who succumb to this ideology wind up diminishing the quality of their wine according to Gianfranco Soldera, arch-traditionalist from Montalcino:

> In Montalcino in the past twenty years many people aimed at selling wine rather than making it. These people were supported by the press, which has

a strong influence over consumer taste. So what happened was an increase in the production of those wines that are easily identifiable, like Cabernet, and one of the consequences was that the average consumer could pretend to have become a wine expert. This situation brought a proliferation of bad wines that hide their low quality with artificial colors and flavors, and so on. Market expansion implied lower quality. This is especially true in agriculture, where human intervention is so important and the number of variables is high.

Technological advances that raise productivity encounter serious concerns from biodynamic producers. Biodynamic winemaker Christophe Erhardt (then at Josmeyer) linked innovations in agriculture that improved productivity directly to mad cow disease that spread across France and threatened the livelihood of many farmers as a result. In interviews, Erhart claimed that biodynamic theorist Rudolph Steiner actually predicted this consequence and warned against using hormones. The major impetus was the drive for more profit: "And here [in France] we have the mad cow disease, you see. And it's amazing to see that it had been written [about] for eighty-five years and we did it anyway for money, to increase productivity."

When global market forces generate resistance in the form of reactive social movements, they can create new opportunities for local, small-scale artisan products. Consumers respond favorably to these claims. According to Marc Kreydenweiss in Alsace, modern wines ("beer style" wines in his words) were created by "a vision of globalization":

> This vision erases any trace of terroir, so that: You can see that today you can drink a wine from Chile, a wine from Moldavia. You take one among many, you take a wine from the south of France, and you don't know where they come from.

Globalization and terroir are commonly depicted by winemakers as opposing forces, in which demand for homogenous tastes are driven by global market forces and also threaten the authenticity of local wines. Marc Kreydenweiss says:

> Consumers are starting to understand that they have been fooled for the past fifteen or twenty years... Everything is based on the consumers' taste... For me it is a horrendous loss of identity.

Conclusion

This chapter has come full circle back to its beginning concern with concepts and processes in social movements and insurgent movements from within the wine industry. Social movements benefit from drawing sharp boundary distinctions between "us" and "them" in order to convey that their values, goals, and beliefs are in contention with prevailing conditions. Movements achieve this by developing oppositional identities, which assist audiences in understanding their goals and purposes. Identity building is thus a central task for social movements seeking social change, both in terms of reinforcing insider loyalties and for recruiting new believers. This chapter suggested that three movements in the European wine industry mobilized successfully by constructing oppositional identities that incorporated new concepts, practices, and beliefs that changed the ways of thinking about winemaking.

It seems apparent from the history of the emergence of modernist and traditionalist market identities that the outcome of oppositional movements does not follow a linear path: modernist movements can be opposed by movements demanding a return to a nostalgic past.

A final set of lessons for social movement theory suggests that sources of conflict among competing concepts and philosophies arise when oppositional identities emerge in the same domain. Insurgencies of all kinds likely confront resistance, which intensifies when one side rejects the practices of the others. The key point is that movements create new, shared understandings and practices, which introduces the possibility that conflict will erupt. Moreover, to the extent that the concepts and categories are clearly delineated and oppositional, more conflict is likely.

These same processes can be seen in three movement-like waves of insurgency in the wine industry. First, the modernist wave built a collective representation of winemaking techniques and concepts that were heralded as new, innovative, and unfettered by rustic tradition and parochialism. In reaction, traditionalist winemakers responded by contrasting their identity with the modern one that produces a globally recognized product. In distinguishing themselves from those producers promoting modernist winemaking, traditionalist winemakers reject market-driven pressures in order to pursue what they view as a more ethical and authentic product. By contrasting winemaking driven by profit motives with ethical concerns, advocates of biodynamic winemaking parallel conventional types of social movements that actively seek to capture the moral high ground.

Biodynamic producers take the view one step further and argue that biodynamic products are distinct because they are intrinsically more authentic.

Advocates of biodynamic winemaking believe that authentic wine will ultimately have more appeal and obtain more favorable evaluations from critics. If the analyses in this book hold, the trend in winemaking is moving back to the winemaking and biodynamic practices of nearly a century ago, when Rudolph Steiner have his lectures on agriculture.

CHAPTER TWELVE

Coda

WE CLOSE BY SKETCHING SOME directions for deepening our approach, which might help orient future research. We outline how five different areas of study could use our ideas linking social structure, genres, and market identities. First, our findings suggest that conceptual consensus and clarity benefit from a high degree of producer solidarity. Such consensus requires less effort when there is a history of intertwined social relations and dense interaction patterns. Building on these findings, the ideas about conceptual consensus (and the underlying probabilistic rendering of concepts) offer a new avenue for analyzing processes of emergence of social norms. Second, scholarship on identities might apply the idea of conceptual ambiguity to clarify the conditions under which new identities are constructed, maintained, and sometimes disputed. Third, studies of authenticity might consider how ambiguity shapes evaluations of authenticity in a variety of fields, including politics, social movements, and cultural norms. Fourth, conceptual ambiguity might have an impact on the dynamics of movements seeking change. For instance, differences in the clarity of movements' identities might explain why some movements gain traction while others fade away. Finally, a consideration of how oppositional identities shape categories of social agents could open new avenues of inquiry for those studying group conflict and its resolution.

12.1   Social Cognition

An overarching theme of our study is that the social structure of producers shapes the emergence and persistence of genres. We view genres as agreed-upon concepts. A concept is a mental representation defined over sets of relevant features. Taken together, the values of these features can be seen as a space. Because the meaning expressed by a concept refers to positions in such a space, Hannan et al. (2019) call it a semantic space. The contemporary view of concepts regards them as probability distributions over the semantic space. Such a distribution tells which positions (combinations of relevant features) are likely for instances of a concept. That is, they describe expectations associated with concept membership. With this kind of construction, concepts lack sharp boundaries. Particular objects, such as producers and products, can vary in the degree to which they exemplify a concept. One way of describing such variation is in terms of typicality.

Retailers, critics, and consumers and even producers have to make judgments about what wines fit what genres and how to categorize particular wines, for example, "What kind of wine is this?"[1] The *categorization probability* is the likelihood that a person will judge an object to be an instance of a particular concept. Take a glass of wine. The person judges its color, aroma, and taste. What is the probability that the person will judge that this wine is a Barolo? This is what we mean by the categorization probability.

The centrality of the concept likelihood in thinking about concepts shows up in the Bayesian categorization probability. This probability, denoted by $P(c|x)$, expresses the observer's subjective certainty that an object with the position in the semantic space (pattern of feature values) x is an instance of the concept c. If this probability is high, then the observer is confident in the concept assignment, the categorization. If it is low, then the observer has considerable doubt about the matter.

The now-standard approach links categorization probabilities to concept likelihoods using Bayes's theorem. Suppose that the person making the judgment perceives that some object is at position x in the semantic space. Then the probability that this person will categorize the object as an instance of the concept c is given by

$$P(c|x) = \pi(x|c)\frac{P(c)}{P(x)}. \tag{1}$$

Here $P(c)$ is the subjective probability that sampled objects will be instances of c in the context, and $P(x)$ is the subjective probability that sampled objects will have the feature values denoted by x in that context.[2] The theoretically most important term in this equation is $\pi(x \mid c)$, the concept likelihood. In our construction, this is the concept. It tells the focal person's expectations about values of relevant features (x) if an object belongs to the concept (c).

The Bayesian formulation in equation (1) treats the categorization probability as proportional to the concept likelihood. As we sketched in chapter 5, two kinds of uncertainty about an object can be seen in terms of categorization probabilities. As we noted above, a categorization probability for a position in the semantic space gives the agent's subjective confidence that an object with certain feature values is an instance of the concept. The lower this probability, the greater is the uncertainty about membership. When multiple concepts come into the picture, an object might be characterized as a possible instance of several of them. This makes it difficult to form expectations. This difficulty, we argue, grows with conceptual ambiguity, defined as the evenness of the distribution of categorization probabilities over the set of concepts. In other words, the most difficult cases for forming expectations are those that are likely instances of several concepts. Such objects are also likely to be categorized in multiple concepts, to be category spanners. But it is the underlying uncertainty that matters. It has its effects even before objects are categorized.

According to the formulation developed by Hannan et al. (2019), both kinds of conceptual uncertainty affect valuations of objects. In general, people prefer experiences with objects with more certain membership (so long as the concept has a positive valence). On top of this effect, people find ambiguous objects hard to interpret, meaning that experiences with them go less fluently. And disfluency in turn depresses valuation.

We have deployed these ideas to analyze reactions of critics and buyers to the wines produced by wineries that span genres. In doing so, we had to assume a high degree of consensus among the interested parties in the meanings of the genres, the expectations associated with genre membership. We concentrated on consensus among producers because the other parties are unlikely to arrive at consensual meanings about products if the producers themselves cannot agree.

A key link in our theory connects solidarity of social structure to conceptual agreement. There is ample sociological justification for assuming this link. A next important step would turn this postulate into a theorem, an implication of an argument. The model of social influence and categorization proposed by Hannan et al. (2019, chapter 14) moves in this direction. This model addresses learning from the categorizations of others. A key idea is that people cannot share their concepts (probability distributions) but can share their categorizations. However, the model assumes that parties to a social interaction already possess the relevant concepts and share labels for them. The situations modeled are those in which one agent wants to know which of the relevant concepts apply to an object and lacks complete information about its feature values. In such contexts, it makes sense for the agent to pay attention to the categorizations of others whom the agent believes have concepts similar to her or his own. And here is a possible link to social structure. People are more likely to trust the categorizations of others in highly solidary communities.

But building the link between community structure and genre emergence requires a model of the *acquisition* of concepts in social interaction, how one person learns the concepts used by others in their community. We think this would be an exciting direction for research. Concept learning has become a hot topic, due not doubt to the incredible progress made in machine learning. The relevant research, as far as we know, considers single agents learning concepts in the course of making sense of variety in incoming information with some kind of feedback. The work we envision could build on this research by embedding the learning process in a structure of social interaction. Some important first steps in such a direction have been made by Goldberg and Stein (2018) and Guilbeaut et al. (2021).

12.2   Identities

A second major theme of the book connects market identities with genres. This connection provides the link between challenges to genre conventions and collective response by producers whose identities are seen as at risk. But identity is a complicated subject, and there is much more that can be done. In particular, more attention should be paid to the multiplicities of identities for agents.

Consider the tension that some producers experience over the decision to affiliate with a collective identity. This showed up repeatedly in interviews with organic and biodynamic producers. The concrete choice they face is whether to announce their genre affiliations on their labels. Some producers expressed concern that broadcasting a category membership will diminish the value of their individual identity, or narrowcast them. Consider the view of André Ostertag:

> We have the certification to give proof that we are biodynamic if people want it. But we did not want to be put in a too-specific niche.
>
> Wine is not just an agricultural product. It's also a cultural product. I hope people want to buy my wines because of their taste or style, because they like them. Not because they are biodynamic.

When we asked him to elaborate about why he would not label his wines as made from biodynamic-certified grapes, he added: "Because my ego is bigger."

Jean Boxler, who works using organic methods, expressed a similar sentiment:

> You can drink organic wine from Chile or Australia, and not only Alsace. If you hide your name behind the organic farming logo, the most important thing becomes organic farming, and you—you are nothing. We have a style that we cultivate, and that is important for us to preserve.

Jean and Pierre Trimbach told us that they had not used chemical fertilizers or treatments against rot in their vineyards since 1952 and added, "If we do organic farming, we will do it, and we are not going to shout it out loud. Today the most important is what's in the bottle."

A related concern with using genre labels on wines is a worry about projecting an inauthentic identity and exploiting the rising popularity of unconventional methods for economic gain. Marcel Deiss voiced this concern to us:

> I have not used logos for many years because I didn't want to appear to support people who want to transform this [biodynamics] into something commercial. Some people do it without believing in it.

More generally, producers in any market have a multiplicity of identities, each tied to a specific audience. If an identity serves as the basis of relatively durable expectations, then we have to be clear about whose expectations these are. Psychology concentrates on personal identities for which one's audience is oneself—what are the person's expectations about how he or she will behave over a range of situations. In sociology, identities are seen as attributed to agents by audiences.[3] And this is where the multiplicity arises. In one case, discussed above, the set of attributed identities consists of the agent's self-identity (as self-attribution) and genre-based identities, which can be either self-attributions (identifying with a genre) or external attributions, such as categorizations by critics.

Issues of ambiguity and interpretability arise when an audience shares two or more concepts in a domain. If audiences are partitioned by genre and if those in one component of the partition do not possess concepts used by members of the other component of the partition, then the fact that members of two or more of these audiences recognize an object as typical of one of their concepts does not lead to confusion. In a sense, the spanning is invisible to members of these audiences. For instance, audiences in nations to which products are exported might not make the same genre distinctions as those in the origin country. What might look like confusing combinations of feature values in one country might seem innocuous in the other. In future research on these issues, it would be very useful to direct attention to structures that might segment audiences.

A second facet of audience multiplicity arises when audiences are nested, not segmented. If a broad domain, such as wine, exists for an audience, then some audience members might form only very-high-level concepts, say, red, white, rose, and sparkling. Others might learn and use concepts at different levels of specificity. For instance, some might conceptualize the color/sparkling distinctions but also national and/or varietal distinctions. Others might conceptualize distinctions that pertain to producers, not only wines. Patterns of feature values that would be confusing for some of these audiences will not be for others. The relevant research in economic sociology has treated such audiences as homogeneous, assuming that each member possesses the same cohort of concepts, those that are used in the data sources, for example, the genres assigned to films by some source such as the American Film Institute. Our study has relied on this kind of simplification of the audience. The obvious next steps will relax the unrealistic assumption of homogeneity.[4] Doing so will require learning the concepts actually used by audience members. Moving in this direction will be costly. But we think that the potential gain will more than compensate for the cost.

12.3   Authenticity

Some of our key informants formulated issues of genre membership in the language of authenticity. Exploring this angle gives another way to connect with current research. Authenticity, long discussed in moral philosophy and arts worlds, has become a central concept in theories of social movements and organizations. The most influential line of current research on authenticity follows Glenn Carroll and collaborators (Carroll and Swaminathan 2000; Carroll and Wheaton 2009). This work starts with the distinction between two forms: moral and type authenticity.[5] In the case of moral authenticity, claims are based on the moral or ethical correctness of the choices embedded in the object. Choices to engage in organic or biodynamic farming exemplify this meaning. Type authenticity stems from typicality in the genre made relevant by the context. In the vignette with which we began the book,

Bob Dylan's choice to switch from acoustic to electronic instruments part-way through a performance in a folk festival was seen as inauthentic by part of the audience because of its atypicality in that genre. As we have recounted it, the traditionalist countermovement was based on claims to type authenticity.

The main point of Carroll and Wheaton's (2009) analysis is that authenticity claims matter most when they are embedded in observable features of producer organizations. We see clear instances of this pattern in our study. We argued that the choice to employ biodynamic farming is highly visible. The vineyards of biodynamic (and organic) farmers are easily distinguishable from those whose owners use chemical herbicide, for instance. At the extreme, the presence of plow horses in the vineyards surely marks a farm as biodynamic. Use of the biodynamic preparations is not easily visible to the final consumer, but it is generally made clear to visitors to the winery (such as professional critics). Likewise, the strongest signal of fealty to the code of tradition in making Barolo and Barbaresco is sole reliance on botti for aging. Again this choice is easily observable to visitors, who can then transmit the information to consumers.

Seen from a social movement perspective, a claim of authenticity that is also accepted by a relevant audience is a necessary component for mobilization. Such validation by outsiders reinforces loyalty of insiders to maintain the core goals of a movement. Distinguishing an authentic belief system also encourages outsiders to acknowledge the movement as a valid representative of those goals. In the case of wine producers, the relevant outsiders involved are critics and consumers, especially high-end wine enthusiasts. The key determinant of authenticity is recognition by both insiders and outsiders of the movement's boundary (and its content), even if they disagree with the goals and purposes of the movement.

Research in psychology has formulated issues of authenticity in terms of essentialism (Newman 2016). This work builds on extensive psychological research that shows that people have a strong tendency to reason in terms of essentialism, to believe that objects and types have some primary attributes. Verhaal and Carroll (2019) conducted experiments to learn whether people respond more to producers's essentialist claims ("our product comes from ingredients from a unique site") or expositional claims ("our product is made in a traditional production facility"). The types of claims differ in verifiability. The experimental evidence using descriptions of products in the American microdistillery industry shows some support for essentialism but finds more robust support for the exposition component of authenticity.

We find it interesting that the notion of terroir cuts across the divide between essentialist and expositionalist claims. Terroir is surely an essentialist concept. The very label of the concept and its reference to unique combinations of soil and climate exemplify essentialist thinking. But the notion also includes cultural practices of production as part of the specification of terroir. Here we encounter potentially verifiable claims about observable practices. More intense study of claims to terroir across markets might, we think, contribute to a deeper understanding of authenticity in product markets.

Considering authenticity issues as they bear on terroir moves the analysis beyond the standard account that focuses on individual agents. Not only wines or wineries can be characterized by varying levels of authenticity; so too can genres and their categories. Some new issues arise at the categorical level. Consider our analysis of the traditional genre of Barolo/Barbaresco. We learned that the producers categorized as traditional contained two types, which we labeled arch-traditionlist and pragmatic traditionalist. Our interviews with the arch-traditionalists such as Beppe Rinaldi, Maria Teresa Mascarello, and Teobaldo Cappellano revealed a strong moralistic streak to their traditionalism. They can indeed be seen as claiming moral authenticity. The pragmatists do not make such claims; we view them as claiming type authenticity. So the nature of the ascriptions of authenticity vary within the traditionalist category. Does this matter? It might. Pragmatism can easily lead to the erosion of distinctiveness of the genre as producers adapt to changing circumstances. Those imbued with motivations that we characterize as morally authentic are more likely to resist the siren calls of the market and remain true to their vision of their genre. Such dedication to a narrow vision is a kind of inertia. And, as with organizational inertia, an emphasis on moral authenticity may risk progression toward cultural obsolescence. Clearly we have much to learn about the interplay of authenticity and genre dynamics.

12.4   Sharpening Social Movement Arguments

Social movement theory can also learn from the probabilistic account of concepts and categories and concepts on which our analyses are based. First, the claim that spanning identities lowers evaluations has been examined in a variety of social movement industries that have varying degrees of affiliation to an ideology or identity, as we detailed in the previous chapter. While the emphasis on identity tends to focus on movement claims and self-descriptions, the conceptual scheme here describes an iterative process, in which identities are created, constructed; and, if successful, recognized. Moreover, the probabilistic theory on which we build brings a new level of precision for addressing these and other issues.

Framing theory of social movements specifies that movements or actors whose claims resonate more closely with an audience will meet with success. Efforts to test this theory empirically have been elusive, in part because movements analyzed are (by definition) already visible and active. The emphasis in this book has been to explore the dynamics of how market identities—in different time periods and locations—have emerged, become dominant, and eventually contested. Our results suggest that possessing a distinct oppositional identity, one that is recognized and verified by the relevant audience, goes a long way in shaping success in product markets. Social movement theories might adopt a similar strategy to analyze variation among movements whose identities are viewed as more or less focused.

12.5   Oppositional Identities and Conflict

Studies of conflicts and their resolution regularly analyze confrontations among various entities with established identities: ethnic groups, terrorist organizations, rebel forces, vigilante organizations, and so on. Our work offers a newer, perhaps more flexible approach that moves away from essentialist assumptions of group identity. Instead our perspective places an emphasis on identifying the interactive dynamics that shape boundaries.

What are some of these processes? In previous chapters, we documented how social movement processes underlie the emergence and reformulation of identities among biodynamic, modernist, and renewed traditionalism among wine producers. As innovation in techniques (or a return to older traditions) were adopted by some subset of wine producers, new lines of cleavage emerged that had not existed previously. In some cases, contention grew over which group has the more credible claim to be producing a true Barolo or more authentic Riesling.

We have seen that strong community solidarity among producers tends to sharpen genre distinctions, which in turn generates strong opposition. It seems likely that genre distinctions backed by less solidary producers would not generate such opposition. At the same time, the weaker genres would be much less durable.

Our research found that conflict can arise over seemingly small, random, or experimental differences in practices or norms. Conflict sharpens the identities that demarcate group boundaries, making them visible and more easily recognized by outsiders and insiders alike. By paying attention to the processes embedded in theories of concepts and categories, the usual causal picture of the emergence of group conflict can be turned upside down. That is, small, often inconsequential departures from ordinary practices can cause conflict if one or the other side resists these changes. Over time, recurring conflict allows for new identities to emerge—among resisters and defenders.

These ideas could inform studies of all kinds of group conflict in which the process of conflict itself creates new identities and boundaries. Our perspective suggests that actors holding conflicting positions might initiate the realignment of identities and groups. In the study of revolutions, the constant movement back and forth across identities and positions has been well documented but not well understood. Our perspective also suggests that conflict that sharpens identities can make such group conflict more intractable. The converse also holds: to the extent that identities are fuzzier and less clearly delineated, conflict situations may be more easily resolved.

Appendix: Data Sources

OUR DATA COME FROM A combination of fieldwork and archival sources. In our fieldwork we conducted interviews with winemakers, the editors and critics of wine publications, and telephone surveys of wineries in our archival list. The archival data were collected from materials in specialized publications that provide critical reviews and ratings, retail prices at the winery, and methods of production.

We did not conduct our fieldwork following formal ethnographic methods. Our guiding goal consisted of gaining knowledge of historical events that had received limited or no coverage in the media and a better grasp of the interpretation of these events developed by the informants themselves. We also aimed at understanding more how the winemakers and the critics view their work and the context in which they carry out their activities. The format of these interviews was semistructured, and we entered each conversation having in mind a few questions to ask our informants, ranging from biographical details about their winery to the description of their winemaking operations in the vineyard and the cellar to identify their style. During the interviews, we asked new questions as a result of what our informant said. In most cases, the interviews were audiotaped (always with the consent of the informant) or written notes were taken when taping was not possible (for example, when an interview took place in the vineyard and audio-recording quality would be too poor due to background noise). We transcribed the interviews based on taped files and translated them from Italian or French when the informant did not speak English.

Our fieldwork allows anecdotal generalization in which our conclusions about each research setting are inferred using a nonprobability sample. In probability or random sampling, every unit in the population being studied has the same probability of being chosen, which allows the sample to represent the population adequately. We followed instead judgmental or purposive sampling. In this approach, the researcher chooses the sample based on who she or he thinks would be appropriate for the study. This is used when the focus of the research is on a specific field or a small population, or relevant information can be obtained from a limited number of sources in the area being researched. In these cases, if the researcher used a random sample, she or he might or might not be able to obtain that information depending on who was sampled. When we designed the project, we could not develop enough knowledge based only on secondary accounts, and we needed to collect primary data from informants, which led us to select the targets of our interviews.

We continued with interviews until we reached what some qualitative researchers call theoretical saturation, a point in which the researchers have done a comprehensive examination of the phenomena being studied and additional cases are not providing more conceptual insights. Using a nonprobability sample cannot guarantee that the sample is unbiased and represents the whole population from which it is drawn. Although our approach is open to this critique, we did select cases with the goal of covering multiple locations within the regions that we studied, as well as cases that vary in organizational size, age, and winemaking style.

Interviews

The research presented in this book builds on 118 recorded interviews done over the course of nine years. In Italy, we conducted a total of ninety-three interviews, seventy-seven with wineries and seventeen with wine critics, magazine editors, and restaurant sommeliers. We conducted the seventy-seven interviews at the wineries during visits between 2005 and 2013. Of these interviews, we did a greater share in the Langhe (forty-nine) than in Montalcino (twenty-eight).

Piemonte

The production area for Barolo and Barbaresco covers the territory of fourteen communes, and we visited wineries in eleven of them and six other locations: Alba, Barbaresco, Barolo, Bra, Castagnole Lanze, Castiglione Falletto, Dogliani, Grinzane Cavour, La Morra, Monchiero, Monforte d'Alba, Neive, Novello, Serralunga d'Alba, Sinio, Treiso, and Verduno. When headquartered in locations outside the production area for Barolo and Barbaresco, the wineries own or rent vineyards in one or more of the fourteen authorized communes.

The wineries that we visited in Piemonte and the dates of the visits are listed in table A.1.

Table A.1 Interviews with producers of Barolo and Barbaresco

Domaine	Interview	Date
Elio Altare	Elio Altare	November 2005
Ascheri Giacomo	Matteo Ascheri	December 2013
Produttori del Barbaresco	Aldo Vacca	November 2005, June 2017
Bovio Gianfranco	Marco Boschiazzo	December 2013
Brovia	Alex Sanchez	June 2017
Comm. G. B. Burlotto	Fabbio Alessandria	December 2013
Ca' Rome' Romano Marengo	Paola and Guiseppe Marengo	December 2013
Dott. G. Cappellano	Teobaldo Cappellano	November 2005, June 2008
	Augusto Cappellano	December 2013
Cavallotto Fratellii	Alfio Cavallotto	June 2011, June 2017
	Giuseppe Cavallotto	June 2011
Ceretto	Alessandro Ceretto	June 2017
	Roberta Ceretto	June 2017
Fratelli Cigliuti	Renato Cigliuti	February 2007
Domenico Clerico	Domenico Clerico	November 2005, December 2006
	Oscar Arrivabene	June 2017
Elvio Cogno	Walter Fissore	December 2013
Poderi Aldo Conterno	Giacomo Conterno	November 2005
Cantina Giacomo Conterno	Roberto Conterno	December 2006, July 2011
Paolo Conterno	Giorgio Conterno	December 2006
Conterno Fantino	Claudio Conterno	December 2006
Poderi Luigi Einaudi	Elena Raimondi	February 2007
Fontanafredda s.r.l.	Danilo Drocco	November 2006
	Giovanni Minetti	November 2006
Gaja	Angelo Gaja	December 2006
Elio Grasso	Gianluca Grasso	November 2005, July 2011
Bruno Giacosa	Dante Scaglione	November 2006
Marchesi di Grésy	Marco Dotta	November 2006
Le Ginestre	Barbara Audasso	November 2006
Cantina Mascarello Bartolo	Maria-Teresa Mascarello	November 2005, June 2008, June 2011
Mascarello Giuseppe e Figlio	Mauro Mascarello	November 2006

Massolino Vigna Rionda	Franco Massolino	June 2017
Moccagatta	Sergio Minuto	December 2013
Poderi e Cantina Oddero	Isabella Boffo	June 2017
Pelissero	Cristina Pelissero	December 2013
E. Pira–Chiara Boschis	Chiara Boschis	June 2017
Principiano Ferdinando	Ferdinando Principiano	June 2017
Prunotto Cantina di Bussia	Albiera Antinori	November 2006
	Gianluca Torrengo	November 2006
Rinaldi Giuseppe	Giuseppe Rinaldi	November 2005, June 2008
Rivetto dal 1902	Enrico Rivetto	December 2006
Cantina Gigi Rosso	Maurizio Rosso	November 2006
Sandrone Luciano	Luciano Sandrone	November 2006
Paolo Scavino	Enrica Scavino	November 2006
Schiavenza	Luciano Pira	December 2013
Sottimano	Anna Sottimano	December 2013
Stroppiana Oreste	Dario Stroppiana	November 2006
La Spinetta	Giorgio Rivetti	November 2005, November 2006
Cantina Terre del Barolo	Matteo Bosco	November 2006
G. D. Vajra	Marina Vajra	March 2007
Vietti	Mario Cordero	November 2006
	Luca Currado	November 2006
Roberto Voerzio	Roberto Voerzio	December 2006, June 2008

Montalcino

The Disciplinare regulating the production of Brunello di Montalcino requires that the grapes are grown within the administrative boundaries of the commune of Montalcino, and all the wineries we interviewed are located there except for Querciabella, which does not produce Brunello di Montalcino and is headquartered in Greve in Chianti.[1]

The wineries that we visited in Montalcino and and the dates of the visits are listed in table A.2.

Alsace

The denomination AOC Vins d'Alsace allows vinification of grapes to be grown in 119 villages in the region. Our interviews with the wineries in this region cover the territory of nineteen different communes in the Haut-Rhin and Bas-Rhin subregions of Alsace: Ammerschwihr, Andlau, Barr, Beblenheim, Bennwihr, Bergheim, Bergholtz, Epfig, Guebwiller, Husseren-les-Chateaux, Kientzheim, Niedermorschwihr, Orschwihr,

Table A.2 Interviews with producers of Brunello di Montalcino

Domaine	Interview	Date
Altesino s.r.l.	Elisabetta Gnudi Angelini	December 2012
Il Colle di Carli	Caterina Carli	December 2012
Castello Banfi	Rudy Buratti	December 2005
Fattoria dei Barbi	Paolo Salvi	July 2017
Biondi Santi Tenuta Greppo	Franco Biondi Santi	December 2005
San Giuseppe di Viola di Campalto	Stella di Campalto	December 2012
Borgo Scopeto e Caparzo	Elisabetta Gnudi Angelini	December 2012
Caprili	Giacomo Bartolommei	December 2012
Castello Romitorio	Tullia Abi Zima Battaglia	December 2012
La Cerbaiola	Giulio Salvioni	December 2005, December 2012
Cerbaiona	Nora Molinari	December 2012
Ciacci Piccolomini d'Aragona	Paolo Bianchini	December 2012
Col D'Orcia	Conte Francesco Marone Cinzano	December 2102
Cupano	Lionel Cousin	December 2012
	Ornella Tondini	December 2012
Donatella Cinelli Colombini	Donatella Cinelli Colombini	July 2008
Tenuta Fanti	Filippo Baldassarre Fanti	July 2008
Eredi Fuligni	Daniela Perini	December 2012
Il Maroneto	Alessandro Mori	November 2017
Tenuta Silvio Nardi	Emilia Nardi	July 2008
Siro Pacenti	Giancarlo Pacenti	July 2008, July 2017
Pian dell'Orino	Caroline Pobitzer	December 2012
	Jan Erbach	December 2012, July 2017
Le Potazzine	Giuseppe Gorelli	July 2008, December 2012
Poggio Antico	Alberto Montefiori	December 2012
La Ragnaie	Riccardo Campinoti	December 2012
San Polino	Katia Nussbaum	December 2102
	Luigi Fabbro	December 2012, July 2017
Podere Salicutti	Francesco Leanza	July 2008, November 2018
Sesti Castello di Argiano	Giuseppe Sesti	December 2012
Case Basse di Soldera Gianfranco	Gianfranco Soldera	December 2005, July 2008
Val di Suga (Tentamenti Angelini)	Mario Calzolari	December 2012
Valdicava	Pierfilippo Abbruzzese	July 2017

Table A.3 Interviews with producers of Alsace AOC wines

Domaine	Interview	Date
Dom. Laurent Barth	Laurent Barth	December 2010
Dom. Christian Binner	Audrey and Christian Binner	November 2009
Dom. Bott-Geyl	Jean-Christophe Bott	December 2010, June 2015
Dom. Albert Boxler	Jean Boxler	December 2010
Dom. Camille Braun et Fils	Christophe and Chantal Braun	December 2010
Dom. Marcel Deiss	Marcel Deiss	November 2009
Dirler-Cadé	Jean-Pierre Dirler	December 2010
Dom. Pierre Frick	Jean-Pierre Frick	December 2010
Dom. Rémy Gresser	Rémy Gresser	November 2009
Hugel et Fils	Etienne Hugel	November 2009
Dom. Josmeyer	Christophe Ehrhardt	November 2009
Dom. André Kientzler	André Kientzler	November 2009
Dom. Marc Kreydenweiss	Marc Kreydenweiss	November 2009
Dom. Albert Mann	Maurice Barthelme	December 2010
Dom. Ostertag	André Ostertag	November 2009
Dom. Martin Schaetzel	Jean Schaetzel	November 2009
Dom. Schlumberger	Thomas Schlumberger Jean-Marie Winter	December 2010
Dom. Gérard Schueller et Fils	Bruno Schueller	December 2010
Dom. Jean Sipp	Jean-Guillaume Sipp	June 2015
Dom. Vincent Stoeffler	Vincent Stoeffler	December 2010
Dom. Marc Tempé	Marc Tempé	November 2009
Maison F.E. Trimbach	Jean and Pierre Trimbach	December 2010
Dom. Weinbach	Catherine and Laurence Faller	November 2009
Dom. Zind-Humbrecht	Olivier Humbrecht	November 2009
Dom. Valentin Zusslin	Jean-Paul Zusslin	November 2009

Orschwihr, Pfaffenheim, Ribeauville, Riquewihr, Turckheim, Wettolsheim, Wintzenheim, and Zellenberg. We conducted twenty-six interviews during three visits to wineries in 2009 (thirteen interviews), 2010 (eleven interviews) and 2015 (two interviews)—see table A.3.

Critics and Other Informants

The wine critics and experts we interviewed include: Marc De Grazia, Gianni Fabrizio, Thomas Matthews, Gigi Piumatti, Giacomo Tachis, Daniel Thomases, Alessandro Torcoli, and Franco Ziliani; the former directors of the Consorzio Langhevini Claudio Salaris and of the Consorzio Brunello di Montalcino Stefano Campatelli; and Eugenio Gamba from the master cooper workshop Fabbrica Botti Gamba. We interviewed sommeliers at the following restaurants and wine shops: Aimo e Nadia, Cracco-Peck, Don Carlos, Joia, Savini and Solci in Milan, and Greg St. Clair, the Italian wine buyer for the retailer K&L in Redwood City, California. We interviewed the wine critics, experts, and sommeliers via telephone as well as visits in person in Alba, Castell'Alfero, Firenze, Pollenzo, San Casciano, and Palo Alto. We also interviewed a set of winemakers and critics who provided guest lectures in a course on the wine industry taught over several years at the Stanford Graduate School of Business.

Notes

Preface

1. Many of our interviews took place in the winter, when things are slow in the winery and the winemakers could make time for our visits.

Acknowledgments

1. These papers include Negro, Hannan, and Rao (2010, 2011); Negro and Leung (2013); Negro, Hannan, and Fassiotto (2015).

1. Genres and Market Identities

1. The classical view of concepts dates back to the Greek philosopher Aristotle, at least. In the classical view, concepts have necessary and sufficient conditions. Any object must be either a (full) instance of a concept or not.

2. We follow the convention in formal linguistics of using a notation that distinguishes the terms used by the members of the communities under study (the so-called object language) from the terms used by the analysts. We do so with fonts, marking the terms in the object language in a sans-serif font. However, this becomes tiresome when the same terms are used repeatedly. So in the case of terms like modern, traditional we use this formatting convention when the terms are first introduced in discussion but then revert to using the same font as the main text.

3. For useful overviews, see D'Andrade (1995), Laurence and Margolis (1999), Murphy (2002).

4. The dictionary website lexico.com claims that the first usage of this term appeared in the *Winnipeg Free Press* in the early 1970s. The *Oxford English Dictionary*, which added this word in its online edition in September 2007, defines it as "the quality or fact of a wine being typical of its geographical provenance and of the grape variety (or varieties) from which it is made."

5. This means that the mental representation of the wine in the semantic space is close to the concept. Objects whose mental representations lie further from the concept are less typical.

6. The only exceptions are a small number of producer cooperatives in which producers grow and harvest grapes from their own vineyards and deliver them to a central, cooperatively owned winery that does the vinification.

2. Barolo and Barbaresco

1. These data were compiled from the database provided by the Consorzio di Tutela for the Langhe, the administrative and trade association responsible for representing the two wine denominations (www.langhevini.it), as well as the National Federation of Consorzi (www.federdoc.com).

2. This standard term refers to wineries that grow their own grapes and vinify and market them. Three nonestate producers of Barolo/Barbaresco are larger: the industrial-scale Terre da Vino and the cooperatives Terre del Barolo and Produttori del Barbaresco.

3. These labels are used to control levels of production. A number of these strips that corresponds to its allowable yield gets allocated to each winery in the DOCG.

4. The complete detailed rules can be found at http://catalogoviti.politicheagricole.it/scheda_denom.php?t=dsc&q=1011.

3. The Barolo Wars

1. Clerico recalled that in 1987 he organized a meeting in Monforte inviting fifty producers and experts to taste his Barolo 1984. The

regulatory commission that awards DOCG status had rejected his wine that year. Before the wine could be submitted for further evaluation in September, he organized an event in which participants "tasted wines all evening."

2. When we visited La Spinetta in 2006, the ultra-hygenic cellar contained only brand-new barriques.

3. His vines were planted 45 cm (about 17.7 inches) apart. He told us that the traditional spacing was 80–100 cm (31.5 to 39.4 inches).

4. Release prices are set by the importer/distributor and are close to actual retail prices, but some variation can occur.

4. Mobilization of Collective Market Identities

1. Maria Teresa Mascarello told us that, before the 2001 elections, the Carabinieri—the national gendarmerie—confiscated a bottle with the Berlusconi label in a shop in Alba for displaying political propaganda in an unauthorized space.

2. When fermentation begins, the solid matter (skins and seeds) rise to the top of the container. Extraction of flavor and color from the skins requires that they be consistently mixed with the juice. The traditional method is the so-called punch down in which a worker uses a wooden pole to break up the "cap" of solids. Modernists tended to rely on machines called rotofermentors for this purpose.

3. This domaine no longer uses barriques.

4. As far as we can ascertain, Giacomo Conterno favored an ultra-traditional genre while his brother wanted a somewhat softer Barolo, but not a modern one.

5. Elio Grasso's son Gianluca joined the family winery in 1995 and started to work on a new wine, the Barolo Runcot Riserva, which is aged in barriques.

6. We identified 387 wineries. This number can be larger than the number of certified producers in any given year because some wineries can go out of business. It can also be smaller than the total number of wineries releasing Barolo and Barbaresco in the market. Some producers, like Teobaldo Cappellano, do not send samples to be reviewed. But it is the most comprehensive population of wineries that we are aware of.

7. The majority of the ratings range between these two extreme values. The median value of these ratings, obtained by at least 50 percent

of the wines, is three stars. WS uses a 100-point scale. In actuality, the publication uses only the upper range of the scale. In the legend provided by the tasters, wines below 50 are not classified, and those between 50 and 74 are not recommended. As a result, we expect to see a concentration above the 75-point score. For Barolo and Barbaresco wines rated by WS, the median score is 90. Most of the ratings range between 85 and 96, which cover the categories of "very good" (for scores between 85 and 89), "outstanding" (scores between 90 and 94), and also "classic" (great wines rated 95 or more).

8. We performed t-test comparisons of ratings between rows, that is, comparisons between traditionalist producers before versus after changing to barriques, and between traditionalist producers after changing to barriques versus modernist producers, for each critic. All the comparisons are statistically significant at conventional values of p = 0.05 or lower.

9. We used fractional-polynomial prediction plots, which allow a wide range of shapes that include the shapes provided by ordinary polynomials like linear and quadratic functions and more.

10. These are fractional-polynomial prediction plots as described for the previous figures in this chapter.

11. The differences are even more pronounced for the newest vintage on the market, 2014. The average U.S. market price for Altare's Arborina was $84, and for Rinaldi's Brunate, it was $249.

12. Of course, these changes do not reflect the mass market but rather the purchasing decisions of specialized consumers.

5. Genre Spanning, Ambiguity, and Valuation

1. The technical details are contained in Chapters 11 and 12 of Hannan et al. (2019).

2. This set must contain concepts at the "same level" and not, for instance, subconcepts of other concepts in the set, for example, Barolo and traditional Barolo.

3. We follow Le Mens, Kovács, Hannan, Nunes, and Pros (2020) in a slight deviation from the measure of ambiguity proposed by Hannan et al. (2019). According to this alternative construction, the conceptual ambiguity of an object is given by the entropy of the vector of these categorization probabilities. Entropy is a standard measure of the inverse of information content of a message. In formal terms, an

object is ambiguous if its set of assigned categorization probabilities conveys little information about its likely feature values.

$$A(o \mid x) = -\sum_{C \in \wp_{(\kappa)}} P^*(\text{IS-A}(C, o) \mid x) \ln P^*(\text{IS-A}(C, o) \mid x),$$

where $\wp(\kappa)$ denotes the powerset of the set of relevant concepts and $P^*(\text{IS-A}(C, o \mid x))$ refers to the probability that an object at position x is categorized in the set of concepts C and not categorized in the other potentially relevant sets of concepts.

4. Our approach builds on an active research program within cognitive psychology examining inferences about unobserved features of objects when their positions are known on some feature dimensions, but the category of the object is uncertain. Research that documents this pattern includes Murphy and Ross (1994), Griffiths et al. (2012), and Konovalova and Le Mens (2016, 2018).

5. A classic example of the importance of context has been suggested by scholars of race and ethnicity who contrast the ease with which South Africans would be likely to classify a person or group as being "colored" compared to the use of this concept by someone in the United States or France.

6. The full model also builds distinctions based on the evaluator's mode of cognition. In the interest of simplicity, we do not discuss these more elaborated models. For those familiar the relevant research, we can state that we assume deliberative cognition because the valuations come from contexts that prime for this.

7. See Hannan et al. (2019, Chapter 12) for details.

8. Because the number of stars assigned is an ordered variable, we estimated an ordered logit regression for these data. A suitable interpretation of the regression coefficients is in terms of odds ratios (they can be obtained by exponentiating the ordered logit coefficients).

9. This effect is obtained holding constant a number of factors, including the fixed characteristics of each winery that produced the wine, the town of production, the quality of the vintage in which the wine was produced, the years of experience of the winery since first bottling, and whether the wine is a regular release or a reserve wine.

10. Hannan et al. (2019) define the contrast of a category as an inverse function of the average ambiguity of its members. Specifically, the contrast of a category is defined as $1/(1 + \bar{A})$, where $\bar{A}$ denotes the average ambiguity of the members. Thus high contrast means that audience members generally perceive producers or products to

be either nearly fully in or fully outside the category. In simpler terms, high contrast means low fuzziness.

11. Simmel (1978 [1900], 256) described this state as promoting blasé attitude, which means experiencing "all things as being of an equally dull and grey hue, as not worth getting excited about." The essence of blasé attitude is an indifference toward the distinction between things (Simmel 1971, 330).

12. We controlled for two additional variables: a linear indicator of vintage year and the quality of the vintage as rated in the *Wine Advocate Vintage Guide* compiled by Robert Parker.

13. These are so-called marginal means. A margin is a statistic—in this case, the average response in terms of ratings—based on a fitted model calculated over data in which the contrast variable varies over a range of values and the other variables are fixed at their means.

6. Brunello di Montalcino

1. Gaggio (2011) provides rich historical detail.

2. Confusingly the family name and the name of their wine estate did not hyphenate the names, but the labels did.

3. For members that do only grape production, the vote is determined by the weight of the production, which benefits large and high-yield producers.

7. Tradition, Modernity, and the Scandal

1. We spent a memorable dinner with Soldera, who on learning that one of us lives in California, launched into a seemingly interminable rant that one cannot make wine in California because true wine does not admit irrigation.

2. www.winemag.com/2013/08/12/the-two-faces-of-brunello-di-montalcino/.

3. The origin of the label is obscure. Some attribute it to American wine writer Burton Anderson; others point to Robert Parker and Luigi Veronelli.

4. We could not find an authoritative account of what transpired. We have pieced together the following account from a few reports in the press, blogs (especially Franco Zilliani's VinoWire),

Kerin O'Keefe's writing on Brunello (O'Keefe 2008, 2012), and our interviews.

5. Franco Zilliani told us in 2008 that Gaja had proposed a change in the Disciplinare for Barbaresco after a German lab had produced evidence that his Barbaresco Costa Russi contained Barbera and that the members of the Barbaresco Consorzio rejected his proposal.

8. Alsace

1. Proposals to the national regulator to designate some crus as Premier Cru have been in the works for years and are still under consideration.

2. Moreover, Ostertag is the only person we interviewed who interrogated us about our research project. In reaction to our brief sketch, he insisted that he wanted to know the vision behind the project. "You must have a vision" he insisted. A very interesting conversation then ensued.

3. Several winemakers told us that cooperatives are reselling wines in bulk and even declassifying Grand Crus.

9. Biodynamic and Organic Winemaking

1. www.wine-business-international.com/wine/marketing-wine-tourism/price-organic-conversion

2. Alsace is close to the Swiss town of Dornach, center of the worldwide Anthroposophical Society, whose headquarters—called Goetheanum—were opened in 1920 by Steiner and his associates.

3. We recorded the number of stars assigned to wineries for the vintages covered by the guides between the first edition published in 1988 and the seventh edition from 2008. The number of wineries rated grew unevenly over time from thirty-eight in 1988 to sixty in 2008, reaching a maximum of sixty-six in the 1999 edition.

4. Starting in 1984, GM published special bulletins with general notes on leading wineries and a few selected wines, but no comprehensive ratings. These earlier editions provide us with winery-level information, particularly price levels and the number of bottles produced. From the 2003 edition, the guide provides comprehensive wine ratings.

5. We obtained such data for 142 of a total of 155 wineries. Our informants also indicated when they began bottling, which we use to determine the time at risk of conversion. We used these data to code memberships in the two unconventional categories. We code the distinction between organic and biodynamic production as mutually exclusive: "organic" means "organic-but-not-biodynamic" throughout. Because of the inherent ambiguity in adherence to sustainable, or lutte raisonnée, practices (with several producers claiming adherence and no strict method to ascertain these claims), we do not try to distinguish membership in the "sustainable" camp. These producers are part of the "conventional" genre in our analyses.

6. We explored two alternative measures of winery quality besides Parker's assessment. Readers interested in more technical details about these measures and the statistical analyses generally described in this chapter can find them in Negro et al. (2015).

7. There are two unusual cases. Eugène Meyer was the first producer who began to use biodynamic methods before the start of the study period, in 1969. Jean-Pierre Frick told us that Meyer converted because he had been poisoned by pesticides: "he went blind for a week. He couldn't see anything and so he said to himself, 'I will no longer work with such products.'" Henry Bannwarth started using organic methods in 1970. We excluded both from the analysis because our informants suggested to us that these early conversions were somewhat idiosyncratic

8. In technical terms, these results are maximum likelihood estimates of time-constant hazard regressions.

9. In hazard models with interaction terms between the three quality measures and the time trend, we do not find the effects of winery quality to vary significantly over time.

10. Cognitive psychologist James Hampton has done a series of experiments that show this. For instance, in these experiments subjects agreed that "chairs are furniture" and that "car seats are chairs," but few agreed that "car seats are furniture" (Hampton 1982).

10. Why Biodynamics? Category Signals and Audience Response

1. A signal can be productive in the sense that adopting the signal improves performance. But it does not need to be so; the signal just

needs to be able to distinguish types of producers whose quality differs prior to investing in the signal. If a signal is productive, however, and for the signal to operate effectively, the gains resulting from productivity increases must be lower than the costs of signaling (Spence 1974).

2. Our argument relates more directly to Spence's model than to others, particularly Podolny's (1993) status-signal model. Spence begins with quality differentials and derives signals; Podolny begins with the status signal and derives differences in quality.

3. Political scientists make this argument about the efficiency of investing in industry associations for political action by individual firms; see, for example, Lohmann (1993).

4. Take a more specific example, the signal of compliance to fair-labor standards in the apparel industry. Nike and Reebok invested in factory standards in Indonesia that were superior to the local legal requirements. They hired auditors of the working conditions in their plants, but the audits were not accessible to outsiders. The companies gained more credibility on this issue once they joined a coalition of other manufacturers, activists, and labor groups, which organized the audits.

5. Cole's fieldwork among Oregon wineries suggests that managing biodynamic vineyards costs 15 percent more than managing a sustainably farmed property and hiring a consultant can cost $1,000 per visit. Certification is a few hundred dollars, and applicants also pay a licensing fee of 0.5 percent on gross sales. Cole notes: "For the same price, organic certification sounds like a safer bet" (Cole 2011, 58).

6. That is, we use fixed-effects estimators at the winery level, which let us examine the effects of changes in practices. Readers interested in more technical details of the statistical analyses described in this chapter can find them in Negro et al. (2015).

7. We cannot reject the null hypothesis that the effects of the two category memberships are equal ($X^2 = 0.18$, p $= 0.68$ with 1 df).

8. The point estimates in the second column are obtained by also including the blind rating assigned by RVF as an additional control variable for the nonblind rating. In this way, the effect of the signal ought to be isolated from the intrinsic features of the product (Negro and Leung 2013).

9. The difference between the effects of the two categories is not statistically significant (F $= 0.40$, p $= 0.40$).

10. WS used a 100-point scale throughout. GM used a 100-point

scale until 2007, then switched to a 20-point scale. For comparability, we converted the latter to the 100-point scale. The median score is 87 for both GM and WS, and the fraction in the upper range is similar: the top 10 percent of wines receive a score of 90 or higher in GM and 91 or higher in WS. The publications differ somewhat in the lower range distribution: the value of the first decile in the GM ratings is 73, and it is 80 in WS.

11. We find no evidence that biodynamics has a stronger effect for lower-quality members, as would be the case if there were a mechanism in which lower-quality producers have more to gain than their higher-quality counterparts.

12. *Hachette* uses a 1-to-4 star rating system, and *Wine Advocate* uses a 100-point scale to rate wines. The estimations followed the other analyses described in this chapter. One exception is the exclusion in the analysis of data from the *Wine Advocate* of the late harvest dummy—late harvest wines are normally more expensive, and the publication did not review any wines below the $25 price point.

13. The difference between the two coefficients of the two unconventional categories is statistically significant ($F = 6.01$, $p = 0.01$).

14. One difference is that we added as a control the critical scores obtained from WS to account for the impact of quality of the focal wine on prices.

15. The price regressions control for Parker's winery ratings and the WS rating of each wine. The estimates indicate that the status accorded to a winery by Parker is significantly associated with increases in prices in the U.S. market, as does quality measured in blind ratings. Formal certification also affects prices significantly, positively for biodynamic and negatively for organic wines in the American market (see also Delmas and Grant (2014)).

16. In markets like these where competing producers sell differentiated products, (1) changes in prices that are proportionate to changes in costs and (2) stationary demand curves (i.e., firms are moving along the same downward sloping demand curve and not switching curves), result in decreasing profits (Dixit and Stiglitz 1977). Because the elasticity of demand exceeds 1, revenues as well as profits are lower.

17. The published retail price in October 2020 for the latest vintage, 2017, of its flagship wine begins at roughly $12,000 per bottle, according to our search on wine-searcher.com.

18. This specification is very similar to that of ViniVeri, discussed in Chapter 4.

19. This means using cuttings from existing vines in the vineyard instead of purchasing clones from nurseries.

20. Chaptalization, legal in France, is addition of sugar to raise alcohol content.

11. Community Structure, Social Movements, and Market Identities

1. Note that Trimbach uses sustainable agriculture for the lower-price wines and organic agriculture for their reserve and Grand Cru wines. He is contrasting "natural" agriculture, in which nothing, even organic fertilizer, can be added, with these other alternative modes of agriculture.

12. Coda

1. If we want a formal representation, we use a membership relation IS-A(c, x). This relation is true if the focal person judges that an object, represented mentally as the set of features values x, is an instance of the concept c and is false otherwise.

2. These probabilities are often called base rates. Consider the role of $P(c)$. If instances of the concept are very rare in the context, meaning that $P(c)$ is small, then a person will be reluctant to categorize objects as instances of the concept.

3. The line of research in social psychology on social identities addresses choices by individuals about which social affiliations to include in their identities.

4. Goldberg, Hannan, and Kovács (2016) conducted one type of disaggregated study by analyzing interindividual differences in patterns of consumption of film and music. They find an overall pattern in which objects that are assigned to multiple genres get lower valuations. However, about a quarter of the sample consume and prefer such nonconforming objects. However, this work is also constrained by the empirical need to assume that all people studied have the same concepts. Without data on the actual concepts used, we cannot tell whether those who like the spanning objects like atypicality or whether they have different concepts for which these objects are actually typical.

5. Newman (2019) suggests a third type is needed, which he calls historical. An object is authentic in this sense if it fits with an observer's concepts about some historical period, for example, whether someone views the uniforms used in a reenactment of a famous battle as fitting their concept of military uniform of the period.

Appendix: Data Sources

1. The interview at Querciabella centered on the use of unconventional farming methods—the winery follows a unique vegan version of biodynamics—and not the production of Brunello di Montalcino, which is otherwise the focus of the research conducted in Montalcino.

Bibliography

Ali, Héla Hadj, Sébastien Lecocq, and Michael Visser. 2008. "The Impact of Gurus: Parker Grades and En Primeur Wine Prices." *Economic Journal* 118:158–73.

Almeida, Paul, and Chris Chase-Dunn. 2018. "Globalization and Social Movements." *Annual Review of Sociology* 44:189–211.

Alter, Adam L., and Daniel M. Oppenheimer. 2008. "Easy on the Mind, Easy on the Wallet: The Roles of Familiarity and Processing Fluency in Valuation Judgments." *Psychonomic Bulletin and Review* 15:985–990.

Altman, Rick. 1999. *Film/Genre*. London: British Film Institute.

Appadurai, Arjun. 1986. *The Social Life of Things*. Cambridge: Cambridge University Press.

Asimov, Eric. 2012. "Wines Worth a Taste, but Not the Vitriol." *New York Times*, January 24.

Becker, Gary S., and Kevin M. Murphy. 1992. "The Division of Labor, Coordination Costs, and Knowledge." *Quarterly Journal of Economics* 107:1137–1160.

Behr, Edward S. 2001. "Southern Piedmont Part II: The Great Wines of Barolo (and Barbaresco), How Much Remains of Tradition and Why Does It Matter? With an Intermezzo on Polenta." *Art of Eating* Summer:1–29.

Belfrage, Nicolas. 2006. *Barolo to Valpolicella: The Wines of Northern Italy*. London: Mitchell Beazley.

Benford, Robert D., and David A. Snow. 2000. "Framing Processes and Social Movements: An Overview and Assessment." *Annual Review of Sociology* 26:611–39.

Carroll, Glenn R., and Anand Swaminathan. 2000. "Why the Microbrewery Movement? Organizational Dynamics of Resource Partitioning in the U.S. Brewing Industry." *American Journal of Sociology* 106:715–762.

Carroll, Glenn R., and Dennis R. Wheaton. 2009. "The Organizational Construction of Authenticity: An Examination of Contemporary Food and Dining in the U.S." *Research in Organizational Behavior* 29:255–282.

Caves, Richard E. 2000. *Creative Industries. Contracts Between Art and Commerce.* Cambridge, Mass.: Harvard University Press.

Cohen, Jon, and Giovanni Federico. 2001. *The Growth of the Italian Economy, 1820-1960.* Cambridge: Cambridge University Press.

Cole, Katherine. 2011. *Voodoo Vintners: Oregon's Astonishing Biodynamic Winegrowers.* Corvallis: Oregon State University Press.

Corbi, Gianni. 1986. "Quella Leggina Sul Metanolo." *La Repubblica*, April 5.

Corsi, Alessandro, and Orley Ashenfelter. 2001. "Predicting Italian Wines Quality from Weather Data and Experts' Ratings." *Cahier Scientifique de l'OCVE.*

Crane, Diana. 1987. *The Transformation of the Avant-Garde.* Chicago: University of Chicago Press.

Cuellar, Steven S., Dan Karnowsky, and Frederick Acosta. 2012. "The Sideways Effect: A Test for Changes in the Demand for Merlot and Pinot Noir Wines." *Journal of Wine Economics* 4:219–32.

Cunningham, David. 2013. *Klansville, U.S.A.: The Rise and Fall of the Civil Rights–Era Ku Klux Klan.* Oxford: Oxford University Press.

D'Andrade, Roy. 1995. *The Development of Cognitive Anthropology.* Cambridge: Cambridge University Press.

Darby, Michael R., and Edi Karni. 1973. "Free Competition and the Optimal Amount of Fraud." *Journal of Law and Economics* 16:67–88.

Delmas, Magali A., and Laura E. Grant. 2014. "Eco-Labeling Strategies and Price-Premium: The Wine Industry Puzzle." *Business and Society* 53:6–44.

Delmastro, M. 2005. "An Investigation Into the Quality of Wine: Evidence from Piedmont." *Journal of Wine Research* 16:1–17.

DiMaggio, Paul J. 1987. "Classification in Art." *American Sociological Review* 52:440–455.

Dixit, Avinash K., and Joseph E. Stiglitz. 1977. "Monopolistic Competition and Optimum Product Diversity." *American Economic Review* 67:297–308.

Esposito, Sergio. 2008. *Passion on the Vine.* New York: Broadway Books.

European Commission. 2010. "Commission Launches the Online Vote on the New EU Organic Logo." ec.europa.eu/dgs /health-consumer/ dyna/consumervoice/create-cv.cfm?id=606.

European Commission. 2012. "Organic Farming." ec.europa.eu/agriculture/organic/organic-farming-en.

Feiring, Alice. 2017. *The Dirty Guide to Wine: Following Flavor from Ground to Glass*. Woodstock, VT: Countryman Press.

Gaggio, Dario. 2011. "Before the Exodus: The Landscape of Social Struggles in Rural Tuscany, 1944–1960." *Journal of Modern History* 82:319–345.

Gaja, Angelo. 2008. "Brunello di Montalcino: E' Ora di Cambiare le Regole." *Il Sommelier* 26:52–53.

Gambero Rosso–Slow Food Editore. 1987–2012. *Vini d'Italia*. Rome: G.R.H. Gambero Rosso.

Gault et Millau. 1989–2011. *Le Guide de Vins de France [Vin De France]*. Paris: Gault et Millau.

Geertz, Clifford. 1983. *Local Knowledge*. New York: Basic Books.

Goldberg, Amir, Michael T. Hannan, and Balázs Kovács. 2016. "What Does It Mean to Span Cultural Boundaries? Variety and Atypicality in Cultural Consumption." *American Sociological Review* 81:215–241.

Goldberg, Amir, and Sarah K. Stein. 2018. "Beyond Social Contagion: Associative Diffusion and the Emergence of Cultural Variation." *American Sociological Review* 83:897–932.

Gould, Roger V. 1995. *Insurgent Identities: Class, Community, and Protest in Paris from 1848 to the Commune*. Chicago: University of Chicago Press.

Grabo, Allen, and Mark van Vugt. 2016. "Charismatic Leadership and the Evolution of Cooperation." *Evolution and Human Behavior* 37:399–406.

Griffiths, Oren, Brett K. Hayes, and Ben R. Newell. 2012. "Feature-Based Versus Category-Based Induction with Uncertain Categories." *Journal of Experimental Psychology: Learning, Memory, and Cognition* 38:576–95.

Guilbeaut, Douglas, Andrea Baronchelli, and Damon Centola. 2021. "Experimental Evidence for Scale-Indusced Category Convergence Across Populations." *Nature Communications* 12:1–7.

Hampton, James A. 1982. "A Demonstration of the Intransitivity of Natural Categories." *Cognition* 12:151–64.

Hannan, Michael T., Gaël Le Mens, Greta Hsu, Balázs Kovács, Giacomo Negro, László Pólos, Elizabeth G. Pontikes, and Amanda J. Sharkey. 2019. *Concepts and Categories: Foundations for Sociological and Cultural Analysis*. New York: Columbia University Press.

Hannan, Michael T., László Pólos, and Glenn R. Carroll. 2007. *Logics of Organization Theory: Audiences, Codes, and Ecologies*. Princeton, NJ: Princeton University Press.

Houlihan, Michael, and Bonnie Harvey. 2013. *The Barefoot Spirit: How Hardship, Hustle, and Heart Built Amrrica's #1 Wine Brand*. Plano, TX Tex.: Footnotes Press.

Hsu, Greta, Michael T. Hannan, and Özgeçan Koçak. 2009. "Multiple Category Memberships in Markets: An Integrative Theory and Two Empirical Tests." *American Sociological Review* 74:150–69.

Hutchins, R. K., and L. A. Greenhalgh. 1995. "Organic Confusion: Sustaining Competitive Advantage." *Nutrition and Food Science* 95:1–7.

Konovalova, Elizaveta, and Gaël Le Mens. 2016. "Predictions with Uncertain Categorization: A Rational Model." In *Proceedings of the 38th Annual Conference of the Cognitive Science Society*, edited by J. Trueswell, A. Papafragou, D. Grodner, and D. Mirman, 722–27.

Konovalova, Elizaveta, and Gaël Le Mens. 2018. "Feature Inference with Uncertain Categorization: Re-assessing Anderson's Rational Model." *Psychonomic Bulletin & Review* 25:666–81.

Kovács, Balázs, Gianluca Carnabuci, and Filippo Carlo Wezel. 2021. "Patent Class Contrast and the Impact of Technological Innovations." *Strategic Management Journal* 42:992–1023.

Kovács, Balázs, and Michael T. Hannan. 2015. "Conceptual Spaces and the Consequences of Category Spanning." *Sociological Science* 2:252–86.

Kramer, Matt. 2010. *Matt Kramer on Wine*. New York: Sterling.

Laurence, Stephen, and Eric Margolis. 1999. "Concepts and Cognitive Science." In *Concepts: Core Readings*. Cambridge, MA: MIT Press.

Le Mens, Gaël, Balázs Kovács, Michael T. Hannan, Cecilia Nunes, and Guillem Pros. 2020. "How Do Categories Affect Valuation?" Working Paper.

Levin, Jonathan. 2009. "The Dynamics of Collective Reputation." *The B.E. Journal of Theoretical Economics* 9:Article 27.

Lohmann, Suzanne. 1993. "A Signaling Model of Informative and Manipulative Political Action." *American Political Science Review* 87:319–33.

March, James G. 1994. *A Primer on Decision Making: How Decisions Happen*. New York: Free Press.

Masnaghetti, Alessandro. 2015. *Barolo MGA. Menzioni Geografiche Aggiuntive. L'Enciclopedia delle Grandi Vigne del Barolo. Ediz. Italiana e Inglese*. Florence: Giunti Editore.

McAdam, Doug. 1983. "Tactical Innovation and the Pace of Insurgency." *American Sociological Review* 48:735–754.

McArthur, Leslie Z., and David L. Post. 1977. "Figural Emphasis and Person Perception." *Journal of Experimental and Social Psychology* 13:520–35.

McCarthy, John D., and Mayer N. Zald. 1977. "Resource Mobilization and Social Movements: A Partial Theory." *American Journal of Sociology* 82:212–41.

McVeigh, Rory. 2009. *The Rise of the Ku Klux Klan: Right-Wing Movements and National Politics*. Minneapolis: University of Minnesota Press.

Meloni, Giulia, and Johan Swinnen. 2013. "The Political Economy of European Wine Regulations." *Journal of Wine Economics* 8:244–84.

Ministère de l'Agriculture (France). 2011. "L'agriculture biologique." http://Agriculture.gouv.fr/l-agriculture-biologique.

Murphy, Gregory L. 2002. *The Big Book of Concepts*. Cambridge, MA: MIT Press.

Murphy, Gregory L., and Brian H. Ross. 1994. "Predictions from Uncertain Categorizations." *Cognitive Psychology* 27:148–93.

Negro, Giacomo, Michael T. Hannan, and Magali Fassiotto. 2015. "Category Signaling and Reputation." *Organization Science* 26:584–600.

Negro, Giacomo, Michael T. Hannan, and Hayagreeva Rao. 2010. "Categorical Contrast and Audience Appeal: Niche Width and Critical Success in Winemaking." *Industrial and Corporate Change* 19:397–1,425.

Negro, Giacomo, Michael T. Hannan, and Hayagreeva Rao. 2011. "Category Reinterpretation and Defection: Modernism and Tradition in Italian Winemaking." *Organization Science* 22:449–63.

Negro, Giacomo, and Ming D. Leung. 2013. "'Actual' and Perceptual Effects of Category Spanning." *Organization Science* 24:684–96.

Negro, Giacomo, and Susan Olzak. 2019. "Which Side Are You On? The Divergent Effects of Protest Participation on Organizations Affiliated with Identity Groups." *Organization Science* 30:189–206.

Nelson, Phillip. 1970. "Information and Consumer Behavior." *Journal of Political Economy* 78:311–29.

Newman, George E. 2016. "An Essentialist Account of Authenticity." *Journal of Cognition and Culture* 16:294–321.

Newman, George E. 2019. "The Psychology of Authenticity." *Review of General Psychology* 23:8–18.

OECD. 2001. *Sustainable Development: Critical Issues*. Paris: OECD Publishing.

O'Keefe, Erin. 2004. "'Pioneer' Veronelli Dies." *Decanter*. November 30.

O'Keefe, Kerin. 2008. "Brunello: Image or Substance, Truth or Dare?" *World of Fine Wine* 20.

O'Keefe, Kerin. 2012. *Brunello di Montalcino: Understanding and Appreciating One of Italy's Greatest Wines*. Oakland: University of California Press.

O'Keefe, Kerin. 2014. *Barolo and Barbaresco: The King and Queen of Italian Wine*. Oakland: University of California Press.

Olzak, Susan. 2020. "Ideological Focus, Tactical Performance, and the Survival of Terrorist Organizations." Unpublished Paper.

Parker, Robert M., Jr. 1988–2011. *Parker's Wine Buyer's Guide*. New York: Simon and Schuster.

Podolny, Joel M. 1993. "A Status-Based Model of Market Competition." *American Journal of Sociology* 98:829–72.

Polletta, Francine, and James M. Jasper. 2001. "Collective Identity and Social Movements." *Annual Review of Sociology* 27:283–305.

Rao, Hayagreeva, Philippe Monin, and Rodolphe Durand. 2005. "Border Crossing: Bricolage and the Erosion of Categorical Boundaries in French Gastronomy." *American Sociological Review* 70:968–91.

Reber, Rolf, Norbert Schwarz, and Piotr Winkielman. 2004. "Processing Fluency and Aesthetic Pleasure: Is Beauty in the Perceiver's Processing Experience." *Personality and Social Psychology Review* 8:364–82.

Reeve, Jennifer R., Lynne Carpenter-Boggs, John P. Reganold, Alan L. York, Glenn McGourty, and Leo P. McCloskey. 2005. "Soil and Winegrape Quality in Biodynamically and Organically Managed Vineyards." *American Journal of Enology and Viticulture* 56:367–76.

Rosch, Eleanor H., 1975. "Cognitive Representations of Semantic Categories." *Journal of Experimental Psychology: General* 104:192–233.

Rosch, Eleanor H., and Carolyn B. Mervis. 1975. "Family Resemblances: Studies in the Internal Structure of Categories." *Cognitive Psychology* 7:573–605.

Sanderson, Bruce. 2016. "Gaja Returns to Barbaresco." *Wine Spectator*.

Simmel, Georg. 1971. "Metropolis and Mental Life." In *On Individuality and Social Forms*, edited by Donald N. Levine, 324–39. Chicago: University of Chicago Press.

Simmel, Georg. 1978 [1900]. *The Philosophy of Money*. London: Routledge.

Snow, David A. 2004. "Framing Processes, Ideology, and Discursive Fields." In *The Blackwell Companion to Social Movements*, edited by D. A. Snow, S. A. Soule, and H. Kriesi, 380–412. Malden, MA: Blackwell Publishing.

Spence, A. Michael. 1973a. "Job Market Signaling." *Quarterly Journal of Economics* 87:355–74.

Spence, A. Michael. 1973b. "Time and Communication in Economic and Social Interaction." *Quarterly Journal of Economics* 87:651–60.

Spence, A. Michael. 1974. *Market Signaling: Informational Transfer in Hiring and Related Screening Processes*. Cambridge, MA: Harvard University Press.

Steiner, Rudolph. 2003 [1924]. *Agriculture: An Introductory Reader*. London: Sophia Books.

Tarrow, Sidney. 2013. *The Language of Contention: Revolutions in Words, 1688–2012*. Cambridge: Cambridge University Press.

Tassoni, A., N. Tango, and M. Ferri. 2013. "Comparison of Biogenic Amine and Polyphenol Profiles of Grape Berries and Wines Obtained Following Conventional, Organic, and Biodynamic Agricultural and Oenological Practices." *Food Chemistry* 139:1–4.

Taylor, Verta, Katrina Kimport, Nella Van Dyke, and Ellen Ann Anderson. 2009. "Culture and Mobilization: Tactical Repertoires, Same–Sex Weddings, and the Impact on Gay Activism." *American Sociological Review* 74:865–90.

Taylor, Verta, and Nancy Whittier. 1992. "Collective Identity in Social Movement Communities: Lesbian Feminist Mobilization." In *Frontiers in Social Movement Theory*, edited by Aldon D. Morris and Carol M. Mueller, 104–29. New Haven, CT: Yale University Press.

Tirole, Jean. 1996. "A Theory of Collective Reputations (with Applications to the Persistence of Corruption and to Firm Quality)." *Review of Economic Studies* 63:1–22.

Torjusen, Hanne, Lotte Sangstad, Katherine O'Doherty, and Unni Kjaernes. 2004. "European Consumers' Conceptions of Organic Food: A Review of Available Research." Professional Report 4-2004, National Institute for Consumer Research, Oslo, Norway.

Tyflo. 2011. "But et Objectifs." http://www.tyflo.org/but-objectifs.ph.

Van Dyke, Nella, and Sarah A. Soule. 2002. "Structural Social Change and the Mobilizing Effect of Threat: Explaining Levels of Patriot and Militia Organizing in the United States." *Social Problems* 49:497–520.

Verhaal, J. Cameron, and Glenn R. Carroll. 2019. "Essentialism and Exposition in Authenticity Among Craft-Based MicroDistilleries." Unpublished Paper.

Veronelli, Luigi. 1988–1990. *Catalogo Veronelli dei Vini d'Italia*. Milano: Giorgio Mondadori & Associati.

Veronelli, Luigi [Seminario Luigi Veronelli]. 1991–2019. *I Vini di Veronelli*. Bergamo: Seminario Luigi Veronelli.

Wang, Daniel J., Alessandro Piazza, and Sarah A. Soule. 2018. "Boundary Spanning in Social Movements: Antecedents and Outcomes." *Annual Review of Sociology* 44:167–87.

Wang, Daniel J., Hayagreeva Rao, and Sarah A. Soule. 2019. "Crossing Categorical Boundaries: A Study of Diversification by Social Movement Organizations." *American Sociological Review* 83:420–58.

Wasserman, Sheldon. 1991. *Italy's Noble Red Wines*. New York: Macmillan.

Weissman, Dick. 2005. *Which Side Are You On? An Inside History of the Folk Music Revival in America*. New York: Continuum.

Wine Spectator. 1984–2018. "Wine Spectator." http://www.winespectator.com/.

Wittgenstein, Ludwig. 1953. *Philosophical Investigations*. New York: Macmillan.

Yirode, E. K., S. Bonti-Ankomah, and R. C. Martin. 2005. "Comparison of Consumer Perceptions and Preference Toward Organic Versus Conventionally Produced Foods." *Renewable Agriculture and Food Systems* 20:193–205.

Index